CW01643124

THE SOCIAL UNCONSCIOUS IN PERSONS, GROUPS, AND SOCIETIES

NEW INTERNATIONAL LIBRARY OF GROUP ANALYSIS

Series Editor: Earl Hopper

THE SOCIAL UNCONSCIOUS IN PERSONS, GROUPS, AND SOCIETIES

Volume 3: The Foundation Matrix Extended and Re-configured

Edited by

Earl Hopper and Haim Weinberg

Routledge
Taylor & Francis Group
LONDON AND NEW YORK

First published 2017 by Karnac Books Ltd.

Published 2018 by Routledge
2 Park Square, Milton Park, Abingdon, Oxon OX14 4RN
711 Third Avenue, New York, NY 10017, USA

Routledge is an imprint of the Taylor & Francis Group, an informa business

British Library Cataloguing in Publication Data

A C.I.P. for this book is available from the British Library

ISBN-13: 9781782203551 (pbk)

Typeset by Medlar Publishing Solutions Pvt Ltd, India

CONTENTS

ACKNOWLEDGEMENTS

We are pleased to acknowledge the help and support of many colleagues who have expressed a keen interest in the study of the social unconscious. They are writing papers on various aspects of this topic, and responding to our invitation to focus on clinical work. Our team are very active in their participation in conferences and workshops, especially in their stimulating questions and comments. For her continuing secretarial and administrative assistance, we are grateful to Céline Stakol who has acquired a degree of expertise which remains unknown until she is asked a question about such matters as the date of an obscure publication. In the context of the New International Library of Group Analysis our work has been supported by the Trust for the Study of Social Trauma, the Abe Stern Family Foundation, and the Adler family. Our own families have made the greatest donation to our continuing work which unfortunately has become ever more urgent in the context of the repetition of social trauma.

Earl Hopper, PhD
Haim Weinberg, PhD

ABOUT THE EDITORS AND CONTRIBUTORS

Editors

Earl Hopper, PhD, is a psychoanalyst, group analyst, certified group therapist, and organisational consultant in private practice in London. A distinguished fellow of the American Group Psychotherapy Association, an honorary member of the Group Analytic Society International, and an honorary member of the Institute of Group Analysis, he is a supervisor and training analyst for many psychotherapy organisations in England. He is a former president of the International Association for Group Psychotherapy and Group Processes (IAGP), and a former chairman of the Association of Independent Psychoanalysts of the British Psychoanalytical Society. The author and editor of many books and articles in psychoanalysis, group analysis, and sociology, he is the editor of the New International Library of Group Analysis.

Haim Weinberg, PhD, is an Israeli psychologist, group analyst, and certified group therapist, living in the USA. He is the academic vice president at the Professional School of Psychology, Sacramento, where he leads a group psychotherapy doctoral programme. He is a former president of the Israeli Group Psychotherapy Association, and of the

Northern California Group Psychotherapy Society, a member of the Group Analytic Society International, and fellow of the American Group Psychotherapy Association. He has moderated the group psychotherapy discussion list on the internet for the past twenty years, and is the author and editor of many books and articles in group analysis.

Contributors

Yael Doron, MA, is a psychologist and group analyst in private practice. She teaches at the Israeli Institute of Group Analysis, at Haifa University, at the School of Psychotherapy in Rambam Hospital, and at the Central School for Social Workers.

Shulamit Geller, PhD, is a supervising clinical psychologist and group analyst in private practice in Tel Aviv. She is a member of the faculty of the clinical psychology graduate programme at the Academic College of Tel Aviv-Jaffa. A member of the Israeli Institute of Group Analysis. Her academic interests include the study of psychoanalysis and of social theory.

Helena Klímová, Mgr, is a group analyst and psychoanalytic psychotherapist in private practice in Prague. She is an honorary member of the Group Analytic Society International. Trainer, supervisor, and publicist, she is a co-founder of the Czech Society for Psychoanalytic Psychotherapy, the Institute of Group Analysis (Prague), Prix Irene Committee, and the Rafael Institute. She specialises in the treatment of the transgenerational transmission of the trauma of Holocaust and of totalitarian systems. She has been married for sixty years to Ivan Klíma with whom she has two children, four grandchildren, and two great-grandsons.

Dieter Nitzgen, MA, is a group analyst. He is a training analyst and supervisor for the Institute of Group Analysis in Heidelberg and the German Association of Group Analysis and Group Psychotherapy (D3G). He is a former member of the Association of Freudian Psychoanalysis (AFP), the former head of the Department of Psychotherapy of Rehaklinik Birkenbuck, and a member of the executive committee of the Group Analytic Society International. He is the editor of *Group Analysis*.

Regine Scholz, PhD, is a group analyst and psychotherapist in private practice in Dusseldorf. She is a member of the management committee of the Group Analytic Society International and a founder member of the German Society for Group Analysis and Group Psychotherapy (D3G). She is also a member of the training staff of the Munster Institute of Therapeutic and Applied Group Analysis. She specialises in the treatment of trauma. She is the former editor of *Arbeitshefte Gruppenanalyse (Psychosozial)*, and a member of the editorial committee of *Group Analysis*.

Yoram Schweitzer, MA, is a senior research fellow and head of the Terrorism and Low Intensity Conflict Program at the Institute for National Security Studies (INSS). He was head of the International Terror Section in the Israeli Defence Forces, and was an advisor on combating terror for the Ministry of Defense and the Prime Minister's Office.

Eran Shadach, PhD, is a supervising clinical psychologist and group analyst. He is a member of the faculty of the clinical psychology graduate programme at the Academic College of Tel Aviv-Jaffa, a member of the Israeli Institute of Group Analysis, and a Research Fellow at the International Institute for Counter Terrorism (ICT) in Herzliya. His research focuses on stress and anxiety, and the psychology of terrorists and of terror organisations.

Mohamed Taha, MD, PhD, is a consultant psychiatrist. He is a lecturer in psychiatry, Faculty of Medicine, Minia University, and an international fellow of the Royal College of Psychiatrists, UK. A former PhD fellow at the Centre for Psychoanalytic Studies, Essex University, UK, and a former vice president of the Egyptian Association for Group Therapies and Processes (EAGT), he is a member of the American Group Psychotherapy Association (AGPA).

Sa'ed Tali, MSW, is a senior social worker, a group analyst, and a certified family mediator in Israel. He is a lecturer at Beit Berl College in group facilitation, and the national coordinator at the Ministry of Social Affairs in the Department of the Individual and the Family. Over the last two decades he has been involved in leading groups and consulting activities for promoting dialogue between Jews and Palestinians.

Juan Tubert-Oklander, MD, PhD, was born, studied medicine, and trained as a group therapist in Buenos Aires, Argentina. Since 1976 he has lived and worked in private practice in Mexico City where, having become a Mexican citizen, he trained as a psychoanalyst. A training and supervising analyst at the Institute of the Mexican Psychoanalytic Association, he is a full member of the Mexican Psychoanalytic Association, the Argentine Psychoanalytic Association, and the Group Analytic Society International. He is the author and co-author of numerous books, articles, and book chapters, published in Spanish, English, Italian, French, Portuguese, Czech, and Hebrew.

Martin Weegmann is a consultant clinical psychologist and group analyst in London. He has specialised in the study and treatment of substance misuse, personality disorder, and complex needs. He is the editor and author of many books, articles, and book chapters. He has a long-held interest in Palestinian society.

Linde Wotton, MRCPsych, PGCE, Dip Mus, is a group analyst working in the National Health Service in London as a specialty doctor in psychotherapy. Having trained as a psychiatrist, she qualified as a teacher with a special interest in dyslexia, and studied for a music diploma with the Open University before returning to clinical work as a group analyst. Formerly the London courses director at the Institute of Group Analysis (UK), she is a member of the management committee of the Group Analytic Society International and a member of the editorial committee of *Group Analysis*.

Gad Yair, PhD, is a professor in the Department of Sociology and Anthropology at the Hebrew University of Jerusalem. He holds the Louis and Ann Wolens Chair in Educational Research and is the director of the NCJW Research Center for Innovation in Education. His academic interests include social theory, culture, and education.

Einav Yogev, MA, is a researcher in the Terror and Low Intensity Conflict Program at the Institute for National Security Studies (INSS). She served on the board of Amnesty International in Israel, participated as a mentor in Oxfam's International Youth Partnerships programme, and initiated projects for the British Council in Israel and Lions International. Her main research areas include delegitimisation by terrorist organisations and women's leadership in social and security fields.

INTRODUCTION

Earl Hopper and Haim Weinberg

In *The Social Unconscious in Persons, Groups and Societies: Volume 3: The Foundation Matrix Extended and Re-Configured* we try to develop the theory of the tripartite matrix, consider music as a form of non-verbal communication as a sub-dimension of the matrix, and to present empirical studies of the matrices of peoples in three societies in the Middle East. The first volume of this series addressed the group analytic theory of the social unconscious, attempting to clarify the definition of the concept itself, indicating some of its main elements, and comparing it to the Jungian collective unconscious, the Morenoian co-unconscious, and to the study of the link and the bond by Pichon-Rivière (Hopper & Weinberg, 2011). The second volume considered the sociocultural transmission of myths, and presented several empirical studies of the foundation matrices of contemporary societies, emphasising the importance of social trauma and the continuing consequences of them (Hopper & Weinberg, 2016). We hope that the study of these three volumes will provide an appreciation of the depth and breadth of this field of inquiry, which is at the very heart of the project of group analysis.

In this Introduction to Volume 3 we share our own thinking and continuing—if not continuous—discussion about particular aspects of the social unconscious in theory, empirical research, and in clinical work. We will also try to provide bridges to the chapters by an international collection of colleagues whose professional "formation" draws on several intellectual traditions and core and clinical trainings. This "collection" has become a team which includes the authors of the chapters in the preceding two volumes. We are especially pleased to acknowledge the important contributions to this Introduction by our colleagues Dieter Nitzgen (2008), Tom Ormay (2012), and Juan Tubert-Oklander (2013, 2014).

Why the matrix?

One of the most significant contributions of S. H. Foulkes to the theory of group analysis was his concept of the *matrix*. This was his way of considering group-specific factors and avoiding various problems arising from the application of unmodified theories of classical psychoanalysis to the study of groups and to the development of group therapy, which usually involved the analysis of each individual in the group or taking the group as a whole as if it were an individual patient. The matrix was also the basis for his emphasis on the sociality of human nature.

Foulkes approached the group situation with the same attitude of curiosity and openness that Freud adopted when dealing with his patients. The therapeutic aim was subordinate to the analytic investigation of what occurs in the clinical situation. Striving zealously to attain a therapeutic goal was unadvisable. The best way to treat the people was to help them understand what it means to work together in a group and to develop new ways of being with, and relating to, other human beings, in a climate of non-judgemental truthfulness, compassion, mutual trust, and co-operation. In part this approach was the basis for distinguishing group *analysis* from group *psychotherapy* more generally, which carries many of the same issues and questions that characterise the continuing discussions of the similarities and differences between psychoanalysis and psychotherapy.

The intellectual perspective that underlies group analysis is a polemic against the tendency in Western societies for people to think in terms of the materialistic metaphysics that underlies the Newtonian model of the universe as a vast space in which there are only pieces of matter which have shape, volume, and mass, but which are inherently inert. Shapeless, volume-less, and mass-less energy acts on these "particles" through inherently dynamic "forces" that set them in motion, through which they accelerate, decelerate, deform, and/or deconstruct. Although such particles are "real", these forces are not necessarily so. The only way to know reality is through the sense organs guided by rational thinking in the context of a particular culture, which constitutes a kind of paradigm with many unconscious aspects. This view of the universe is closely related to the Cartesian belief that an individual is an autonomous and self-contained subject who is identified with the human organism and perhaps with its brain in particular. Starting from such assumptions, it is inevitable that a group should be understood as "nothing but" an imaginary construction of its members who regard the perceptions of their interactions to be a supra-individual entity, but which is merely a product of their own perceptions (a point of view which was sometimes entertained by Bion himself).

If we start from a different ontology, one which includes not only material events, but also relations, values and norms, semiotic systems, verbal and non-verbal communications, styles, and thinking and feeling, etc. as real entities—in the sense that they are "capable of producing real effects", then quite another picture emerges. The group is not merely an illusion or just a name for the interactions among the individual members of it, but a reality in itself, albeit not a material reality. In this context, group processes can be seen as personal, interpersonal, and transpersonal processes, thus severing the alleged identity between mind and brain. Actually, this idea is completely captured by Durkheim in his theory of a "social fact". It is also captured later by Lewin in his application of field theory to human affairs, which was a way of acknowledging the influence of quantum mechanics with respect to the importance of waves as opposed to particles.

This hyper-complex reality cannot be conceived, perceived, or considered from a single vantage point. In order to get some idea of the whole, multiple points of view and multiple frames of references are required. Such cognition is necessarily constructive and collective, and ruled by the gestalt principle of the figure-ground distinction: if the individual member is taken as the figure, the group becomes ground, frame, and context for the perception of it; but if the group becomes the figure, the individual members of it become its ground. Of course, Bion discussed this in terms of binocular vision. Viewing, knowing, enquiring, and thinking about the human person is an active process of constructing images, thoughts, and entities, a process that necessarily includes the observer as a part of the field of inquiry.

History of the concept of matrix

The idea of condensing many mathematical relationships of similar structure into an orderly table can be traced to Chinese philosophers around the time of the birth of Jesus. Relationship and condensation are two important elements of any matrix. We know that in 1683 these ideas were outlined by Saki, the Japanese mathematician, and in 1693 were reformulated by Leibnitz, one of the outstanding proponents of the "new" philosophy in seventeenth-century Europe. There can be little doubt that the concept of matrix arrived in Europe via the Silk Route, but the influence of the Crusades cannot be entirely ignored.

In 1873 the word "matrix" was used to refer to the organisation of relationships. In 1904, James Joseph Sylvester (1973) used the Latin word "matrix", meaning "womb", derived from "mater" or "mother" in order to conceptualise a matrix as a condenser which contains smaller or sub-matrices. Thus, he foresaw modern systems theory in which a system contains smaller subsystems and is itself a subsystem of an even larger system. He regarded a matrix as the organisation of systems, and explained that the matrix was like a womb from which many interconnected systems of relationships were born.

Burrow (1926), writing about the social and phylogenetic foundations of our consciousness, referred to the matrix as a vehicle of our cohesion (Pertegato & Pertegato, 2013). However, his increasing emphasis on biology, at the expense of the sociocultural and political dimensions of the foundation matrix, differentiates his work from that of Foulkes. This is reminiscent of the use of the "social unconscious" by Fromm as a biological notion based on an homology of human societies with human organisms, which was then developed by Foulkes in reference to sociocultural arrangements of which people were unaware.

Foulkes (1975) argued that the matrix is in part societal and cultural, and in part biological and instinctual, the former inherited through sociocultural transmission, and the latter through transgenerational reproduction. The structure of the species is reflected in our society and culture, and to a lesser degree and in a different way, vice versa. However, Foulkes's most succinct definition of the matrix is as follows:

> *The Matrix* is the hypothetical web of communication and relationship in a given group [to which was added elsewhere the dimension of "values and norms"]. It is the common shared ground which ultimately determines the meaning and significance of all events

> and upon which all communications and interpretations, verbal and non-verbal, rest. (1964, p. 292)

In other words, the matrix becomes the *context* for the meaning or meanings of group events, including communicational events. It is also a construct that permits the location of causal explanations of such events. As we have outlined in our previous volumes, many colleagues have contributed to the development of the conceptual theory of the matrix and its clinical applications in both small and larger groups.

The mind in group analysis

Foulkes intended to develop *a process theory of mind* and to break the old association between mind and the individual organism, especially its brain (1973):

> It seems difficult for many at the present time to accept the idea that what is called "the mind" consists of interacting processes between a number of closely linked persons, commonly called a group. … These interactional processes play in a unified mental field of which the individuals composing it are a part. … *This network is a psychic system as a whole network, and not a superposed social interaction system in which individual minds interact with each other*. This is the value of thinking in terms of a concept which does not confine mind, by definition, to an individual. … This enabled me to say that *it is mental processes, not persons, that interact*. (pp. 224–228, italics added)

We (Hopper & Weinberg, 2011) have conveyed our own disagreement about the value of the concept of a group mind. Basically, for Hopper, the introduction of "matrix" was intended to avoid the organismic and "personistic" connotations of the term "mind"—namely, the assumption of an organised and unitary entity, with a conscious identity, purpose, and intention. He was reluctant to fall back on the concept of the Cartesian subject applied to a Cartesian group. Furthermore, he wished to disassociate himself from those theorists who applied the concept of mind to a social system based on a conservative ideology, which emphasised the integrity and stability—if not the permanence—of the system, based on homeostatic mechanisms, fostering the maintenance of the *status quo*, and regarding social change as an indication of instability—if not social pathology.

These are of course valid points. However, it has been argued that after Freud, Nietzsche, Marx, and Durkheim, no one can seriously maintain that the Cartesian conception of a unitary, autonomous, and pristine subject is valid, especially when applied to social systems. There can be no doubt that human groupings harbour and consolidate around different interests, feelings, and points of view that must necessarily be negotiated. Individuals must be regarded as "multividuals", possessed of inner societies comprised of living parts who also have to negotiate their agreements and disagreements. Nonetheless, while accepting these reservations, it must also be acknowledged that many colleagues continue to hold the Cartesian conception of individuals in groups.

Another objection to the concept of group mind was based on the fact that in English and in the English philosophical and scientific tradition, mind is conceived as a functional entity, something like an inner organ and intimately related to the brain, of which it is supposed to be an epiphenomenon. In German, however, the corresponding terms are *Seele* (soul) and *Geist* (spirit), which carry very different connotations. Neither Freud nor Foulkes, whose native language and culture were German, had much difficulty in conceiving the group as a *Massenpsyche*, as Foulkes shows in the following quotation:

> Looked at in this way it becomes easier to understand our claim that the group associates, responds and reacts as a whole. The group as it were avails itself now of one speaker, now of another, but it is always the transpersonal network which is sensitized and gives utterance, or responds. *In this sense we can postulate the existence of a group "mind" in the same ways as we postulate the existence of an individual "mind"*. (1957, p. 118, italics added)

Nonetheless, that the word "mind" is in quotation marks shows that Foulkes was as ambivalent about the value of the concept of the individual mind as he was about the group mind:

> I do not talk of a group mind because this is a substantivation of what is meant and as unsatisfactory as speaking of an individual mind. The mind is not a *thing* which exists but a series of events, moving and proceeding all the time. (1973, p. 224).

In the context of psychoanalysis in Britain, this notion of mind as a collective process is akin to Marjorie Brierley's (1944, 1951) reformulation of metapsychology as a process theory. However, Foulkes went even further than this when he argued that such processes are not limited by the boundaries of the human organism, but are actually interpersonal and transpersonal.

This perspective was not dissimilar to the one developed by the anthropologist and epistemologist Gregory Bateson (1972, 1979). For him, the basic question was how to distinguish between the world of substance (i.e., that of physical science, in which only "forces and impacts" can be causes) and the world of form (i.e., of biology and the social sciences, in which a unit of information is a cause):

> The explanatory world of *substance* can invoke no differences and no ideas, but only forces and impacts. And, per contra, the world of *form* and communication invokes no things, forces or impacts but only differences and ideas. (A difference which makes a difference *is* an idea. It is a "bit", a unit of information.) (1972, pp. 271–272)

This functional definition of the collective mind as an organised system of ideas also implies *intentionality*. In the same way that all psychic acts tend towards an "aim", living processes are not merely a sequence of events with one direction and one goal, the result of linear causality. Living processes involve what cyberneticists call "circular causality", which self-regulates and self-corrects in order to attain the goal. This requires a continuous input of information about the circumstances and the effects of their particular actions, including responses from other living systems. However, since living human social systems are rarely homogeneous, neither are their intentions. Intentionality involves negotiation, which is one of the main functions of mind!

It follows that in the course of a complete group analytic inquiry it is always necessary to consider the goals, beliefs, values, and norms, etc. of the group and its contexts. It is also necessary to appreciate the political and ethical aspects of human life (Hopper, 1996, 2009).

The habitus, the foundation matrix, and the social unconscious

The "habitus", the "foundation matrix", and the "social unconscious" are closely related and perhaps even intertwined concepts. Foulkes was inspired by Elias (1939) who introduced the concept of habitus in reference to the usually unconscious socially learned dispositions, skills, and ways of acting that are acquired through the activities and experiences of everyday life. Bourdieu (1977) developed the concept of habitus by explaining its dependency on history and human memory (or actually forgetfulness). He focuses on those aspects of culture that are anchored in the body or daily practices of individuals, groups, societies, and nations, including the totality of learned habits, bodily skills, styles, tastes, and other non-discursive knowledge that might be said to "go without saying". A certain behaviour or belief becomes part of a society's structure when its original purpose can no longer be recalled but nonetheless becomes internalised by its members. Thus, the habitus of a society can be understood in terms of various aspects and dimensions of a collective mind, including normative, physical, and psychological demeanour.

We use the concept of the social unconscious in order to refer to the social, cultural, and communicational constraints and restraints of which people are to varying degrees unconscious. The social unconscious emphasises shared anxieties, fantasies, defences, myths, and memories of the members of a particular social system. Its most important building bricks are chosen traumas and chosen glories. The field theory of the social unconscious includes its sociality, relationality, transpersonality, transgenerationality, and collectivity.

One way to specify the elements of the social unconscious of a specific society is to consider the signifiers that are characteristic of it. When such signifiers are heard or read by a member of that society, a set of conscious and unconscious associations are evoked, leading to emotional reactions and behaviours including inner threats, anxieties, and defences.

It is possible to become more conscious of signifiers when a member of a specific society reacts to them in a way that is perplexing and mystifying to someone from outside that society. In fact, we become more aware of our social unconscious when we have the feeling that a stranger "cannot understand it". Certain visual images (e.g., a picture of the Wailing Wall for Israelis), auditory vignettes (e.g., the music of a national anthem), insulting names (e.g., "nigger" for African-Americans), collective memories (e.g., the Holocaust or the Shoah for Jews), etc. are all likely to provoke responses and associations that are typical for someone who grew up in a specific society. Although language in general offers many examples of social signifiers, food is especially important, perhaps because it is associated not only with mother's milk, but also with cultural tears: for example, soul food for African-Americans, bagels for Jewish emigrants and refugees from Poland, *dolce de leche* for emigrants from Argentina, etc.

In the study of the social unconscious, collective memories by people of the same society are of special interest and importance. The term "collective memory" was coined by Halbwachs (1980), referring to the shared pool of information held in the memories of two or more members of a group. "A 'collective memory', as a set of ideas, images, and feelings about the past, is best located not in the minds of individuals, but in the resources they share" (Irwin-Zarecka, 1994, p. 4).

Collective memories are actively co-created in the minds of people in various kinds of relationships to one another. They are "… more than just an aggregate of individuals' personal memories …" (Zerubavel, 2003, p. 28). "While the collective memory endures and draws strength from its base in a coherent body of people, it is individuals as group members who remember" (Halbwachs, 1980, p. 48). Co-constructed collective memories are communicated from one generation to another, repeated and amplified through public discourse and the written and electronic media, and iterated by leaders and other citizens.

We prefer to use the concept of the foundation matrix in reference to a particular society or nation state. When a "people" becomes institutionalised, new social facts come into existence, and, thus, it is misleading to refer to the social unconscious of their more institutionalised social system. "The foundation matrix considers individual (persons) and groups as one single, inseparable process in which biological, social, cultural and economic factors meet and merge. The foundation matrix includes all dimensions of communication—including the non-verbal, e.g., facial expressions, gestures, postures and mimetically transferred meanings" (Scholz, in this book). Many aspects or dimensions of a foundation matrix can be considered. Although Foulkes mentioned biological aspects, he focused on relations, values and norms, communication, etc. More specifically, Le Roy (1994) has discussed family systems, gender relations, and generational relations. Dalal (2001) has emphasised the socio-economic structure, including power relations.

This perspective helps to clarify and to locate the status and range of various theories and concepts for the analysis of the foundation matrix, the social unconscious, and habitus. In order to describe and analyse a foundation matrix, mainly social science concepts are required; to describe and to analyse personal matrices, mainly *psychoanalytical* or psychodynamic concepts are required; and to describe and analyse the dynamic matrix, group analytic or group dynamic concepts must be used. In other words, there are registers of concepts for the description and analysis of the components of the tripartite matrix, ranging from the more sociological to the more psychoanalytical, and vice versa, with specifically group analytic concepts mediating between them. For example, basic assumptions, including their patterns of valence and/or personifications, are properties of a dynamic matrix. It is important to recognise that patterns of valence and personification are matters of the personal matrices of the members of a particular group, which lead them to be vulnerable and sensitive to role suction and/or inclined to personify a particular role that is generated in the dynamic matrix. However, in some societies their foundation matrix and their dynamic matrix are virtually the same, for example, traditional tribal societies or a people without a specific territory and state.

National and social character

The study of the social unconscious of the personal matrices of the members of a specific society echoes the socio-psychoanalytic notion of a national character.[1] Freud (1939a) claimed in *Moses and Monotheism* that a "national character" can be identified, and posed the idea of the ontogenetic recapitulation of phylogeny, which claims that individuals at birth possess a sort of collective memory of the life experience of their forbears. Fromm (1941) later used the term "social character". Fenichel (1947) was interested in this topic in connection with character disorders.

Sociological and anthropological modifications of the psychoanalytical studies of national character were very popular in the middle of the twentieth century, for example, Benedict's (1947) study of the Japanese national character, Gorer's (1948, 1949) studies of the American, Russian, and English, Gooch et al.'s (1945) study of the German, Inkeles and Bauer's (1959) studies of the Russian, etc. It is important to acknowledge the work of Erik Erikson, for example, *Childhood and Society* (1950). The work of Margaret Mead warrants special attention, although her tribal societies were much more homogeneous than the industrial societies indicated above.

This project flourished in the 1950s, primarily in the United States, under the heading of "Personality and Culture". Derived from Malinowski's (1927) *Sex and Repression in a Savage Society*, to which

Foulkes referred in 1948, this work was really a kind of polemic against classical Freudian psychoanalysis, based on an attempt to privilege the efficacy of nurture as opposed to nature, and sociocultural relations as opposed to instincts and unconscious phantasies.

Such studies almost disappeared from the sociological and anthropological literature, perhaps as a late reaction to WWII and National Socialism, which created an aversion towards the psychological characterisation of populations. In a multicultural postmodernist world, it became politically incorrect to talk about "national character", especially when the stereotypes were negative. Furthermore, these studies were often regarded as psychological reductionism, but this really depended on what was taken as problematic: the personality or the culture.

It is interesting that studies of the German, Dutch, Austrian, and Danish national character have recently re-emerged (Kuipers, 2012; Kuzmics & Axtmann, 2007). We would also draw attention to the recent concept of the *ethnic unconscious* (Herron, 1995; Javier & Rendon, 1995), which refers to "… material that is derived from identification with a particular group of people who have sufficient characteristics in common to give themselves a categorical name, although they also have actual and potential differences … The ethnic unconscious is repressed material that each generation shares with the next and is shared by most people of that ethnic group" (Herron, 1995, p. 525). Perhaps this development is related to the increased rate of mass immigration into Europe and the United States?

From the point of view of the study of habitus, the foundation matrix, and the social unconscious, we are interested in understanding the commonalities among the personal matrices of the members of a particular society characterised by a particular habitus and foundation matrix. For example, as constraints on the relationships between frustration, aggressive feelings, and aggression, Hopper (1965) has considered normative orientations towards authority and towards the expression of emotions in Britain compared to the United States, and in working class women compared to middle class women. Hopper (1996, 2009) has also discussed societal variations in definitions of maturity and processes of maturation in connection with what Fromm called "the revolutionary character". However, we are especially interested in the influence of traumatic events and their transgenerational transmission. For example, Penna (2016) has described certain character types within the context of the Brazilian foundation matrix, such as the cordial man, the rogue, and the mulatto. Similarly, it has been argued that Israelis tend to suffer from a "freier complex", feeling hypersensitive to the possibility that they will be taken advantage of by other people, not wanting ever to be anyone's bar of soap, with implicit connotations of the traumatic experience of the melted fat of Auschwitz (Abramovitch, 2007; Raufman & Weinberg, 2017a).

Society and culture viewed psychoanalytically

Following the paradigm of classical Freudian psychoanalysis in its most reductionist form, Eissler (1963) assumed that the history of groups and nations can be studied as if it were the psychosexual history of the individual. He believed that nations can suffer from traumas which can be repressed, which leads to symptoms, irrational acts, etc., expressed in various sociocultural patterns and pathologies. Kohut (1985) was also concerned with the historical influences on the development of culture, and was especially interested in the application of self psychology to the study of groups and nations. For him, the nuclear self of an individual is attuned to what he conceptualised as the nuclear self of his society. It is important to recognise that the self emerges within an interpersonal network and context. The self is formed in accord and in parallel with the self of the nation. Kohut identified a cultural "self-object", which can be a work of art or a cultural figure. He also argued that the group self, which is based on the shared psychological experience of individuals in the group, merges with the leader's self-objects (Stone, 2009).

Winnicott (1967) developed the idea that play is not a matter of either inner psychic reality or external reality. He used the term "cultural experience" as an extension of the idea of transitional phenomena. "The space where the cultural experience is located is in the *potential space* between the individual and the environment. … Cultural experience begins with creative living first manifested in play" (p. 100). Although this space is part of the ego organisation it is not part of a body-ego. These experiences belong to object-relating "at the place where … *continuity* is giving place to *contiguity*" (p. 109).

This view of cultural experience is completely different from the Freudian one, and, for that matter, from Kohut's development of it. After all, the social unconscious is not simply a matter of the internalisation of sociocultural objects, but a function of a transitional space in the context of interpersonal and transpersonal relations. Ogden (1994), for instance, conceptualised the "analytic third" as "the intersubjectively generated experience of the analytic pair … (p. 3). Stern (2004) reminds us that the intersubjective field is "the domain of feelings, thoughts, knowledge that two (or more) people share about the nature of their current relationship" (p. 243). The intersubjective field is a co-creation of the collective psyche of the people involved in the relationship. This is the space of the social unconscious!

Altman (2010) has argued that in addition to the intrapsychic aspects of a patient's fantasies (one-person psychology) and interpsychic aspects of objects and intersubjective relation systems (two-person psychology), it is necessary to consider a "social third" (three-person psychology), which is a product of social, cultural, national, and historical factors on the psyche of the individual subject. He suggested that a psychoanalysis that integrates this perspective of a "social third" will be able to examine the transgenerational transmission of trauma. The social third refers to cultural and historical forces that shape individuals and the relationship systems among them, as well as larger social and cultural systems. They also influence the definitions of what is normal and what is pathological. This is very close to how we understand the social unconscious.

These frames of reference in contemporary psychoanalytical thought overlap with the more group oriented perspectives developed by Pichon-Rivière (Losso, De Setton, & Scharff, 2017) and by Kaes (1993). It must also be acknowledged that virtually from the beginning group analysis has stressed the multipersonal formation of the relational field and the transgenerational transmission of its mentality. The group has been regarded as a transitional object in a transitional space. Thus, group analysis itself offers a kind of revision of classical psychoanalytic theories of society and culture as well as personal development (Hopper, 2003). It is not entirely clear why contemporary schools of thought in psychoanalysis tend to be unaware of the group analytic project (Hopper, 2017).

Learning about the social unconscious, the habitus, and the foundation matrix

Although it is possible to explore the social unconscious, the habitus, and the foundation matrix of any society, and for that matter of any social system, in dyads and small groups (Hearst, 1993; Hopper, 2003), several special techniques are particularly useful:

1) The study of large groups, perhaps in excess of thirty-five people in workshops and conferences. The regressive power of the large group creates processes of equivalence through which many aspects of the wider society can be explored (e.g., Weinberg & Weishut, 2012).
2) The study of social dreaming through a social dreaming matrix as invented by Gordon Lawrence (1998). This is a source of information about the common and sometimes interrelated preoccupations of the members of the matrix of which they are unconscious.
3) The study of trans-cultural processes in workshops, as developed by the European Association for Transcultural Group Analysis.
4) The study of myths, fairy tales, and folklore of a specific society, as they reflect and echo parts of the social unconscious of the members of it (Raufman & Weinberg, 2017b).
5) The study of more formal aspects of various types of communication, such as music, clothing, manners, language, plastic art, architecture, dance, graphics, or family relationships—in other words, everything that hermeneuts call a "text" as a bearer of meaning (Tubert-Oklander & Beuchot Puente, 2008).

In our discussion of social and national character, we indicated that describing and analysing the social unconscious of a specific society risk stereotyping its citizens. However, we are interested in the unconscious dynamics of their typicalities and commonalities, which can also be the basis for the study of their differences. For example, if Israelis are usually more aggressive than the citizens of other European countries, we need to describe the situations in which this occurs. It is likely that these situations are perceived as threatening and dangerous to many Israelis, because they arouse unconscious memories of hundreds of years of persecution, including those of the more recent Holocaust/Shoah. Thus, what might be a stereotypical description of Israelis as aggressive and rude can be transformed into a more elaborated description and explanation of their tendency to experience daily dangers as threats to their very existence.

We (Hopper & Weinberg, 2011) have argued that "The recognition and understanding of the social unconscious constitutes another painful blow to our narcissistic grandiosity, omnipotence and omniscience" (p. li). However, the exploration of the social unconscious of the people of a specific society and the understanding of their foundation matrix can open up another narcissitsic wound. People need to feel proud of their "belonging groups", including their societies. Being an American, Brazilian, Israeli, Egyptian, German, etc. tends to be idealised and to become a source of pride. This is important for the maintenance of national identity and a sense of belonging. However, the exploration of the dynamics of any society might have contradictory effects: a positive one in feeling connected to other people through positive common themes, but a negative one in becoming aware of their collective black holes. What forms of collective instrumental adjustments are likely to follow the recognition of collective denial? It must be recognised that as Elias and Scotson (1994) argued, the citizens of any society can internalise group charisma and/or group disgrace (Hopper, 2003).

The first part of *The Foundation Matrix Extended and Re-Configured* is concerned with the development of the theory of the matrix. It begins with a comprehensive review of the ideas of Foulkes about the social unconscious and the matrix. Dieter Nitzgen and Earl Hopper trace the emergence of the concept of the tripartite matrix, which is comprised of the foundation matrix of a contextual society, the dynamic matrices of its constituent groupings, and the personal matrices of the participants in them. They conclude that the social unconscious cannot be located in any *one* part of the tripartite matrix, but virtually by definition is located in *all* of them. The concept of the tripartite matrix is based on an open systems perspective in time and space, and can be analysed in terms of various properties and dimensions of the components of it.

In the next chapter, Regine Scholz explains how she distinguishes the social unconscious from the foundation matrix in connection with large group identity. She argues that foundation matrix is more fluid, while the social unconscious and especially large group identity are more stable. Various dimensions of these phenomena are characterised by their own respective rates and patterns of change.

Gad Yair reconnects us with the concept of the national habitus. He suggests that this concept offers a bridge between social theories and group analysis. Echoing our studies of the social unconscious, Yair offers numerous examples of the efficacy of social trauma within a national habitus. He concludes that a "national habitus should be considered in terms of the interplay of four analytic levels: a mythological past; known and verified historical events; contemporary geopolitical risks and challenges; and a future strewn with risks". The study of social identities and especially of national identities can hardly be separated from the study of a national habitus.

Building on the ideas of Pichon-Rivière and the work of Bleger, Juan Tubert-Oklander identifies six levels or modes of experience and mental functioning in the group. Avoiding the usual confusion of the psyche of the individual person with the matrices of their groups and contextual social systems, he provides an analysis of the matrix in terms of proto-mental processes. It seems that not only did Foulkes and Pichon-Rivière develop their ideas at almost the same time, but their ideas also almost completely overlap.

The second part of this volume is concerned with non-verbal aspects of the communication dimension of the foundation matrix. Although the perception of reality and the ways in which people think are influenced by the language they use, the differences between verbal and non-verbal communication are subtle, complex, and context dependent. Each of the two chapters in this section is concerned with music and the social unconscious. The first is by Helena Klimova. Developing her ideas about the collective false self, she elaborates the theme of how music and song in totalitarian regimes become ritualised, contributing to a powerful massification process. By organising the sense of time in a rhythmic way, music supplies the group with energy while providing a structure of security, unconsciously shaping the collective self.

The second chapter in this section is by Linde Wotton. She views the matrix as a musical process, building on the ideas of Foulkes about the "music" of the group emerging from the creative space of relations among the members of it. Our innate musicality is fundamental in the transmission and elaboration of the sociocultural inheritance. Each infant and caregiver create a unique musical improvisation that is rooted in both their bodies and their relationship. She claims that the shared musical process forms both the "social" and the "individual" person simultaneously.

The third part of this volume is concerned with the description of the foundation matrices of specific peoples in the Middle East, the origins of Western culture, and the arena of many past and current conflicts. The first chapter is about the social unconscious of Israeli Jewish people. It is by Haim Weinberg, one of the co-editors of this volume, from his point of view as an Israeli living in California, who has become more aware of various unconscious assumptions that govern the behaviour of Israelis.

He details the main themes, myths, defences, and anxieties that Israeli people unconsciously re-enact in terms of their experience of hundreds of years of persecution.

Yael Doron, another Israeli, writes about "black holes" as a collective defence against extremely painful shared anxieties associated with collective memories. In order to illustrate this idea, she brings an example from a therapy group in Israel about a new member of the group who had been injured inadvertently in the army through "friendly fire". The group re-enacted this situation by rejecting and attacking the member until he felt compelled to leave the group. The author shows how "friendly fire" is located in the dark web of the foundation matrix, deep within the hidden areas of collective black holes.

The next two chapters focus on the social unconscious of the Palestinian people. They focus on ruptures in collective memories. The first chapter is written by Sa'ed Tali, an Israeli Palestinian. He discusses the lack of chosen glories in the Palestinian social unconscious, at least in recent times, which might explain some of the violent acts of those who are called Shaid (martyrs). The second chapter is written by Martin Weegmann, a British group analyst, who can be regarded as an "outsider". He argues that Palestinians must fight not to forget and not to be forgotten. It is interesting to compare the similarities and differences between Sa'ed's and Martin's perspectives, and to speculate about the reasons for them. Sa'ed admits that he felt constricted while writing his chapter, acknowledging his fear of expressing ideas that the members of his community might find offensive to them, thus submitting to the Palestinian collectivistic culture. It would seem that Martin had more freedom to write about the pain and suffering of the Palestinian people. Each writer sees the Israelis as the "other" of the Palestinians, and vice versa.

The next chapter is by Mohamed Taha, an Egyptian psychiatrist, who applies Kleinian and Bionian ideas to the understanding of the social unconscious of Egyptians. The Tahrir Square revolution of 2011 ignited hopes in Egypt and throughout the Arab world for the development of democracy. Taha himself believed that this would completely change his country. However, his analysis of the four basic assumptions that characterise the Egyptian foundation matrix leads us to wonder whether a quick revolution can change such unconscious processes.

Volume 3 concludes with a chapter representing a pioneering, creative, and daring attempt to understand the foundation and dynamic matrices of ISIS. Eran Shadach and Shulamit Geller from Israel argue that this matrix includes a "reversed family structure", defined in terms of defiant relationships with the community and its values, which prevent learning from experience and coping with mental pain. They argue that at the level of the dynamic matrix, ISIS is characterised by illusional and delusional qualities. At the level of the foundation matrix, ISIS re-enacts the myth of the Abrahamic family.

Note

1. It could be said that although not really psychoanalytically informed, the observations by de Tocqueville (1838) of the developing national character of the early American people were in essence group analytical.

References

Abramovitch, H. (2007). The cultural complex: linking psyche and society. *Jung Journal: Culture & Psyche, 1*(1): 49–52.

Altman, N. (2010). *The Analyst in the Inner City: Race, Class and Culture through a Psychoanalytic Lens, second edition*. New York: Routledge.

Bateson, G. (1972). *Steps to an Ecology of Mind*. New York: Ballantine.

Bateson, G. (1979). *Mind and Nature: A Necessary Unit*. New York: Bantam.

Benedict, R. (1947). *The Chrysanthemum and the Sword: Patterns of Japanese Culture*. London: Secker & Warburg.

Bourdieu, P. (1977). *Outline of a Theory of Practice*. Cambridge: Cambridge University Press.

Brierley, M. (1944). Notes on metapsychology as process theory. *International Journal of Psychoanalysis, 25*: 97–106.

Brierley, M. (1951). *Trends in Psycho-Analysis*. London: Hogarth.

Burrow, T. (1926). The laboratory method in psychoanalysis, its inception and development. *American Journal of Psychiatry, 5*(3): 348.

Dalal, F. (2001). The social unconscious: a post-Foulkesian perspective. *Group Analysis, 34*: 539–555.

de Tocqueville, A. (1838). *Democracy in America*. New York: Saunders.

Eissler, K. R. (1963). Freud and the psychoanalysis of history. *Journal of the American Psychoanalytic Association, 11*: 675–703.

Elias, N. (1939). *The Civilizing Process, Vol. I. The History of Manners*. Oxford: Blackwell, 1969.

Elias, N., & Scotson, J. (1994). *The Established and the Outsiders*. London: Sage.

Erikson, E. H. (1950). *Childhood and Society*. New York: W. W. Norton. [Reprinted London: Paladin, 1987.]

Fenichel, O. (1947). *The Psychoanalytic Theory of Neurosis*. New York: W. W. Norton.

Foulkes, S. H. (1948). *Introduction to Group-Analytic Psychotherapy*. London: Maresfield, 1984.

Foulkes, S. H. (1957). Psychodynamic processes in the light of psychoanalysis and group analysis. In: *Therapeutic Group Analysis* (pp. 108–119). London: Karnac, 1984. [Originally published as "Group-analytic dynamics with special reference to psychoanalytic concepts", *International Journal of Group Psychotherapy, 7*: 40–52.]

Foulkes, S. H. (1964). *Therapeutic Group Analysis*. London: Maresfield, 1984.

Foulkes, S. H. (1973). The group as a matrix of the individual's mental life. In: *Selected Papers: Psychoanalysis and Group Analysis* (pp. 223–233). London: Karnac, 2004.

Foulkes, S. H. (1975). *Group-Analytic Psychotherapy: Method and Principles*. London: Gordon & Breach. [Reprinted London: Karnac, 2012.]

Freud, S. (1939a). *Moses and Monotheism*. *S. E., 23*: 1–138. London: Hogarth.

Fromm, E. (1941). *Escape from Freedom*. New York: Holt, Rinehart & Winston.

Gooch, G. P., Ginsburg, M., Willoughby, L. A., Butler, E. M., Stirk, S. D., & Pascal, R. (Eds.) (1945). *The German Mind and Outlook*. London: Chapman & Hall.

Gorer, G. (1948). *The American People: A Study in National Character*. New York: W. W. Norton.

Gorer, G. (1949). *The People of Great Russia: A Psychological Study*. London: Cresset.

Halbwachs, M. (1980). *The Collective Memory*. L. A. Koser (Trans. and Ed.). Chicago, IL: University of Chicago Press.

Hearst, L. (1993). Our historical and cultural cargo and its vicissitudes in group analysis. Seventeenth S. H. Foulkes Annual Lecture. *Group Analysis, 26*: 389–405.

Herron, W. G. (1995). Development of the ethnic unconscious. *Psychoanalytic Psychology, 72*: 521–532.

Hopper, E. (1965). Some effects of supervisory style: a sociological analysis. *British Journal of Sociology, XVI*(3): 189–203. [Reprinted in Hopper, E. (2003), *The Social Unconscious: Selected Papers*. London: Jessica Kingsley.]

Hopper, E. (1996). The social unconscious in clinical work. *Group Analysis, 20*(1): 7–43. [Reprinted in Hopper. E. (2003), *The Social Unconscious: Selected Papers*. London: Jessica Kingsley.]

Hopper, E. (2003). *The Social Unconscious: Selected Papers*. London: Jessica Kingsley.

Hopper, E. (2009). Building bridges between psychoanalysis and group analysis in theory and clinical practice. *Group Analysis, 42*(4): 406–425.

Hopper, E. (2017). Interview by editor Nikos Lamnidis. *Oedipus—Biannual Greek Psychoanalytic Journal*. Spring issue.

Hopper, E., & Weinberg, H. (Eds.) (2011). *The Social Unconscious in Persons, Groups, and Societies: Volume 1: Mainly Theory*. London: Karnac.

Hopper, E., & Weinberg, H. (Eds.) (2016). *The Social Unconscious in Persons, Groups, and Societies: Volume 2: Mainly Foundation Matrices*. London: Karnac.

Inkeles, A., & Bauer, R. A. (1959). *The Soviet Citizen: Daily Life in a Totalitarian Society*. Cambridge, MA: Harvard University Press.

Irwin-Zarecka, I. (1994). *Frames of Remembrance: The Dynamics of Collective Memory*. New Brunswick, NJ: Transaction.

Javier, R. A., & Rendon, M. (1995). The ethnic unconscious and its role in transference, resistance, and countertransference: An introduction. *Psychoanalytic Psychology, 72*: 513–520.

Kaes, R. (Ed.) (1993). *Transmission de la vie psychique entre generations*. Paris: Dunod.

Kohut, H. (1985). *Self-Psychology and the Humanities: Reflections on a New Psychoanalytic Approach*. C. B. Strozier (Ed.). New York: W. W. Norton.

Kuipers, G. (2012). The rise and decline of national habitus: Dutch cycling culture and the shaping of national similarity. *European Journal of Social Theory, 16*(1): 17–35.

Kuzmics, H., & Axtmann, R. (2007). *Authority, State and National Character: The Civilizing Process in Austria and England, 1700–1900*. Aldershot, UK: Ashgate.

Lawrence, W. G. (1998). *Social Dreaming @ Work*. London: Karnac.

Le Roy, J. (1994). Group analysis and culture. In: D. Brown & L. Zinkin (Eds.), *The Psyche and the Social World*. London: Routledge.

Losso, R., De Setton, L. S., & Scharff, D. E. (Eds.) (2017). *The Linked Self in Psychoanalysis: The Pioneering Work of Enrique Pichon Rivière*. London: Karnac.

Malinowski, R. (1927). *Sex and Repression in Savage Society*. London: Routledge, 2001.

Nitzgen, D. (2008). The 32nd S. H. Foulkes Annual Lecture: The group analytic movement sixty years on: revisiting *Introduction to Group Analytic Psychotherapy* by S. H. Foulkes. *Group Analysis, 41*: 325–346.

Ogden, T. (1994). The analytic third: Working with intersubjective clinical facts. *International Journal of Psychoanalysis, 75*: 3–19.

Ormay, T. (2012). *The Social Nature of Persons: One Person is No Person*. London: Karnac.

Penna, C. (2016). Reflections upon Brazilian social unconscious. In: E. Hopper & H. Weinberg (Eds.) (2016), *The Social Unconscious in Persons, Groups, and Societies: Volume 2: Mainly Foundation Matrices*. London: Karnac.

Pertegato, E. G., & Pertegato, G. O. (2013). *From Psychoanalysis to Group Analysis: The Pioneering Work of Trigant Burrow*. London: Karnac.

Raufman, R., & Weinberg, H. (2017a). *The Hidden Language—Fairy Tales and the Social Unconscious*. London: Karnac.

Raufman, R., & Weinberg, H. (2017b). Working with a multicultural group in times of war—three metaphors of motion and mobility. In: R. Friedman & Y. Doron (Eds.), *Group Analysis in the Land of Milk and Honey*. London: Karnac.

Stern, D. N. (2004). *The Present Moment in Psychotherapy and in Everyday Life*. New York: W. W. Norton.

Stone, W. N. (2009). *Contributions of Self Psychology to Group Psychotherapy: Selected Papers*. London: Karnac.

Sylvester, J. J. (1904). *The Collected Mathematical Papers of James Joseph Sylvester*, *I*. H. F. Baker (Ed.). New York: AMS Chelsea, 1973.

Tubert-Oklander, J. (2013). *Theory of Psychoanalytical Practice: A Relational Process Approach*. London: Karnac.

Tubert-Oklander, J. (2014). *The One and the Many: Relational Psychoanalysis and Group Analysis*. London: Karnac.

Tubert-Oklander, J., & Beuchot Puente, M. (2008). *Ciencia mestiza. Psicoanálisis y hermenéutica analógica* (Hybrid science: Psychoanalysis and analogical hermeneutics). Mexico City: Torres.

Weinberg, H., & Weishut, D. J. N. (2012). The large group: Dynamics, social implications and therapeutic value. In: J. L. Kleinberg (Ed.), *The Wiley-Blackwell Handbook of Group Psychotherapy* (pp. 457–479). New York: Wiley-Blackwell.

Winnicott, D. W. (1967). The location of cultural experience. In: *Playing and Reality* (pp. 95–103). London: Tavistock, 1971.

Zerubavel, E. (2003). *Time Maps: Collective Memory and the Social Shape of the Past*. Chicago, IL: University of Chicago Press.

PART I

THEORY

CHAPTER ONE

The concepts of the social unconscious and of the matrix in the work of S. H. Foulkes

Dieter Nitzgen and Earl Hopper

The concept of the social unconscious has not been studied with respect to the work of S. H. Foulkes taken as a whole. Apart from the abstract survey of his ideas implicit in the Introduction to *The Social Unconscious in Persons, Groups and Societies: Volume 1: Mainly Theory* (Hopper & Weinberg, 2011), the development of the *concept* of the social unconscious from its Jungian and Freudian origins to Foulkes's mature group analytic theory has been neglected. No serious attempts have been made to link the concept of the social unconscious to the "matrix", which Foulkes called the "corner-stone of our working theory" (Foulkes & Anthony, 1957, p. 217). Accordingly, the purpose of this chapter is to support with citations from the work of Foulkes the argument outlined by Hopper and Weinberg (2016) in their Introduction to *Volume 2: Mainly Foundation Matrices*, that the main elements of his more mature theory of the social unconscious include sociality and socialisation, relationality, transpersonality, transgenerationality, and collectivity, ultimately subsumed by the matrix. This field theory of the social unconscious and the matrix was a product of Foulkes's continuous and persistent thinking about these elements and their interconnections over a period of four decades.

The social a priori

From the beginning of his work Foulkes asserted "… the … importance of society …" (1948, pp. 11–16). He fervently hoped that group work "on psycho-analytic lines" (cf. Foulkes & Lewis, 1944) could be an antidote to the "mass techniques" employed by "the totalitarian states" (Foulkes, 1960, p. 46; cf. Foulkes, 1966). In his first book, he referred to the contribution of Erik Erikson (cf. Erikson, 1946), who was one of the first psychoanalysts to emphasise "the relationship between Group Identity and Ego-Identity, Ego-Pathology and historical change and ego-damaging social pathology" (Foulkes, 1948, p. 11). In 1950, Foulkes wrote: "Conditions under which modern man lives force him to cope with mass and group problems to an extent hitherto unknown" (p. 46). Moreover, "[T]he totalitarian states themselves make vast-scale experiments in solving these problems" and thereby created "nightmare conditions" (ibid.). Through a consideration of the social, political, and psychic consequences of these political experiments, "[P]sycho-analysis [can complete] its basic studies of neuroses by investigating more explicitly" … "man's *enslavement by historical conditions which claim autonomy*" (ibid., p. 12; italics ours).

Although the concept of the social unconscious was framed in terms of the "*social a priori*", Foulkes was neither the first nor the last to have been influenced by this idea (Dalal, 2011, p. 254; italics ours). Indeed. As Foulkes explained to the British Psychoanalytical Society in 1946, not very long after the end of World War II, "[I]n my approach, the qualifying word 'analysis' does not refer to psychoanalysis alone, but reflects at least *three different influences*, all of which *operate actively*" (E. Foulkes, 1990, p. 129; italics ours): "… the principles evolved by Kurt Goldstein and Ahémar Gelb" (ibid.), Freudian psychoanalysis (ibid., p. 130), and "sociological analysis" or what Karl Mannheim termed "socio-analysis" (ibid., p. 131). Accordingly, what made group analysis *unique* was its inter-disciplinarity (cf. Mies, 2012).

Long before he entered psychoanalytic training and well before he encountered members of the Institute of Social Research in Frankfurt, Foulkes had already disposed of a theoretical notion of a social a priori (cf. Nitzgen, 2008, 2011). This was provided by his "revered teacher" in neurology and psychiatry, Kurt Goldstein (cf. Fuchs, 1936, p. 212), who argued that whatever happens in the *organism* depends on what he called the "total situation" of its material environment (Goldstein, 1934, p. 20). Their reciprocal interdependence was the vantage point from which all scientific investigations had to proceed, that is, always from a *specific* organism within a specific *situation* (cf. Geroulanos & Meyers, 2014).

Despite this affinity to the views of left-wing psychoanalysts such as Bernfeld, Fenichel, and Friedländer (cf. Nitzgen, 2011, pp. 9–11; Nitzgen & Hoffmann, 2014), Foulkes's perspective was much more systemic than Marxist.[1] In 1943 he wrote: "When we study communities, ancient and modern, intelligently, we become aware of the fact that they can only be understood as a working whole" or as a "whole *social system*" (Foulkes, 1944, p. 36; italics ours). Therefore, none of their "individual manifestations" can be "taken out of the total context" (ibid.). In other words, even at that time, Foulkes was concerned not only with the effects of a society on the members of it and the groupings within it, but also with the enabling and inhibiting effects of "society" in general. He was making a general theoretical point rather than a specific political one!

Originating mainly in the works of German "holistic" biology, namely from Jakob van Uekküll (cf. Harrington, 1996), this perspective served to orientate the group analytic approach in terms of both theory and practice. For Foulkes, however, the "total situation" was always a social situation structured by human communication. Although a dedicated psychoanalyst, he argued that what Freud had called "free association is in no way independent of the total situation" (Foulkes, 1948, p. 71). By transforming individual into group associations, Foulkes not only provided a mode of access to unconscious processes in groups, he also integrated the Freudian *method* of access to unconscious processes into a holistic or a systemic frame of reference.

For the construction of the social a priori in group analysis, the early sociology of Norbert Elias was crucial. His sociological vision of society (in)formed the group analytic social a priori, and, thus, confirmed Foulkes's basic conviction that "the group is a more fundamental unit than the individual" members of it (Foulkes & Anthony, 1965, p. 235; cf. E. Foulkes, 1990, p. 212). Nonetheless, it took almost a decade before Foulkes was able fully to conceptualise *unconscious* processes of communication in groups. This enabled him to add psychoanalytical substance to what Elias had recognised as the reciprocity of social exchange, and to show that the reciprocity of *dialogue* was based on the group members' "*instinctive* understanding of each other" (Foulkes & Anthony, 1965, p. 29). This understanding rested on the "common communicational ground" (E. Foulkes, 1990, p. 291) of their collective sociocultural heritage. Thus, the social a priori in group analysis is not only *complex* in terms of its roots, it is also *consistent* in its theoretical construction and application in clinical practice.

Through a Freudian lens

Based on the social a priori in general and on the sociological perspective of Elias in particular, the *idea* of a social unconscious can be found in Foulkes's work from the very beginning of it. In his paper "On Introjection", his first to be published in English, he focused on the importance of the introjection of objects from the external world (1937). Moreover, in a booklet originally published in Canada, he addressed issues of crime and delinquency in the context of society (Foulkes, 1943). In his first paper about groups, written in 1944 together with Eve Lewis, a Jungian therapist, Foulkes maintained that in the analytic group it is as if the "collective unconscious" acted as a *condenser* (Foulkes & Lewis, 1944, reprinted in Foulkes, 1984, p. 34; italics ours), an insight that he repeated in his first book (1948, p. 167). Although they used the Jungian term "collective unconscious", it is likely that this reflected the influence of Lewis. Otherwise, as a Freudian psychoanalyst who had been working in Frankfurt before he came to London, Foulkes might well have used "sociocultural" or a similar notion. Nonetheless, he conceived the group situation as a "collective of human beings" whose study he likened to "what Anthropologists call Field Work" (ibid., p. 16).

As a term and a concept, the "social unconscious" was not used by Foulkes until 1950 in "Group Therapy: Survey, Orientation, Classification". He approached the notion of the social unconscious from the point of view of the unfolding of the *therapeutic process* within the group analytic *situation*, which he considered in terms of its totality. Although the therapeutic process in the group is "in a sense … the same as the making conscious of the unconscious" (ibid.), it "brings into operation and perspective *a totally different area* of which the individual is *equally unaware*" (ibid.). "Although access to the *social* unconscious is only possible *while dealing intensively with the* (repressed) *unconscious in the Freudian sense*, it is the group situation *itself* which brings *a totally different area* into *operation and perspective*" (ibid.). He continued, "The individual is as much compelled by these colossal forces as by his own *id*, and defends himself against their recognition without being aware of it, but in *different ways and modes*" (1960, p. 52; original italics). This is, of course, an echo of Freud's comment: "We approach the id with analogies: we call it a chaos, a cauldron full of seething excitations" (1933a, p. 73). Linking the *seething excitations* of the *id* with the *colossal forces* of society underlined Freud's and Foulkes's conviction that the "ego behaves essentially passively in life, and that ... we are 'lived' by unknown and uncontrollable forces" (Freud, 1923b, p. 23).

From an epistemological point of view, however, supplementing the concept of body ego with the concept of what Hopper (2003a) called "society ego" creates several problems. For example, in his conceptualisation of the social unconscious Foulkes referred to Freud' s first and second model of the topographical structure of the psychic apparatus, and, thus, to two very different notions of the unconscious: *repression* and the *system Ucs* (Freud, 1915d); and the *agencies* of the *ego*, the *superego*, and the *id* (cf. Freud, 1923b). Without entering the complex metapsychological details of this problem, we can ask whether the unconscious is "the result of primal repression" or "the deepest element in the psyche" (Laplanche, 1987, p. 28). In other words, "Is the id something primordial and primal or does it *become* a stranger who lives within us as the result of the very process which constitutes the psychic apparatus and of repression?" (ibid.; italics ours). For Foulkes, this internal "*stranger*" represents not only the *drives*, but also the *forces* of society. Such forces were regarded as virtually an *agency* of their own, similar to but different from the biologically based id. In this context, Foulkes evoked Freud's image of the "censor" (Freud, 1916–17, p. 429) who stands at the intersection between the two systems and agencies, and who fulfilled the double function of "an outside, political censor" and a "doorkeeper" at the "room of consciousness" (Foulkes in Foulkes & Anthony, 1965, p. 265). However, it is important to see that these internalised social forces were not only connected to the construction of the superego (or even the ego ideal), based on figures in the external world, but also became part of the ego itself.[2]

Foulkes insisted that access to unconscious psychic facts as well as to unconscious social facts (or to be absolutely precise, psychic facts as well as social facts of which people are unconscious) was to be achieved in groups by the same *method* of investigation, namely "free floating group discussion" (1948, p. 71) or "free group association" (Foulkes & Anthony, 1965, p. 56). This "communication under reduced censorship" (ibid., p. 42) applies to "the content of contributions, ... to the expression of personal and interpersonal feelings" ibid., p. 59), to the "patient's relationship to others including the conductor", and, thus, to "those social relationships [that] are not usually revealed, or are not even conscious" (ibid., p. 56).[3]

To summarise: in the 1950s, separating from a Jungian perspective, Foulkes supplemented Freud's concept of the dynamic unconscious rooted in the id with his notion of a social unconscious rooted in the society and its constituent groupings, thereby emphasising the unity of the group *analytic* (italics ours) perspective. However, in so far as he focused on sociality and socialisation of individual persons, Foulkes's conceptualisation of the social unconscious was more an attempt to modify classical psychoanalytical thinking than it was to develop a theory of the group as such. Moreover, after he introduced the concept of the social unconscious, Foulkes did not elaborate on it in any significant way. Although he gave up considering the social unconscious as an "agency", he never stopped thinking in terms of conscious, preconscious, unconscious, and non-conscious biological, social, and psychic *processes*. This is the main reason why he continued to refer to the social unconscious, albeit very infrequently, even *after* its conceptual integration into a truly group analytic framework (cf. E. Foulkes, 1990, p. 252).

The coming of the matrix

As of the early 1950s, Foulkes's conceptualisation of the social unconscious was definitely more Freudian than Jungian, and in so far as it focused on sociality and socialisation, his concept was more psychoanalytic than group analytic. What was (and perhaps still is) the Foulkesian group analytic equivalent of the social unconscious? (cf. Foulkes in Foulkes & Anthony, 1965, pp. 16, 52, 263). We can answer this question in the context of the gradual development of the notion of the group *matrix* from the late 1940s to the 1960s.

Starting with a view of the group as a "social network" (1948, p. 14) and the insight that "understanding, like communication, is a social process" (ibid., p. 169), Foulkes claimed towards the end of his first book that it was "in the process of *communication* and the struggle for it that all the other dynamisms meet" (ibid., p. 169; italics in original). "[W]*orking towards an ever more articulate form of communication* … [is in fact] … *identical with therapeutic process itself*" (ibid.; italics in original). Consequently, the "concept of *communication*" (Foulkes in Foulkes & Anthony, 1957, p. 224; italics ours) became the centre of his theoretical and clinical attention (cf. Foulkes, 1960, pp. 269–278).

In other words, the group matrix was seen as a social network whose participants are in communication with one another. In parallel with the development of this perspective, Foulkes gradually replaced his *organismic* understanding of the group-as-a-whole in favour of a more *systemic* one. This reflected development in field theory (cf. Lewin, 1947, 1951) which focused on the human organism as responsive to and in interaction with the environment. Drawing on his previous work with Goldstein (1934) and building on this holistic approach, Foulkes began to elaborate the concept of the group matrix, which he called "*our* concept" (1960, p. 118; italics ours), claiming that it is "at the centre of all our thinking about groups" (Foulkes & Anthony, 1957, p. 242).

As of 1957, the matrix was defined as the operational basis of all relationships and communications (Foulkes, 1957, p. 118). However, in the 1960s, the matrix became the "... the hypothetical web of communication and relationship in a given group ..." (Foulkes, 1964, p. 292), and also "... the common shared ground which ultimately determines the meaning and significance of all events and upon which all communications and interpretations, verbal and non-verbal, rest" (ibid.). Yet, in 1965, Foulkes extended this definition (cf. Nitzgen, 2015). The matrix now became "the operational basis of all *mental* processes in the group in the same way as the individual's mind is the operational basis of all mental processes in the individual" (Foulkes & Anthony, 1965, p. 258; italics ours; cf. Foulkes, 1971). Foulkes considered the individual as a "nodal point" (1948, p. 14) "suspended" in the group matrix (1957, p. 118) like the neuron in anatomy and physiology: "the neuron being the nodal point in the total network of the nervous system which always reacts and responds as a whole" (Foulkes, 1957, p. 118, quoting Goldstein). Looked at in this way, "... it becomes easier to understand that the group *associates, responds* and *reacts* as a whole" (ibid.; italics ours). In summary, he argued that "... each individual (is) an artificial, though plausible, abstraction, basically and centrally determined, inevitably, by the world in which he lives, by the community, the group, of which he forms a part" (1948, p. 10), and that "they can at no stage be separated from each other, except by artificial isolation" (ibid; cf. Foulkes 1990, p. 148).

In the 1970s, Foulkes went even further than this. He now characterised the group matrix as a "*unified mental field*" (E. Foulkes, 1990, p. 226; italics ours), in which the mental "boundaries" of the group members "do not run parallel with the boundaries of their *physical* person" (1960,

p. 118; italics ours). He emphasised that by adopting this view he was "enabled" to think and to say that "it is *mental processes*, not *persons* that interact" (E. Foulkes, 1990, p. 228; italics ours). In brief, although he originally described the group as a "living *organism* as distinct from the individuals composing it" (1948, p. 140; italics ours), he eventually came to regard an individual "not as a *closed* but as an *open system*" (1960, p. 118; italics in original). Moreover, "… what is called the 'mind' consists of interacting processes between a number of closely linked persons, commonly called a group" (p. 224). The "… 'mind' is not confined, by definition, to an individual" (p. 226).[4]

It is important to see that although in the early years of his work, Foulkes used the concept of individual as synonymous with the concept of person, he began to realise that the individual organism who has been socialised through participation within his family, education system, and society in general should be called a "person" (Hopper, 2003a). In this conceptual context, *individuals interact*, but *persons relate* to one another within interpersonal and ultimately transpersonal relations and networks.[5] This shift from "individual" to "person" was consistent with the distinction that he made between "brain" and "mind": whereas the individual has a brain, the person has a mind. Thus, it was not only possible, but also entirely appropriate to think in terms of a collective mind of a group of persons, virtually by definition.[6]

Based on these theoretical distinctions and developments, Foulkes felt a growing need to distinguish more clearly between the "matrix of *interpersonal* relationships" (Foulkes & Anthony, 1957, p. 242) and the matrix as a "*transpersonal network*" (ibid., p. 243; italics in original) (cf. Nitzgen & Hoffmann, 2014). Whereas *interpersonal* relationships "literally occur in-between two or more people" (Foulkes & Anthony, 1957, p. 242; italics ours), *transpersonal* processes "may be conceived as passing right through the individual members" (ibid., p. 243). Through elaborating the dialectics between interpersonal relationships and transpersonal processes, Foulkes was able to make what he called "a totally new assumption", and to take "a further decisive step regarding method as well as theory of the matrix" (Foulkes & Anthony, 1965, p. 29).

The community in the consulting room

According to Foulkes, the group always "*associates, responds* and *reacts* as a whole" (1960, p. 118; italics ours). However, to comprehend this complex statement and to appreciate its originality, it is necessary to focus on the *associative* process of the group as a whole. Contesting Freud's established psychoanalytic understanding of associations based on "memory traces" in the brain (cf. Freud, 1950a), he claimed: "We now treat associations on the common ground of *unconscious instinctive* understanding of each other" (1965, p. 29; italics in original). Thus, group associations were conceived as "quasi associations to a *common context*" (ibid.; italics ours). He stated: "We no longer take as our basis of operation the conditioning by old experiences based on traces in the brain" (ibid.), and argued that "We accept that ideas and comments expressed by different members [of a group] have the value of *unconscious interpretations*" (ibid.; italics in original).

Having moved beyond his earlier view of group communication in terms of a "network" (1948), he realised that the group matrix was more than a simple circuit of the communications of the members of it. Moreover, although clinically effective, understanding group communication as a "retransformation" of libidinal "energies into exchangeable value (cash as it were)" (ibid., p. 169) was of limited *theoretical* value. Its *ahistorical* character left the dynamics of the group without a symbolic memory function, and, thus, as unrelated to history and society as a whole. However, by conceiving it as the *common ground* of virtually *all* communications, past and present, the matrix became the locus and container of *collective memories* (Foulkes & Anthony, 1965, p. 265).[7]

Thinking about the group matrix as the "common shared ground" (1964, p. 292) of all communications in the group, Foulkes changed the core metaphor for the group matrix. A "social network" of (horizontal) communication (1948, p. 14) became the "*mother soil* in which all dynamic processes take place" (E. Foulkes, 1990, p. 212; italics ours). The concept of the matrix then developed into a four-dimensional entity with time as the fourth dimension. Therefore, the matrix became firmly *rooted* or *grounded* in both historical time and space, and in *interpersonal* and *transpersonal* space (Foulkes & Anthony, 1957, p. 243; 1965, pp. 258–259). In other words, the matrix became simultaneously both *social* and *mental* (E. Foulkes, 1990, p. 228).[8]

On cultural inheritance and/or transmission

In the 1960s, Foulkes took yet another important step regarding group analytic theory. Borrowing from Julian Huxley (cf. Foulkes, 1960, pp. 155–156), he claimed that "[C]*ultural* inheritance is seen as having superseded *biological* inheritance in the development of the human species" (ibid., p. 291). In 1954, Julian Huxley had stated that whereas "biological evolution depends on natural selection ... psychosocial or cultural evolution depends on cumulative tradition, which was made possible when mind and its products became capable of self-production and self-variation" (Huxley, 1957, pp. 44–45). According to what Huxley (1964) called an "evolutionary humanism", one of the "most important tasks of our time" was to facilitate "the development of a set of integrative, directive and transmissive mechanisms for human societies and for their continuity down the generations" (p. 122).

Foulkes (1960, p. 291) also emphasised the significance of the "concept of transmission", and envisaged a group analytic theory of "cultural inheritance" based on sociocultural transmission (cf. Foulkes & Anthony, 1965, p. 27). He wrote:

> The culture and values of a community are inescapably transferred to the growing infant by its individual father and mother as determined by their particular nation, class, religion and region. They are transmitted verbally or non-verbally, instinctively, and emotionally twenty four hours a day and night. Even the objects, movements, gestures, and accents are determined in this way by the representatives of the cultural group. (ibid.; italics ours).

In effect, there are ongoing processes of transmission that operate on conscious, preconscious, unconscious, and non-conscious levels, processes which we can also conceive as a continuing *dialogue* between the generations. Therefore, in any given group or group-like system not only do the group members resonate horizontally with each other in the matrix of the group, but they also resonate "down the generations" in the (potentially) infinite time-space of the socio-historical field. Moreover, these patterns of resonance are simultaneous. For Foulkes, the scope and means of their communication range from "objects, movements, gestures, and accents" to verbal language and thus include the full *semiotic* scale from preverbal signs to symbols.[9]

These theoretical and clinical advances of the 1960s not only validated Foulkes's "basic conviction" that "[T]he group is a more fundamental unit than the individual" (ibid., p. 235), but also confirmed his early intuition that "the community is represented in the treatment room" (ibid., p. 27). In other words, "the therapeutic analytic group" is a token community or a microcosm of it with access to the "social, interpersonal unconscious" (Foulkes, 1960, p. 296).

It must be acknowledged, however, that there are two important conceptual limitations in Foulkes's model of cultural inheritance or transmission. One is that it lacks *sociological* substance and complexity. Assuming that "the culture and values of a community" are transferred by the "individual" parents (Foulkes & Anthony, 1965, p. 27), Foulkes did not even mention other social agents and/or agencies involved in the process of socialisation, for example, kindergarten, schools, professional educationlet alone consider them as problematic (cf. LeRoy, 1994; Rouchy, 1990), The second limitation in the model is the neglect of the maternal other as the (first) representative of the sociocultural order, that is, as the Lacanian m(Other) (cf. Lacan, 1953) or the Winnicottian "environmental mother" (Winnicott, 1963b), although Foulkes made frequent references to the importance of pre-oedipal phenomena and the work of Klein.

The matrix reloaded[10]

The further elaboration of the concept of group matrix was connected with, if not based upon, the development of the group analytic model of sociocultural inheritance and transmission. What Foulkes had initially called the group's "common ground" (Foulkes & Anthony, 1965, p. 29) was not elaborated further until 1970, when, in his opening address to the First European Symposium on Group Analysis in Lisbon, he introduced the notion of the foundation matrix. He described it as a "pre-existing, relatively static part" of the general overall matrix (E. Foulkes, 1990, pp. 212–213) and/or "a firm pre-existing community or communion" (ibid., p. 212) (cf. Hopper & Weinberg, 2016; cf. Scholz, 2011, 2014). He wrote: "… even [a] group of total strangers, being of the same species and more narrowly of the same culture, share a fundamental mental matrix or a foundation matrix" (1975, p. 228).

He then explained that on top of this "part" of the matrix there are "various levels of communication which are increasingly dynamic", and, thus, which are called the "dynamic matrix" (E. Foulkes, 1990, pp. 212–213). Through their "… closer acquaintance and initial exchanges", they "… add consistently" to the foundation matrix, thus forming "… a current, ever moving, ever-developing dynamic matrix" (ibid.). The foundation matrix is the common ground and the "mother-soil" from which these more specific dynamic processes both develop and "take their place" (E. Foulkes, 1990, p. 212; cf. p. 228). In a nutshell, these sentences cover the formation of Foulkes's work since 1948!

In his Lisbon presentation, however, Foulkes emphasised that between the foundation and the dynamic matrices there are various "levels" of cultural inheritance or transmission which an observer might regard as "... either more biologically or more culturally [determined]" (ibid., p. 213). He stated that "certain complexes and values" are not so much "inborn" as "they are *transmitted* by very early experiences" (ibid.). In this statement Foulkes both alluded to and confirmed Huxley's view regarding the predominance of "cultural inheritance".[11] He also clarified his often-quoted statement that the foundation matrix is "based" not only on the properties of the species, but also on "... culturally firmly embedded values", and, by implication, on the structure of the society as a whole. Thus, the foundation matrix is connected not only to the collective unconscious, but also to the social unconscious.

In other words, the foundation matrix of any group or group-like social system is based on the structure of the species and the social organisation of the wider contextual society. However, Foulkes lacked satisfactory concepts for the former (the structure of the species) and for the latter (the social organisation of the wider contextual society) and, therefore, he used "foundation matrix" somewhat ambiguously, involving both species elements and societal elements, and in reference to the society as-a-whole as well as to the manifestations of it in its constituent groupings. Another source of ambiguity is that whereas the realm of the social relates to the "social unconscious", based on repression as well as denial, the realm of the biological does not pertain only to the "collective unconscious".[12] It is important to acknowledge the restraints of the non-conscious as well as the species based innately symbolic (Hopper & Weinberg, 2011).

The social unconscious in terms of the tripartite matrix

Eventually, Foulkes conceptualised the matrix of any group or group-like social system in terms of a tripartite structure involving the contextual foundation matrix of a particular society, the dynamic matrices of its constituent groupings, and what he came to call the "personal matrices" of the participants in a particular grouping in a particular contextual society. Although he had already differentiated the *dynamic* matrix from the *foundation* matrix (cf. E. Foulkes, 1990, pp. 212–213), and then anticipated the concept of the *personal* matrix in his paper "The Group as Matrix of the Individual's Mental Life" (ibid., p. 228), he did not actually introduce the concept of the personal matrix until his last book. He wrote: "Just as the individual's mind is a complex of interacting processes (personal matrix), mental processes interact in the concert of the group (group matrix)" (Foulkes, 1975, p. 130), "relating to each other in manifold ways and on a variety of different levels" (ibid., p. 130).

Despite the logic of this sequence, which can only be seen in retrospect, the concept of the personal matrix was inchoate. Nevertheless, from the few sentences he devoted to the subject, the personal matrix can be equated with "the workings of the ... mind of an individual person" (Powell, 1994, p. 13) based on "culturally embedded values and reactions" (Foulkes, 1975, p. 131). For Foulkes, as we have outlined, these values and reactions have been "*developed* and *transmitted*" in the process of socialisation, especially in the *nuclear family*, in the *social network*, *class*, etc., and have been *maintained* or *modified* by the *intimate plexus* in which the person now moves (ibid., p. 132, italics ours; cf. Foulkes & Anthony, 1984, p. 27). By conceptualising the mind of an individual person in terms of a personal matrix in the context of the collective mind of a grouping, characterised by a dynamic matrix, in the context of a society, characterised by a foundation matrix, Foulkes finally met the requirements of his own anticipations, namely, that the overall configuration of the matrix should be conceptualised in terms of multi-relational processes. From the Foulkesian group analytical point of view, the matrix of any group can be analysed in terms of patterns of relations, values and norms, verbal and non-verbal communication, styles of thinking and feeling, etc., depending on what is taken as problematic (Hopper & Weinberg, 2011, 2016).

Whereas the concept of the matrix is indeed the cornerstone of the theory of group analysis, the concept of the personal matrix is the capstone of the theory of the tripartite matrix as a whole, and, thus, of the group analytic edifice as a whole.[13] First of all, the concept of the personal matrix subverts the "strict subject-object juxtaposition" (Foulkes in Foulkes & Anthony, 1965, p. 23; cf. E. Foulkes, 1990, p. 152) of the ego and the world implied in classical, Cartesean philosophy (E. Foulkes, 1990, p. 152; cf. Mies, 2012, pp. 8–11), as well as the (ego-) psychoanalytical notion of the so-called "autonomous ego" proposed by Heinz Hartmann (cf. Hartmann, 1939; cf. Hartmann, Kris, & Loewenstein, 1946). Second, by conceiving the individual mind in terms of a multi-personal mental matrix, Foulkes implicitly also continued Cassirer's philosophical project to think in terms of *relational* rather than *substance*-related or "material" concepts (Cassirer, 1910; cf. Nitzgen, 2013). Third, the personal matrix serves as an essential link between the dynamic and the foundation matrix. By the "artificially created, strange but potentially very intimate group network in the 'T'-situation" (Foulkes, 1975, p. 132), *personal* matrices of the group members all feed into (and are modified by) the *dynamic* matrix of the group. Simultaneously and recursively the foundation matrix is activated, and, in turn, feeds into the dynamic matrix in a recursive, circular loop. Based on what can be called a "circular causality" (T. Fuchs, 2008) operating between all of its parts, the group matrix as a whole links time and space in such a way that the past can be re-presented in the present, and the present can be manifest simultaneously in several spaces.[14]

Finally, the model of the tripartite matrix implies a relocation of the social unconscious within the general theory of group analysis. The social unconscious can no longer be *located* in any *one* part of the group matrix. Instead, it has to be *located* in all of them (in much the same way that having dismissed the idea of the localisation of brain functions, Goldstein favoured the hypothesis that they were located in the functional brain as a whole). Furthermore, the parts of this tripartite matrix can "at no stage be separated from each other, except by *artificial isolation*" (Foulkes, 1948, p. 10). (In much the same way that having dismissed the "old juxtapositions" of an "inside world and an outside world, constitution and environment, individual and society, phantasy and reality, body and mind", he now, in the 1970s, dismissed the new conceptualisation of the tripartite matrix.)

This vision of a "supra-personal mental matrix" (E. Foulkes, 1990, p. 227) explodes any notion of a social unconscious as an agency located *within* the individual person. In fact, the social unconscious must be considered as a property of the tripartite matrix as a whole, that is, in terms of the fully combined—if not necessarily fully integrated and cohesive—personal, dynamic, and foundational matrices. This is why Foulkes finally gave up his "Freudian" conceptualisation of the social unconscious for a strictly group analytic one. In terms of his model of the sociocultural process of transmission operating on conscious, preconscious, unconscious, and non-conscious levels, the notion of the dynamic social unconscious is implicit, and, thus, preserved. Or in Hegel's terms "*aufgehoben*".

Clinical evidence of the restraints and constraints of the social unconscious

Foulkes rarely illustrated his work on the social unconscious with clinical vignettes of his own. However, he gave a detailed critique of the work of a colleague in supervision with him which serves this purpose. On the occasion of the International Congress of Group Psychotherapy in Zurich in 1957, Dr James Anthony had presented a case that fifty years later he (Anthony, 2010, p. 84) described as "a group of murderous mothers". These mothers were treated at the Maudsley Hospital as "a psychopathic and borderline group who at various times, consciously and frighteningly, had threatened to kill their children". About the presentation in Zurich, he wrote: "I felt for the first time Foulkes's criticism of me, stating publicly that he did not feel that I had fully understood the psychopathology of these women, that I had not taken into consideration the historical and Hitlerite era in which they had lived, and that ... I had not followed group-analytic lines" (ibid.).[15]

Actually, Foulkes (1960) published his critique in a paper, part of which was reprinted in 1964 in chapter XX of his book on *Therapeutic Group Analysis*, saying that although this group was carried out "entirely independently" by Dr Anthony, it was "connected" with his own unit in the Maudsley. He emphasised that although it "emerged from the group analytic approach" (1960, p. 259), and agreed that the mothers were of "a very disturbed personality development", he was not sure Dr Anthony moved in his work in the same direction as *my original interest* has been (ibid.). This interest was mainly stimulated by the fact that "these mothers had *conscious* death wishes, manifest murderous impulses towards their children" which were neither "repressed or disguised" nor expressed "merely by obsessional impulses" (ibid.; italics ours). Although Foulkes (ibid., p. 289) understood that for these mothers the group unconsciously represented "the inside of the mother, the womb", he also emphasised that "the emergence of such an orientation into open consciousness, as an ego-syntonic attitude, was an expression of the progressive demoralization of the whole of our culture since the advent of Hitler, Stalin, and under the impact of two World Wars and the murder of literally millions of innocent people" (ibid.; italics ours). For Foulkes, these social-historical facts challenged the conventional psychoanalytic knowledge that "the relationship of a mother to her child contains a greater or lesser degree of hostility and destructiveness, almost a *normal* ingredient which is usually ... ignored" (ibid.). Although Foulkes had *hoped* that a group of such mothers "would show much of the psychopathology of this particular syndrome" (ibid.), he was, to his disappointment, unaware that "Dr Anthony's work took ... this course" (ibid.). Although he and Dr Kreitmann (who treated a similar group; cf. Foulkes, 1960, p. 260) had arrived at a "diagnostic differential classification" of these types of mothers, subsuming them under "the better known obsessional and depressive type of disturbance" (ibid., p. 259), they had failed to provide "a more dynamic account of their observations" (ibid., p. 260).

By this critique Foulkes meant, we assume, that Anthony and Kreitmann should have taken into account the connection between the *psychic* facts of the murderous mothers and the *social-historical* facts of the "demoralization of the *whole of our culture*" (ibid., p. 259; cf. Snyder, 2010).[16] In terms of the concept of the social unconscious, this discussion of the case of the murderous mothers illustrates the emerging group analytic perspective that the internal representations of the body, that is, the unconscious body ego, develop in parallel with the internal representations of the mother–infant dyad in the context of the family in the context of the wider society, which includes the state itself. In parallel, but entirely and inevitably intertwined!

Notes on "social psychopathology"

During his time at Northfield, still thinking in terms of an organismic homology, Foulkes advanced the idea of a *"social psychopathology"* (Foulkes, 1960, p. 99; italics ours). He argued that the form of "man's neuroses and their treatment changes decisively in accordance with the community in which they arise" (ibid., p. 207; italics ours). This, he claimed, was *"experimentally* confirmed at Northfield" (ibid.; italics ours) because it could be observed "that the patient's mind, concerns, attitudes and even symptoms changed according to the dynamics of the hospital as a whole" (ibid.). In order to illustrate this, he referred to the hospital bandsmen who at a particular moment towards the end of the war were unable to play together (cf. 1948, pp. 127–128; 1960, pp. 211–214). According to Foulkes, "[T]he disturbances of this group were in a clear interaction with the larger group of the hospital" (1960, p. 213). The band's failure was only a *symptom* of a disturbance in Northfield as a whole. For Foulkes, this disturbance was connected to a particular conflict: "While *our idea* was to make them better for civilian life, *they* were afraid of showing any improvement for fear they might [be] retain[ed] in the army" (ibid.; italics ours).

According to the principles of this nascent *social* psychopathology, Foulkes maintained that "Every individual symptom, process, syndrome, even diagnostic category, is tested afresh in the light of the social situation" (ibid.). Such a "testing", he asserted, "will help us very greatly to *know better what we already know*, as well as *to make quite new observations* of equal importance" (ibid.; italics ours). Therefore, "[I]t will allow us to make important contributions to the theory and practice of both group and individual psychology" (ibid.). The idea of testing psychopathological hypotheses in a particular social situation helps to clarify that in Foulkes's view in their providing a mere "classification" of symptoms and character traits, Anthony and Kreitmann ignored the "social situation", namely the impact of the totalitarian regimes of Hitler and Stalin on this "syndrome". In contrast to this, a "social psychopathology" would have acknowledged and taken into consideration the close relationship between "Group Identity and Ego-Identity, Ego-Pathology and historical change" to which he (1948, p. 11) had referred in his first book. Methodologically, it would therefore be a "*comparative psychopathology*" (Foulkes, 1960, p. 297; italics ours) taking into account a variety of social-historical situations and the interdependence of conscious and unconscious social and psychic facts. Although Foulkes was able to elaborate a framework for this extensive and demanding project, he could not provide the clinical details for it. Nonetheless, he did provide us with a basic theoretically informed clinical principle: "The group analyst orients himself in the light of the total/socio-historical/situation and its context" (E. Foulkes, 1990, p. 181) which "determine the meaning and significance of all communications" (ibid., p. 260).

Notes

1. This does not mean that dialectical thinking was alien to Foulkes. Taken from Otto Fenichel, his psychoanalytic view of character was based on the dialectics of internal demands and external restraints (cf. Nitzgen, 2011, pp. 10–11). Also, Foulkes thought in terms of a dialectics of interpersonal relations and transpersonal processes (cf. Foulkes & Anthony, 1985, pp. 27–29).

2. Ormay (2012) has argued that this society ego or societal part of the ego is based on the "nos" which he conceptualised as a kind of social instinct rooted in the id and connected with the "social brain".
3. It would be misleading to reduce the meaning of *social relationships* to what today is referred to as *relational* and/or *interpersonal*. For Foulkes, these relationships encompass both the *interpersonal* and *transpersonal* relations between the subject and the *personal* as well as the *symbolic social O/other*.
4. These notions of open systems and mind were based on discussions with Hopper about groups as social systems which could be considered as ranging from close to open, the latter only seeming to be a contradiction in terms (Hopper, 1975).
5. It is noteworthy that whereas Winnicott and others who worked in the Independent tradition of psychoanalysis began to use the notion of the person, Foulkes was slow to do so.
6. Concerning the contribution of Elias (1939) see the discussion of the development of this point by Dalal (2011) and Lavie (2011).
7. This particular aspect was elaborated by Mies (2011) and Scholz (2011, 2014). For further discussion of the concept of collective memories, which are sometimes called "social memories", see Doron in this volume, and Weegmann in this volume.
8. This has been discussed in terms of a "social historical field" by Castoriadis (1988, p. 150). See also the Introduction to *The Social Unconscious in Persons, Groups, and Societies: Volume 2: Mainly Foundation Matrices* edited by Hopper and Weinberg (2016).
9. Accordingly, Mies has spoken of a "semiotic" turn in group analysis (2012, p. 15).
10. cf. Nitzgen (2010). In 2014 Scholz wrote of the "Foundation Matrix Reloaded".
11. This has been largely overlooked in group analytic literature (cf. Ormay, 2012).
12. Regarding their relation, the criticism of intersubjectivity offered by Castoriadis seems relevant: no conceivable "cooperation" or "communicative action" of individuals could ever create language. Language, through "learning on" biological properties of the human being, is "not a biological datum either, it is a fundamental institution" (Castoriadis, 1988, p. 144).
13. Among the first of our colleagues to use the term "tripartite matrix" was Martin Bhurruth (2008).

14. For discussions of equivalence, see Hopper, 2003b, p. 94, endnote 1; pp. 150–151; and Beck, 1990.
15. Anthony's group was also mentioned in Slavson's textbook on analytic group psychotherapy (1964). Discussing endogenic and induced forms of anxiety in groups, Slavson referred to the most prominent of the mothers in the group as an "obviously obsessionally psychotic woman" (p. 318).
16. It is noteworthy that this passage is the only one in his entire work in which Foulkes refers directly and explicitly to the millions of victims of the political crimes of the Shoah and the Stalinist regime (cf. Snyder, 2010).

References

Anthony, E. J. (1957). A group of murderous mothers. Proceedings of the Second International Congress on Group Psychotherapy (Zurich) (pp. 137–142). Basle, Switzerland: S. Karger, 1959.

Anthony, E. J. (2010). My psychoanalytic and group-analytic life with S. H. Foulkes. *Group Analysis, 43*(1): 81–85.

Beck, W. (1990). Equivalence in groups. *Group Analysis, 23*(3): 285–290.

Bhurruth, M. (2008). Matriculating the matrix. *Group Analysis, 41*(4): 352–365.

Cassirer, E. (1910). *Substance and Function and Einstein's Theory of Relativity*. W. C. Swabey & M. C. Swabey (Trans.). New York: Dover, 1953.

Castoriadis, C. (1988). *Philosophy, Politics, Autonomy*. D. A. Curtis (Ed). New York: Oxford University Press, 1991.

Dalal, F. (2011). The social unconscious and ideology: in clinical theory and practice. In: E. Hopper & H. Weinberg (Eds.), *The Social Unconscious in Persons, Groups and Societies: Volume 1: Mainly Theory* (pp. 243–264). London: Karnac.

Elias, N. (1939). *The Society of the Individuals*. Oxford: Blackwell, 1991.

Erikson, E. H. (1946). Ego development and historical change. In: *Psychoanalytic Study of the Child*, 2: 359–396.

Foulkes, E. (Ed.) (1990). *S. H. Foulkes, Selected Papers. Psychoanalysis and Group Analysis*. With a foreword by M. Pines. London: Karnac.

Foulkes (Fuchs), S. H. (1936). Zum Stand der heutigen Biologie. Dargestellt an Kurt Goldstein: der Aufbau des Organismus. *Imago, 22*: 210–241. [English version, Biology in the light of the work of Kurt Goldstein. In: E. Foulkes (Ed.), *S. H. Foulkes, Selected Papers* (pp. 39–56). London: Karnac, 1990.]

Foulkes (Fuchs), S. H. (1937). Über Introjektion. *Internationale Zeitschrift für Psychoanalytische Psychologie, ihre Grenzgebiete und Anwendungen XXII*: 420–446.

[English version, On Introjection. *International Journal of Psychoanalysis, 18*: 239–293. Reprinted in E. Foulkes (Ed.), *S. H. Foulkes, Selected Papers* (pp. 57–78). London: Karnac, 1990.]

Foulkes, S. H. (1943). Psycho-analysis and crime. *Canadian Bar Review, 22*: 22–61. [Reprinted in L. Radzinowicz & J. W. C. Turner (Eds.), *English Studies in Criminal Science, Pamphlet 7*, Department of Criminal Science, Faculty of Law, Cambridge: University of Cambridge, 1944. Abridged version in: E. Foulkes (Ed.), *S. H. Foulkes, Selected Papers* (pp. 119–126). London: Karnac, 1990.]

Foulkes, S. H. (1948). *Introduction to Group Analytic Psychotherapy*. London: Karnac, 1983.

Foulkes, S. H. (1950). Group therapy. Survey, orientation, classification. In: *Therapeutic Group Analysis* (pp. 47–54). London: Karnac, 1984.

Foulkes, S. H. (1960). Application of group concepts to the treatment of the individual in the group. In: B. Stokvis (Ed.), *Topical Problems of Psychotherapy, Vol. 2*, Basle, Switzerland: S. Karger.

Foulkes, S. H. (1964). *Therapeutic Group Analysis*. London: Karnac, 1984.

Foulkes, S. H. (1966). A Soviet view of group therapy: discussion of a paper by N. V. Ivanov. In: E. Foulkes (Ed.), *S. H. Foulkes, Selected Papers* (pp. 159–168). London: Karnac.

Foulkes, S. H. (1971). Access to unconscious processes in the group-analytic group. In: E. Foulkes (Ed.) *Selected Papers of S. H. Foulkes: Psychoanalysis and Group Analysis* (pp. 209–222). London: Karnac, 1990.

Foulkes, S. H. (1975). *Group-Analytic Psychotherapy—Methods and Principles*. London: Interface, Gordon & Breach. [Reprinted London: Karnac, 1986.]

Foulkes, S. H., & Anthony, E. J. (1957). *Group Psychotherapy. The Psychoanalytical Approach*. [Reprinted London: Karnac, 2014.]

Foulkes, S. H., & Anthony, E. J. (1965). *Group Psychotherapy. The Psychoanalytical Approach. Second edition*. [Reprinted London: Karnac, 1984.]

Foulkes, S. H., & Lewis, E. (1944). Group analysis. A study in the treatment of groups on group analytic lines. In: Foulkes, S. H., *Therapeutic Group Analysis* (pp. 20–37). London: Karnac.

Freud, S. (1915d). Repression. *S. E., 14*: 141 ff. London: Hogarth.

Freud, S. (1916–17). *Introductory Lectures on Psycho-Analysis. S. E., 15–16*. London: Hogarth.

Freud, S. (1923b). *The Ego and the Id. S. E., 19*: 1 ff. London: Hogarth.

Freud, S. (1933a). *New Introductory Lectures on Psycho-Analysis. S. E., 22*: 1 ff. London: Hogarth.

Freud, S. (1950a). A project for a scientific psychology. *S. E., 1*: 281–397. London: Hogarth.

Fuchs, T. (2008). Sind psychische Krankheitern Gehirnkrankheiten? In: Vogeley, K., Fuchs, T., & Heinze, M., *Psyche zwischen Natur und Kultur* (pp. 67–80). Berlin: Parodos.

Geroulanos, S., & Meyers, T. (2014). *Experimente im Individuum. Kurt Goldstein und die Frage des Organismus*. Berlin: August.

Goldstein, K. (1934). Der Aufbau des Organismus. Einführung in die Biologie unter besonderer Berücksichtigung der Erfahrungen am kranken Menschen. T. Hoffmann & F. W. Stahnisch (Eds.). Paderborn, Germany: Wilhelm Fink, 2014. [English version: The Organism: A Holistic Approach to Biology Derived from Pathological Data in Man. New York: American Book Company, 1939; new edition with a foreword by Oliver Sacks: New York: Zone Books, 1995.]

Harrington, A. (1996). *Reenchanted Science, Holism in German Culture from Wilhelm II to Hitler*. Princeton, NJ: Princeton University Press.

Hartmann, H. (1939). *Ego-Psychology and the Problem of Adaptation*. New York: International Universities Press, 1958.

Hartmann, H., Kris, E., & Loewenstein, R. M. (1946). Comments on the formation of psychic structure. *Psychoanalytic Study of the Child, 2*: 11–38.

Hopper, E. (1975). A sociological iew of large groups. In: L. Kreeger (Ed.), *The Large Group: Dynamics and Therapy*. London: Constable. [Reprinted in Hopper, E. (2003), *The Social Unconscious: Selected Papers*. London: Jessica Kingsley.]

Hopper, E. (2003a). *The Social Unconscious: Selected Papers*. London: Jessica Kingsley.

Hopper, E. (2003b). *Traumatic Experiences in the Unconscious Life of Groups. The Fourth Basic Assumption: Incohesion: Aggregation/Massification or (ba) I:A/M*. London: Jessica Kingsley.

Hopper, E., & Weinberg, H. (Eds.) (2011). *The Social Unconscious in Persons, Groups and Societies: Volume 1: Mainly Theory*. London: Karnac.

Hopper. E., & Weinberg, H. (Eds.) (2016). *The Social Unconscious in Persons, Groups and Societies: Volume 2: Mainly Foundation Matrices*. London: Karnac.

Huxley, J. (1957). Man's place and role in nature. In: *New Bottles for New Wine*. London: Chatto & Windus [Reprinted as *Knowledge, Morality, Destiny*. New York, 1960.]

Huxley, J. (1964). *Essays of a Humanist*. London: Chatto & Windus.

Lacan, J. (1953). The function and field of speech and language in psychoanalysis. In: *Écrits* (pp. 30–113). New York: W. W. Norton, 1977.

Laplanche, J. (1987). *New Foundations for Psychoanalysis*. London: Basil Blackwell.

Lavie, J. (2011). The lost roots of the theory of group analysis. In: E. Hopper & H. Weinberg (Eds.), *The Social Unconscious in Persons, Groups and Societies: Volume 1: Mainly Theory* (pp. 155–178). London: Karnac.

LeRoy, J. (1994). Group analysis and culture. In: D. Brown & L. Zinkin (Eds.), *The Psyche and the Social World*. London: Routledge.

Lewin, K. (1947). Frontiers in group dynamics: concepts, method and reality in social science: social equilibria and social change. *Human Relations, 1*: 5–41.

Lewin, K. (1951). *Field Theory and Social Science*. New York: Harper & Row.

Mies, T. (2011). Das kommunikative Unbewusste. Anmerkungen zum Verhältnis von Gruppeanalyse und Psychoanalyse anhand eines Fallbeispiels von Sigmund Freud und Theodore Reik. *Gruppenpsychotherapie und Gruppendynamik, 46*: 151–166.

Mies, T. (2012). Die Gruppenanalyse im interdisziplinären Dialog. Anmerkungen zur Geschichte und Aktualität des Matrix-Begriffs. *Gruppenanalyse, 22*(1): 4–25.

Nitzgen, D. (2008). The group analytic movement sixty years on: revisiting introduction to group analytic psychotherapy by S. H. Foulkes. *Group Analysis, 41*(4): 319–340.

Nitzgen, D. (2010). The matrix reloaded. Ernst Cassirer—Kurt Goldstein—S. H. Foulkes. *Psychosozial, 119*: 25–37.

Nitzgen, D. (2011). The concept of the social unconscious in the work of S. H. Foulkes. In: E. Hopper & H. Weinberg (Eds.), *The Social Unconscious in Persons, Groups and Societies: Volume 1: Mainly Theory* (pp. 3–22). London: Karnac.

Nitzgen, D. (2013). Symboltheoretische Perspektiven der Gruppenanalyse. *Psychososozial, 36*. Jg. Nr. 131, Heft 1: 19–42.

Nitzgen, D. (2015). Group psychotherapy: the psychoanalytical approach by S. H. Foulkes and E. J. Anthony. From the first to the second edition. *Group Analysis, 48*(2): 126–136.

Nitzgen, D., & Hoffmann, K. (2014). Aspekte der Freudianischen Emigration in England. Psychoanalysis and Crime von S. H. Foulkes. *Gruppenpsychotherapie und Gruppendynamik. Zeitschrift für Theorie und Praxis der Gruppenanalyse, 50*(2): 92–110.

Ormay, T. (2012). *The Social Nature of Persons: One Person Is No Person*. London: Karnac.

Powell, A. (1994). Towards a unifying concept of the group matrix. In: D. Brown & L. Zinkin (Eds.), *The Psyche and the Social World* (pp. 11–26). London: Routledge.

Rouchy, J. C. (1990). Identification and groups of belonging. *Group Analysis, 28*(2): 129–140.

Scholz, R. (2011). The foundation matrix and the social unconscious. In: E. Hopper & H. Weinberg (Eds.), *The Social Unconscious in Persons, Groups and Societies: Volume 1: Mainly Theory* (pp. 265–288). London: Karnac.

Scholz, R. (2014). (Foundation) matrix reloaded—some remarks on a useful concept and its pitfalls. *Group Analysis, 47*(3): 201–213.

Slavson, S. R. (1964). *A Textbook in Analytic Group Psychotherapy*. New York: International Universities Press, 1969.

Snyder, T. (2010). *Bloodlands. Europe between Hitler and Stalin*. London: Random House.

Winnicott, D. W. (1963b). Communicating and not communicating leading to a study of certain opposites. In: *The Maturational Processes and the Facilitating Environment* (pp. 179–192). New York: International Universities Press.

CHAPTER TWO

The fluid and the solid—or the dynamic and the static: some further thoughts about the conceptualisation of foundation matrices, processes of the social unconscious, and/or large group identities

Regine Scholz

It is a great pleasure for me to contribute to a volume, whose purpose it is to "work out" conceptualisations of the foundation matrix, the social unconscious, and large group identities. It is also an unexpected one, because I have sometimes felt a bit lonely, insisting on the value of these concepts, at the very least as useful fictions (Scholz, 2003).

In this chapter you will find an elaboration on the concept of foundation matrix, which originally was not much more than a layout: "Instead, I have accepted from the beginning that even a group of total strangers, being of the same species and more narrowly of the same culture, share a fundamental mental matrix (*foundation matrix*). To this their closer acquaintance and their intimate exchanges add consistently so that they also form a current, ever moving, ever developing *dynamic matrix*" (Foulkes, 1973 in E. Foulkes, 1990, p. 228; emphasis original). This outline is followed by a discussion of some arguments by group analytic colleagues against the notion of foundation matrix.

The next step is to scrutinise the fact that—after years of relative neglect—transpersonal concepts of foundation matrix, social unconscious, or large group identity have recently found some popularity. In my opinion they help us to understand and to deal with the conscious and unconscious processes on large scale levels that become visible in the accelerated changes connected to the process of globalisation.

As theories can also be understood as "spotlights" highlighting certain aspects and leaving out others, the three concepts—foundation matrix, social unconscious, large group identity—are discussed regarding their different range of influence. The point is made that the process character of the underlying phenomena becomes less and less visible corresponding with different tempos of change rates. Moreover if the communicational construction is definitely overlooked we end up with distinctly separate entities with no grades in between, a dichotomised world in black and white. This world reflects more the fears accelerated by globalisation processes than the existing and real interdependencies.

I will begin by summarising the main thesis of my chapter in the first volume of this series on the social unconscious (Scholz, 2011). In my view the foundation matrix considers individuals and groups as one single, inseparable process in which biological, social, cultural, and economic factors meet and merge. The foundation matrix includes all dimensions of communication—including the non-verbal, for example, facial expressions, gestures, postures, and mimetically transferred meanings. As there is sometimes a tendency to restrict communication to verbal modalities, I want to emphasise the body as communicative agent. The body is not merely biological, it is socially shaped and thus carries meaning. For example, a man in civilian clothes who once served in the military can be recognised as an ex-soldier long after he has left the military, because his posture and his movements convey some aspects of his mindset and values, which are "unconsciously" understood. The new discipline of cultural neurosciences studies how cultural experiences shape the neurological system (Losin, Dapretto, & Iacoboni, 2009). This leads us to understand the biology of the human body not only in terms of its basic biological make-up shared by the species, but also in terms of verbal and non-verbal communication as well as other aspects of society and culture (Foulkes, 1971).

Le Roy (1994), who did anthropological fieldwork in Zaire, was the first to elaborate on culture as a foundation matrix and the incorporation of cultural codes through primary and secondary groups in a society. As basic dimensions he mentioned the culturally specific forms of family groups, including gender relations and relations between the generations. These dimensions give a certain framework to describe simpler societies and their implicit power relations. To apply this model to more complex societies I included the whole social structure (Scholz, 2003) as the basis of the foundation matrix. In doing so history became visible (because social structures are clearly time bound) as did the power relations inherent in the foundation matrix. The concept thus carries a time dimension on all levels, in which even biology—elsewhere often considered as invariant—is flexible.

Though biology might be the slowest moving dimension, it moves not only with respect to the lifespan of a single person, but also with respect to group levels. For example, when Johann Sebastian Bach served as cantor of the St. Thomas Choir in Leipzig (1723–1750), the voices of the boys broke at the age of seventeen or eighteen years, whereas nowadays they break on average at fifteen years, which means that some boys must leave this world-famous boys' choir at eleven or twelve years of age (Spiegel, 2012). In other words, what we usually call "structure" is nothing but the process with a comparatively slow rate of change.

Some continuing arguments about the utility and validity of the concept of the foundation matrix

The different dimensions mentioned above are not separate, but more or less different perspectives concerning a more comprehensive process, one being the condition of the other and vice versa, existing in and through the other. This conceptualisation is one of Foulkes's main theoretical achievements. However, this view is not shared by all my colleagues who are interested in this subject, and it is worth summarising some aspects of various debates.

For example Weinberg (2006) follows Foulkes's mapping of the matrix—mentioning a personal, a dynamic, and a foundation matrix, the last being "based (not only) on the biological properties of the species, but also on the culturally firmly embedded values and reactions" (Foulkes, 1975a, p. 115). But then Weinberg nonetheless comments: "It seems that the foundation matrix is a biologically based web, connecting individuals from different cultures, and inside cultures" (2006, p. 23), which suggests that the different matrices are different layers rather than different parts or perspectives of an overall process. The author seems to think of biology and culture as two separate entities, when he complains about the confusion created by Foulkes in putting biology and culture together under the same umbrella. Weinberg writes that:

> ... biological characteristics seem to unite us all, making us look more similar and connecting people trans-culturally [simply because they have more in common biologically], [whereas] cultural aspects seem to divide people, pointing to the differences and hinting towards cultural-diversity [just because people from different cultures tend to focus more on their differences]. Compounding these two aspects in the same term is simply confusing. (ibid., p. 76)

In fact, it is Weinberg who seems to be confused, in that human biology is manifest only in its sociocultural forms from which it is not extractible. Again, in their introduction to Volume I, Hopper and Weinberg repeat this point of view when they compare the Jungian conceptualisation of the collective unconscious with the Foulkesian conceptualisation of the social unconscious (Hopper & Weinberg, 2011).

My insistence on the value of the concept of the foundation matrix and the importance of biology within it leads me also to dissent from some ideas of Farhad Dalal, Andrew Powell, and Ralph Stacey concerning the foundation matrix. Dalal dropped the concept of the foundation matrix completely (1998), having nothing to contribute to a post-Foulkesian group analytic theory. This verdict is based on Foulkes's (1971) various referrals to biology—for instance, when he speaks of "the relatively static and unalterable *genetic* foundation matrix" (my italics).

However, I see in Dalal's argument the old nature-nurture debate at work, in which we are reluctant to consider human biology as an integral part of a theory of the unconscious that is aware of its "sociality" at all levels. It was, for example, Norbert Elias who reminded us to pay attention to the body: "Sociologists are somewhat defensive towards biology, because they are afraid [that] sociology could dissolve into biology. However, in my opinion one cannot put up a theory—let's say on human action—without knowing about the structure of the body and how it works" (1990, p. 41, my translation).

Nowadays we know better that and how social contact develops and shapes our brains and our whole biological/physiological make-up (Gantt & Agazarian, 2011; Stern, 1985). From the very beginning our biology is social and vice versa. In fact, Hopper referred to the sociality of human nature, and, not without a shade of irony, to the "nature of hope" (Hopper, 2003).

Another problem is the idea that the foundation matrix is based on the "primordial" level of communication as seen in the contribution from Powell (1994). Although we should consider the relevance of the primordial level, Foulkes's concept of the primordial level of communication is too close to Jung's concept of archetypes and his theory of the collective unconscious. The Jungian collective unconscious is inherited by the species and consists of pre-existent forms, the archetypes, which can become conscious only secondarily (Jung, 1936, p. 43). For Jung the ubiquitous nature of these images proves their hereditary character. I would rather suggest that living in groups, equipped with the same biology and the innate necessity to communicate, humans develop very similar images. Although Foulkes did not develop a theory of symbols and symbolisations (Mies, 2013; Nitzgen, 2013), it is the human ability to symbolise that is heritable (Hopper & Weinberg, 2011; Scholz, 2004).

Another argument against using the concept of the foundation matrix is made by Stacey (2001) who claims that there is no need to postulate either a separate psychic or a separate social level. However, Foulkes did not argue in favour of a separate psychic structure. Perhaps Stacey had in mind the statement by Jung: "In contrary to the personal nature of the conscious psyche there is a second psychic system of collective non personal character besides our conscious mind ...." (1936, p. 45). Moreover, I cannot follow Stacey when he connects the *foundation matrix* to individualistic thinking: "Through the notion of the foundation matrix, Foulkes has brought the individual back to the central position because now mental processes interact in a way *determined* by instincts, predispositions and inner constellations and *decisively shaped* by early family life. This determination and decisive shaping clearly refers to the individual mind" (2001, p. 224). It is Stacey, not Foulkes, who has the implicit idea of the individual and the social as irreconcilable opposites, and the notion of the family as an institution outside the social universe. For Foulkes the mind of an individual is virtually, by definition, a social mind.

Actually, arguing against the value of the concept of foundation matrix is—directly or indirectly—an argument against C. G. Jung's theory of the "collective unconscious". Though from time to time Foulkes uses this term (e.g., 1948; 1968a, p. 182), there is yet no evidence that Foulkes shared the theoretical background of Jung. Foulkes seems to take up the term descriptively, perhaps echoing his collaboration with the Jungian analyst Eve Lewis, who was the co-conductor in his first groups (Foulkes & Lewis, 1944), before he went on to discuss social unconscious, interpersonal unconscious, and transpersonal processes (see Hopper & Nitzgen in this volume).

The use by Foulkes of "collective unconscious" might have come in through another—more hidden—line of thought. In the early 1930s, the sociologist Karl Mannheim already used the term "group analysis", and in a very natural way he also spoke of a collective unconscious in the late 1920s (1929). Mannheim was a sociologist of knowledge, seemingly more concerned with conscious than unconscious processes. He argued that a growing potential for conflicts is linked to the growing complexity and differentiation of societies. It results from the fact that complex societies consist of many subgroups which, because of their different social practices, no longer share a common understanding of the world—that is, who they are, where they come from, and where they are going. These interpretations and the inherent knowledge are distributed among and located in different groups and institutions, each with its unique perspectives on the world. These perspectives result from practical knowledge more than from reasoning, and, therefore, appear to be "natural": that is, unconscious. Its concealed social construction can only be seen from the outside by another group. To reach the optimum of consciousness at a given time it is necessary to bring members of different groups together revealing to each other their hidden aspirations and knowledge. Mannheim called this group analysis (1943, Chapter Five).

In claiming the "copyright" for the term *group analysis*, Foulkes wrote in 1946 that this chapter only recently had come to his notice (1946, p. 131). Even if so, nonetheless "something was in the air" and the fact that both lived and worked in the same context of pre-fascist Frankfurt, and both were connected through Norbert Elias suggests that there is likely more of a connection with Mannheim than Foulkes acknowledged.

I would hypothesise that group analysis was born in Great Britain, but conceived in the vibrant climate of post-World War I, pre-fascist Germany. It was felt that the individual was not to be understood outside his sociocultural-political context. This atmosphere also infected visitors from the United States such as Trigant Burrow, who also in the 1920s developed his own ideas on group analysis and the social nature of human beings when he came back from Europe (Pertegato & Pertegato, 2013; Sandner, 1998). Terms like social unconscious (Fromm, 1930, 1964) and collective unconscious were coined and used in various ways, sometimes without strict theoretical conceptualisation. In fact, with respect to the study of social systems, Foulkes's theoretical endeavour in working out what he meant by group analysis can be found instead in his notion of matrix.

In this concept of matrix, Foulkes understood the sociocultural communicative web as complementary to the neuronal web conceptualised by his teacher, Kurt Goldstein. The most famous definition he gave is: "The matrix is the hypothetical web of communication and relationship in a given group. It is the common shared ground which ultimately determines the meaning and significance of all events and upon which all communications and interpretation, verbal and non-verbal, rest" (1964, p. 292). Here we find individuals as part of an ongoing communicative process, creating the world of which they are products themselves at the same time. Thus challenging the boundaries between the inside and outside, the division between the realms of biology and the world of interactions, the matrix contains in essence an anti-Cartesian approach as already indicated by Foulkes and Anthony (1957) and elaborated by Thomas Mies (2012).

Some aspects of the recent interest in transpersonal concepts

In times of accelerated international integration of social and economic systems called globalisation—fuelled by modern telecommunication and transportation devices as well as by large scale voluntary and involuntary migration processes—ample opportunities and necessities for international contacts are provided. It is a time of big upheavals, characterised by breathtaking new opportunities which are often at the same time full of threats and violence—a fragile, unstable, and therefore frightening situation (Khanna, 2008). In this context, the idea of foundation matrix has belatedly found some popularity—along with closely related concepts such as "the social unconscious", and "large group identity", a term developed in the work of Vamik Volkan. It was Earl Hopper, who in 2001 simply stated: "… we need a concept like the 'social unconscious' in order to discuss social, cultural and communicational constraints and restraints" (p. 11). Vamik Volkan's focus is on the traumas that are inherent in the globalisation process because the shifts in the international and national balance of power are rarely peaceful. He claims that "large group psychology in its own right includes the necessity to find enemies and allies … often accompanied by excessive destructive acts" (2006, p. 17).

These terms—foundation matrix, collective unconscious, social unconscious, large group identity, etc., often are used synonymously, when discussing the characteristics, compatibilities, and antagonisms of different societies, cultures, and civilisations (Huntington, 1996). In fact, I consider this discourse to be potentially misleading, because we have an urgent need for concepts that might help us understand the extensive and deep lying social phenomena inherent in the globalisation process and its inherent traumata, ambiguities, and uncertainties which are rattling the "foundations" of traditional social identities of persons and their groupings of various kinds. Clearly, we have to look at larger contextual entities which connect as well as divide people, the restraints and constraints of which are largely unconscious: it is the notion of the unconscious that connects all three concepts—foundation matrix, social unconscious, and large group identity.

Foundation matrix

One might imagine the foundation matrix as three-dimensional, unfolding its current shape between persons in the two dimensions of space but having its roots in time. It can be visualised as a mainly "subterraneous" multi-stranded network or perhaps better as a "rhizome" (Deleuze & Guattari, 1977) that encompasses the whole of mankind. It is a living system, whose threads or veins/tubes are made of different materials (media), have different colours (qualities) and thicknesses (intensities) built up by communication and fuelled by emotions, based on needs and desires. You find not only "knots" (individuals, persons), but also areas of higher density, that is, more communicational exchange between persons, and also areas of lower density, some of which are only connected in a very loose manner. The areas of higher density might be considered as different types of groups: face-to-face groups, families, tribes, organisations, institutions, nations, religions, and cultures.

The foundation matrix as a living system is a pattern that generates patterns, some with a shorter lifespan, some existing longer, but all in permanent flux. Individuals die, group members withdraw or are excluded, groups of every size and quality gain and lose members, tribes disappear and/or come to form nations, empires rise and decline, cultures emerge, have their climax and their transformations, and sometimes they cease to exist, their members becoming part of other groups. But, despite these changes, there will always be a foundation matrix as long as mankind exists. Cultures as part of the foundation matrix are characterised as slow-moving, uneven, and indefinite, open processes, and not as fixed, unchangeable, and impermeable entities marking the fundamental other. Foundation matrix is a concept that can contain a large number of changes of different speeds.

To illustrate, I would like to pick up and outline the metaphor of "commuting trains" that Claudio Neri (1998) used to describe the transfer between individuals and group. One might say that there are vehicles of different speeds and qualities—some travel by bicycle, some by horse, by car or by different types of trains, some by boat or by ship, and some by helicopter or by plane. Some vehicles can transport more people than others and the "ground" on which they travel—earth, water, and air—is constantly moving itself. But the slower the alterations, the more is it likely that its process character and thus its time dependency will be overlooked. Relatively stable entities are treated as if they were fixed objects and eternal in duration. Concerning the world of planets, this attitude leads to the erroneous assumption that the earth should be a disk.

The concepts of the foundation matrix, social unconscious, and large group identity could all be understood in terms of a continuum from the fluid to the solid: foundation matrix clearly emphasising a process character and then the concepts gradually turning to phenomena that are considered to be more stable.

Social unconscious

Though I usually avoid using the term "social unconscious" (see Scholz, 2011, p. 282), I plead for integrating the concept of a "social unconscious" into the notion of foundation matrix. Social unconscious here is understood as matters and operations that are actively and definitely excluded from large scale group communication and thus from becoming conscious to its members. Excluded from discourse and negotiation, they tend to be static or even untouchable, though nonetheless they are still embedded in the overall processes of the foundation matrix.

It has to be said that this is not the prevalent notion of the social unconscious. More widely shared are ideas as formulated by Weinberg in an early version of his thinking on the subject: "The social unconscious is the co-constructed shared unconscious of members of a certain social system as community, society, nation or culture. It includes shared anxieties, fantasies, defences, myths, and memories. Its building bricks are made of chosen traumas and chosen glories …" (2006, p. 99). He later differentiates the social unconscious from the superego, the social in the unconscious, the collective unconscious, and hidden social norms (ibid., pp. 99 ff.). Here Weinberg clearly postulated a special psychic layer as "the social unconscious" for all members of a given group, which implies that he also postulated the existence of "non-social" psychic structures. This way of thinking is somewhat distant from the Foulkesian notion that "We sometimes talk of group and individual separately … what is in fact one single and inseparable process" (1975b, p. 252). However, it is possible that Weinberg really meant that what the members of a particular grouping have in common is their very personal internalisation of certain social patterns and processes during a particular period of time.

In fact Foulkes himself contributed to these different positions in the group analytic community by using the term "social unconscious" a few times and then in a more descriptive way (similar to his use of the term "collective unconscious"), as in saying: "This reduced censorship … enables us to approach what might be called the social unconscious, i.e., such social relationships as are not usually revealed or are not even conscious" (Foulkes & Anthony, 1957[1], p. 56). Such quotations may be an indirect reflection of the time when he was together with Erich Fromm in the Frankfurt Psychoanalytic Institute (Foulkes, 1968b). However, beyond one or another quotation, basically group analysis lacks a theory of the boundaries of groups as open systems (Hopper, 1975) and how a given group and being a member is represented consciously and unconsciously in the minds of its members. Perhaps one might say that the term "social unconscious" reflects the more stable elements of the global foundation matrix.

Large group identity

The third concept relevant in this context is that of *"large group identity"*. It is inseparably linked to the work of Vamik Volkan (2001).

Volkan calls every historically grown social organisation consisting of a not specified large number of people a large group (deviating from the group analytic use of the term (see Schneider & Weinberg, 2003)). Thus he can look at ethnic or religious groups and/or nations with the same instruments. What he is interested in is the psychic representation of belonging to these entities: "Large-group (ethnic, national, religious) identity is ... the subjective experience of thousands of millions of people who are linked by a persistent sense of sameness while also sharing numerous characteristics with others in foreign groups. The main task that members of a large group share is to maintain, protect, and repair their large group identity" (Volkan, 2001, p. 79). This wording clearly echoes the famous definition of an individual's identity by Erik H. Erikson, describing it as a sustained feeling of inner sameness with oneself (1946). Volkan then connects a "core identity"—that part of individual identity which cannot be transformed easily, that part which is fragmented in psychosis, whose loss means psychological death to large group identity—in saying "... an individual's large group identity is intimately connected to his or her personal core identity" (2004, p. 33). Here we have a very special version of the idea of the social going to the core.

Before going deeper into this matter, I would like to refer to some elements of the discussion of Erikson's thinking. Erikson connected the feeling of personal identity with his stage model of personal development. Identity formation (i.e., integrating earlier identity-elements into one ego identity), becomes the task of adolescence. It is seen as the aim of a successful developmental process (Erikson, 1950). This model is linear, step by step upwards. Elements not contributing to this development retrospectively are seen as failure, are omitted or even labelled psychopathological. People who usually validate our identities fail to appear; they do not become visible as partners in the process of creating and negotiating identities. In its original version the concept of identity is that of a closed system. It has firm boundaries and inside it is cleaned from all trials and detours by repression and denial of all elements that contradict the (idealised) self-image (Luther, 1992). However, Erikson indirectly brought to our attention the fragility of identity processes. His heritage was very fruitful, eventually leading to a notion of identity as a more open system and a result a lifelong process of (hard) work integrating various and conflicting elements in negotiation with others (Keupp, 1999). Some authors go further and consider a coherent (Pines, 1998) personal identity more or less as a healthy illusion (Bromberg, 1996; Watkins & Watkins, 1997).

There were various attempts to develop Erikson's ideas further. For a deeper integration of these concepts into group analytic thinking a clearer understanding of the individualising forces in groups and societies would be a prerequisite. The challenge is to conceptualise large social entities with a multiplicity of actors. Volkan struggles with the problem already inherent in the Eriksonian idea: how to postulate more or less clear boundaries, with some homogeneity/sameness inside and all the rest outside (the group). Volkan translates this into the field of large groups by postulating that the group members share basically the same psychic construction which discriminates them from members of other large groups, who on their side are interconnected in a similar way. There is no significant overlap on any core dimensions which become visible under threat.

In a way this psychological construction fits what Benedict Anderson (1983) described in terms of how nations "invent" their own people by naturalising the bonds between the members *as if* they were tribal, fantasising some kind of ethnic homogeneity. Nations can then be perceived as distinctly different from each other. The processes described by Anderson are anything but intentional or cognitive, they are deeply emotional and widely unconscious—a fact overlooked by Gregory Lobo's (2014) criticism of Anderson's concept—and can only be seen from a historic point where the nation is no longer the unchallenged "natural" home for people, though the time of the nation state does not seem to be completely over.

These ideas in the German philosophical tradition echo the late eighteenth century's ideas of Johann Gottfried Herder (1784–85), who understood nations and national cultures like balls or spheres: single and separate, discrete—closed systems with minimal points of touch to other spheres (see Herder in Bollacher et al. (eds.), 1989). In Herder's thinking the different nations and cultures were equal in right and value. There was no idea of hierarchy or supremacy: not yet. It was a philosophy that perfectly served the needs of rising nation states at the end of the eighteenth century and the beginning of the nineteenth.

What connects Herder's work to that of Vamik Volkan's "psychological" idea of large group identity is the notion that the system has a clear, perhaps even fixed boundary, and that differences within the system can be neglected at times. In fact, Volkan's concept is a modern psychoanalytical version of Herder's theory—and echoes Wilhelm Wundt's (1912) folk psychology. Nonetheless, there is one major and decisive difference, which is also due to the completely different historical situations. Whereas Herder is rather optimistic, claiming equal rights for all nations, Volkan's main concern is societal regression. All his endeavours to describe the qualities of large group identity (1999, 2004) serve just one purpose: to contribute to the understanding of regressive processes in large groups. As indicated by the title of his last book *Enemies on the Couch* (2013), for Volkan these phenomena of idealising one's own group and—if under threat—denigrating or even creating the enemies of it, are actually conceptualised as pathological processes.

In Freudian thinking the concept of regression is embedded in instinct theory, describing the healthy as well as the neurotic development connected to somatic maturation processes and the unfolding and differentiation of instinctive life. For obvious reasons such a theory, which clearly refers to *one* body, cannot easily be translated into large group psychology because we lack a comparable model for the rise and decline of societies (Hopper & Weinberg, 2011; Scholz, 2006, 2011).

However, on a descriptive level the large group's regression can very well be outlined (Volkan, 2004, pp. 60–61). Rather primitive psychic mechanisms prevail: introjections, projections, splitting between us and them, and mild (cleansing a language) or cruel ("ethnic cleansing", killing of traitors) purification acts gain ground. Originating from real or imagined collective trauma, the large group is formed and closes the boundaries, there is a clear division between "us" and "them", no deviation or differentiation is allowed, and revenge becomes more important than solving or regulating problems.

In a different way, but aiming at similar processes, Earl Hopper developed his theory of the fourth basic assumption: in cases of trauma and the accompanying annihilation fear, groups and group-like social systems lose their previous cohesion, become incohesive either in form of aggregates or masses, as in scapegoating, sexualisation of aggression, and in the end encapsulation and bureaucratic processes dominate the scene (Hopper, 2003). Hopper, who originally trained as a sociologist, clearly distinguishes between regressed and non-regressed social systems, and marks the transition between both. He has a clear understanding of different types of groups instead. Hopper insists that groups are social systems, but that not every social system is a group, and he informs us that by definition no social system can be completely open nor can it be completely closed (1975). He also argues that under certain conditions—social trauma—societies can become like large groups in a group analytic sense, that is, these entities lose their organisational structure.

Thinking in terms of distinctly closed psychosocial systems nevertheless is at the bottom of Vamik Volkan's approach to systems/entities that are the products of regression or are on the edge of regression. Part of the regressive move is the fantasised closure of boundaries of the group—a sharp distinction between us and them—and the postulation of a hierarchy of nations/cultures with one's own large group at the top—"Deutschland über Alles"; "les francais d'abord". If trauma is added, the situation can be fuelled with hatred and feelings of entitlement towards revenge in order to (re)gain the "deserved" place.

For the ideologies that are always connected to these emotional constellations, James Wertsch's (2011) idea of templates of trauma narratives seems helpful. Such templates foster the integration of what is otherwise very different traumatic material. For an example, Wertsch describes the Russian template of the peaceful Russian people, who without any reason are being attacked and nearly overwhelmed by vicious forces from the West, finally overcoming this threat by heroic fights. This template is able to "host" so disparate events as the different invasions from Karl XII, through Napoleon, to Hitler, but also to classify the Marxist ideology and thus Stalinism as Western attacks on the Russian people and culture. The benefit of Wertsch's theory is that it does not depend on just one chosen trauma; on the other hand it lacks the connection to the intense archaic emotions that are at the core of Volkan's thinking.

Volkan's whole work can be understood as a constant attempt to identify these destructive forces and processes—seen in purification and cleansing as elements of homogenisation and weakening the moral standards of the large groups—thus developing models and procedures to prevent the worst. Similar intentions seem to be in the background of the recent interest in the social unconscious of different large groups—again using the concept of social unconscious as nearly synonymous with large group identity or foundation matrix.

Summary

There have been several recent attempts to apply the group analytic concept of foundation matrix to national, ethnic, cultural, and/or religious entities. To me these worthwhile attempts must be made with great caution. If we are not precise in our wording and thinking—if we leave the communicational ground of ever-moving, intertwined, and overlapping processes with *multiple* actors in favour of distinct entities with clear boundaries—we are not so far from the new right-wing thinking, in which "culture" replaces "race".

These thinkers give themselves an anti-racist posture, and claim the right to be different. New right-wing thinking makes broad use of anti-capitalist and anti-imperialist criticism and arguments. It is a fine blend of right and left-wing theoretical concepts, but it nevertheless ends up with the idea of distinct different groups and groupings which "cannot" and "should not" be intermingled. The currently relevant concept in this context is that of "ethno-pluralism", a term created by Henning Eichberg (2004), a German sociologist living and teaching in Denmark. The practical consequence is to advocate for a "semantic and mental cleansing", that is, for "the natural and everywhere understandable return of the immigrants to the land of their forefathers" (Krebs, without year). For Krebs this means to bring into fruition "real tolerance and humanity". From a different angle it could be seen as "purification", where the "not-us" are endangered, to be wiped out as dirt: for instance, Anders Breivik (the Norwegian who in 2011 massacred dozens of activist young people, whom he considered to be traitors and therefore even worse than the immigrants) with his idea of a pure Norwegian nation; and before that in the Nineties the so called "ethnic cleansings" in former Yugoslavia tell us a lot about the destructive forces that in this context can be unleashed by irresponsible political leaders. The ideologies behind these atrocities appear to me as a late, but definitely no longer innocent version of Herder's spheres.

I am concerned that our concepts could be used to describe the psychological side of these "spheres", postulating distinct "unconsciousnesses" for each sphere: nation, culture, etc. It is an enormous task to work out the dialectics between the multiple actors—individuals, groups, and subgroups—of these larger entities and the wholes at a given moment and its changes: the task being to think the fluid and the solid at the same time. If we fail in that respect we might unwillingly deliver arguments for causes and concepts that we do not support or even deeply oppose. Nowadays only very few people would articulate as grossly as Jung (1934) did, when he wrote: "The Aryan unconscious has a higher potential than the Jewish."

What remains is the question: why do these deeply inhuman ideologies gain ground again in contemporary times? I would argue that the background is the same one that inspires us to look for concepts that can incorporate the large scale transpersonal processes: the context of globalisation. Rapid changes, the demands to "invent" ourselves anew on personal as well as on collective levels in rather unclear and confusing situations, the violence inherent in these social upheavals—all this creates many tensions, fear, and rage, as well as a longing for clarity. These emotions, if not contained, lead to (over) simplifications, to dichotomised and polarised thinking that seemingly offers security. This mentality knows nothing but black and white; and no grey, no ambiguities. In our field such thinking pushes towards forced distinctions between sociology and psychology, opposing individual and group interventions.

The theoretical consequence is that we have to think more precisely. What does it means that large groups are composed of millions of individuals and their—formal and informal, face-to-face and institutionalised, conscious and unconscious—interconnections? In my opinion, the concept of foundation matrix is a sound base to work on this problem, whereas the idea of spheres or balls in fact doesn't very well mirror the reality of a globalised world where the composition of and sizes of groups and the membership of nations change more quickly than ever. Moreover, the notion of foundation matrix is able to integrate not only these changes but also relatively new phenomena like the fact that meanwhile an estimated 220 million people live in countries not their own, many of them no longer to be identified with a clear national/ethnic/cultural affiliation (Iyer, 2013), whose identities probably are better described by the concept of hybrid identity (Rutherford & Bhabha, 1990). In Bhabha's thinking, culture and identity are considered as unfinished and uneven productions of meaning and value. He makes ambiguities and spaces "in between" the focus of interest, not as a deviation, but as a realm where new possibilities emerge. I would insist that this attitude corresponds very closely with the basic values of group analysis, with the theoretical potential of the concept of foundation matrix to embrace the fluid as well as the solid, and with the demands that the modern world imposes on us of finding new equilibriums while dealing with ambiguities and uncertainties.

Note

1. NB: the second edition of 1965—reprinted in 1984—differs in significant ways from the first edition of 1957, which has been the subject of frequent comments and discussions in the general group analytic literature.

References

Anderson, B. (1983). *Imagined Communities—Reflections on the Origin and Spread of Nationalism*. London: Verso Editions.

Bromberg, P. (1996). Standing in the spaces: the multiplicity of self and the psychoanalytic relationship. *Contemporary Psychoanalysis, 32*: 509–535.

Dalal, F. (1998). *Taking the Group Seriously*. London: Jessica Kingsley.

Deleuze, G., & Guattari, F. (1977). *Rhizom*. Berlin: Merve.

Eichberg, H. (2004). *The People of Democracy. Understanding Self-Determination on the Basis of Body and Movement*. Aarhus, Denmark: Klim.

Elias, N. (1990). *Norbert Elias über sich selbst*. Frankfurt, Germany: Suhrkamp.

Erdheim, M. (1982). Die gesellschaftliche Produktion von Unbewusstheit. Eine Einführung in den ethnopsychoanalytischen Prozess. Frankfurt, Germany: Suhrkamp.

Erikson, E. H. (1946). Ego development and historical change—clinical notes. *Psychoanalytic Study of the Child, 2*: 359–396.

Erikson, E. H. (1950). *Childhood and Society*. New York: W. W. Norton, 1993. Foulkes, S. H (1946). On group analysis. In: E. Foulkes (Ed.), *S. H. Foulkes. Selected Papers* (pp. 127–136). London: Karnac.

Foulkes, S. H. (1948). *Introduction to Group Analytic Psychotherapy*. London: Karnac, 1983.

Foulkes, S. H. (1964). *Therapeutic Group Analysis*. London: Allen and Unwin.

Foulkes, S. H. (1968a). Group dynamic processes and group analysis. In: E. Foulkes (Ed.), *S. H. Foulkes. Selected Papers* (pp. 175–186). London: Karnac.

Foulkes, S. H. (1968b). Some autobiographical notes. *Group Analysis, 1*(2): 117–122.

Foulkes, S. H. (1971). Access to unconscious processes in the group-analytic group. In: E. Foulkes (Ed.), *S. H. Foulkes. Selected Papers* (pp. 209–221). London: Karnac.

Foulkes, S. H. (1973). The group as matrix of the individual's mental life. In: E. Foulkes (Ed.), *S. H. Foulkes. Selected Papers* (pp. 223–233). London: Karnac.

Foulkes, S. H. (1975a). *Group-Analytic Psychotherapy*. London: Gordon Breach.

Foulkes, S. H. (1975b). Problems of the large group. In: E. Foulkes (Ed.), *S. H. Foulkes. Selected Papers* (pp. 249–269). London: Karnac.

Foulkes, S. H., & Anthony, E. J. (1957). *Group Psychotherapy—The Psychoanalytical Approach. Second edition*. London: Karnac, 1984.

Foulkes, S. H., & Lewis, E. (1944). Group analysis. Studies in the treatment of groups on psycho-analytical lines. *British Journal of Medical Psychology, 20*: 175–184.

Fromm, E. (1930). *The Working Class in Weimar Germany: A Psychological & Sociological Approach*. Cambridge, MA: Harvard University Press, 1984.

Fromm, E. (1964). Die Seele des Menschen—Ihre Fähigkeit zum Guten und zum Bösen. In: GA, Bd. II: 159–268.

Gantt, S., & Agazarian, Y. (2011). The group mind, systems-centred functional sub-grouping, and interpersonal neurobiology. In: E. Hopper & H. Weinberg (Eds.), *The Social Unconscious in Persons, Groups and Societies: Volume 1: Mainly Theory*. London: Karnac.

Herder, J. G. (1784–85). Ideen zur Philosophie der Geschichte der Menschheit. In: M. Bollacher, U. Geier, H.D. Irmscher, R. Smend, G.E. Grimm. J. Brummack, Ch. Bultmann, T. Zippert, R. Wisbert, G. Arnold (Eds.), *Werke in 10 Bänden, Bd. 6*. Frankfurt, Germany: Deutscher Klassiker Verlag.

Hopper, E. (1975). A sociological view of large groups. In: L. Kreeger (Ed.), *The Large Group: Dynamics and Therapy*. London: Constable. [Reprinted London: Karnac, 1994, and in E. Hopper (2003), *The Social Unconscious: Selected Papers*. London: Jessica Kingsley.]

Hopper, E. (2001). The social unconscious: theoretical considerations. *Group Analysis, 34*(1): 9–27.

Hopper, E. (2003). *Traumatic Experience in the Unconscious Life of Groups—The Fourth Basic Assumption: Incohesion: Aggregation/Massification or (ba) I:A/M.*London: Jessica Kingsley.

Hopper, E., & Weinberg, H. (Eds.) (2011). *The Social Unconscious in Persons, Groups and Societies: Volume 1: Mainly Theory*. London: Karnac.

Huntington, S. (1996). *The Clash of Civilizations and the Remaking of World Order*. New York: Simon & Schuster.

Iyer, P. (2013). Where is home? http://t.co/ZgjuYcs75G, accessed October 2013.

Jung, C. G. (1934). Zur gegenwärtigen Lage der Psychotherapie. In: *Zentralblatt für Psychotherapie. Gesammelte Werke, Bd. 10*. Patmos-Walter-Verlag Dusseldorf 1974.

Jung, C. G. (1936). The archetypes and the collective unconscious. In: *Collected Works Vol. 9a*. London: Routledge and Kegan Paul 1971.

Keupp, H. (1999). *Identitätskonstruktionen—Das Patchwork der Identitäten in der Spätmoderne*. Reinbek, Germany: Rowohlt.

Khanna, P. (2008). *The Second World. Empires and Influence in the Global Order*. New York: Random House.

Krebs, P. (without year). Wofür wir kämpfen. http://www.thule-seminar.org/wofuer_1.htm, accessed October 2013.

Le Roy, J. (1994). Group analysis and culture. In: D. Brown, D. & L. Zinkin (Eds.), *The Psyche and the Social World* (pp. 180–201). London: Routledge.

Lobo, G. (2014). Spectacular nationism in Colombia: making war make sense. Library of Social Science. http;//www.libraryofsocialscience.com/publishers/titles/nationalism-war-and-sacrifice/index.html, accessed October 2014.

Losin, E. A., Dapretto, M., & Iacoboni, M. (2009). Culture in the mind's mirror: how anthropology and neuroscience can inform a model of the neural substrate for cultural imaginative learning. *Progress in Brain Research, 178*: 175–190.

Luther, H. (1992). Identität und Fragment. In: *Religion und Alltag—Bausteine zu einer praktischen Theologie des Subjekts* (pp. 160–182). Stuttgart, Germany: Radius.

Mannheim, K. (1929). *Ideologie und Utopie*. Bonn, Germany: Friedrich Cohen. [English version, *Ideology and Utopia*. London: Routledge, 1936.]

Mannheim, K. (1943). *Diagnosis of Our Time*. London: Kegan Paul, Trench, Trubner & Co.

Mies, T. (2012). Die Gruppenanalyse im interdisziplinären Dialog. *Gruppenanalyse, 1*(12): 4–25.

Mies, T. (2013). Die Symboltheorie von Norbert Elias—Ein Paradigma für die Theorie der Gruppenanalyse? *Arbeitshefte Gruppenanalyse, Psychosozial, 131*: 63–84.

Neri, C. (1998). *Group*. London: Jessica Kingsley.

Nitzgen, D. (2013). Symboltheoretische Perspektiven der Gruppenanalyse. *Arbeitshefte Gruppenanalyse, Psychosozial, 131*: 19–42.

Pertegato, E. G., & Pertegato, G. O. (Eds.) (2013). *From Psychoanalysis to Group Analysis: The Pioneering Work of Trigant Burrow*. London: Karnac.

Pines, M. (1998). *Circular Reflections: Selected Papers on Group Analysis and Psychoanalysis*. London: Jessica Kingsley.

Powell, A. (1994). Towards an unifying concept of the group matrix. In: D. Brown & L. Zinkin (Eds.), *The Psyche and the Social World* (pp. 11–26). London: Routledge.

Rutherford, J., & Bhabha, H. (1990). The third space. Interview with Homi Bhabha. In: J. Rutherford (Ed.), *Identity. Community, Culture, Difference* (pp. 207–221). London: Lawrence & Wishart.

Sandner, D. (1998). Die Begründung der Gruppenanalyse durch Trigant Burrow. *Luzifer-Amor, 21*: 7–29.

Schneider, S., & Weinberg, H. (Eds.) (2003). *The Large Group Revisited*. London: Jessica Kingsley.

Scholz, R. (2003). The foundation Matrix: a useful fiction. *Group Analysis, 36*(4): 548–554.

Scholz, R. (2004). Das Unbewusste kennt keine Zeit! Das Unbewusste kennt keine Zeit? *Gruppenanalyse, 2*(4): 147–154.

Scholz, R. (2006). Das Thema der Gruppenphasen in der gruppenanalytischen Diskussion. In: R. Heinzel & C. Seidler (Eds.), *Gruppenprozess zwischen Struktur und Chaos—Die Gruppe in Klinik und Praxis, Vol. 2* (pp. 33–46). Opladen, Germany: Barbara Budrich.

Scholz, R. (2011). The foundation matrix and the social unconscious. In: E. Hopper & H. Weinberg (Eds.), *The Social Unconscious in Persons, Groups and Societies: Volume 1: Mainly Theory* (pp. 265–285). London: Karnac.

Spiegel online 22.04.2012: Countdown für die Chorkarriere. http://www.spiegel.de/karriere/stimmbruch-spezialist-countdown-fuer-die-chorkarriere-a-828845.html, accessed April 23, 2012.

Stacey, R. (2001). What can it mean to say that the individual is social through and through? *Group Analysis, 34*(4): 457–471.

Stern, D. N. (1985). *The Interpersonal World of the Infant. A View from Psychoanalysis and Developmental Psychology*. New York: Basic Books.

Volkan, V. (1999). *Das Versagen der Diplomatie*. Giessen, Germany: Psychosozial.

Volkan, V. (2001). Transgenerational transmissions and chosen traumas: an aspect of large-group identity. *Group Analysis, 34*(1): 79–97.

Volkan, V. (2004). *Blind Trust: Large Groups and Their Leaders in Times of Crises and Terror*. Charlottesville, VA: Pitchstone.

Volkan, V. (2006). *Killing in the Name of Identity: A Study of Bloody Conflicts*. Charlottesville, VA: Pitchstone.

Volkan, V. (2013). *Enemies on the Couch*. Durham, NC: Pitchstone.

Watkins, J. G., & Watkins, H. (1997). *Ego States. Theory and Therapy*. New York: W. W. Norton.

Weinberg, H. (2006). Group analysis, large groups and the internet unconscious. PhD Thesis. http://www.group-psychotherapy.com/articles/weinbergh02.htm.

Wertsch, J. V. (2011). Grundlegende Codes und kollektives Gedächtnis. (Underlying codes and collective memory.) *Gruppenpsychotherapie und Gruppendynamik, 47*: 310–326.

Wundt, W. (1912). *Elemente der Völkerpsychologie*. Leipzig, Germany: Kröner. [English version, *Elements of Folk Psychology—Outlines of a Psychological History of the Development of Mankind*. E. L. Schaub (Trans.). London: George Allen & Unwin.

CHAPTER THREE

The national habitus: steps towards reintegrating sociology and group analysis

Gad Yair

> In addition to the constitutional and institutional foundations of the state and its political economy, the nation state has a psychosocial foundation—a "national habitus". The concepts of *homo nationis* and national habitus underscore that modern individuals are historical individuals, in that they have personality structures that are unlike those of individuals in other historical epochs, and that they should be explicitly conceptualised as such, rather than as a trans-historical *homo economicus* or *homo sociologicus*.
>
> (Pickel, 2004)

Just about a century ago, sociologists, anthropologists, and psychologists profitably shared worldviews, read each other's work, and cited across disciplinary divides (Fromm, 1963). Durkheim and Freud, indeed, shared common understandings of unconscious elements and sought analytic ways to tie them to social practices and cultural values (Durkheim, 1951; Freud, 1930a). In the heyday of Parsonian sociology, Freudian psychological elements proved crucial in the functionalist hierarchical model of society (Parsons, 1964)—integrating the success of the schools of "culture and personality" and studies of "national character" (Benedict, 1947; DeVos, 1968; Martindale, 1967; Mead, 1965). However, a short while into the 1960s, the theoretical connections between psychology, anthropology, and sociology were severed. E. Adamson Hoebel, president of the American Anthropological Association declared in 1967 that "In the brief span of less than two decades, anthropological involvement in the systematic study of national character has waxed to a high pitch of enthusiasm and waned to a tiny ripple of continuing interest". Spiro had a similar portrayal regarding the scientific path of the idea of "national character", saying that "[H]aving succeeded in legitimizing the use of personality concepts by anthropology, it might be argued that [national character study's] original mission has come to an end" (quoted by Inkeles & Levinson, 1997). Fifty years after Parsonian grand integrations, sociology, anthropology, and psychology parted ways.

One major reason for the disjunction of the disciplines was the dominance of the psychoanalytic approach that animated the school of "culture and personality" in anthropology. Psychiatrists, sociologists, and anthropologists used to derive national character from child-rearing practices. Examples of this approach were given by attempts to reduce adult obedience in Germany to domineering father–child relations during childhood (Reich, 1970), or to explain violent behaviours in Russia by the effects of child swaddling (Gorer, 1949). Over the long haul, psychoanalytic instruments proved scientifically ineffective. As Martindale (1967) said, while the study of national character is of immense importance, it was "a radical error to derive national character from family structure, toilet training, child care, etc." Another explanation for the demise of studies of national character refers to the traumatic burden that such explanations carried after National Socialism. As Elias said, in writing about the German national character, "The hypersensitivity towards anything that recalls National Socialist doctrine results in the problem of 'national character' being largely shrouded in silence" (1996, p. 2).

The present chapter joins efforts made by group analysts to reconnect the severed analytic ties between sociology and psychology. In this series of volumes on *The Social Unconscious in Persons, Groups and Societies*, Earl Hopper and Haim Weinberg bring together group analysts to ponder the roots of their discipline and discuss the ideas set forth by Foulkes—founder of group analytic psychotherapy—during the heyday of studies of national character. I supplement the collective work of Hopper and Weinberg by relying on main currents in sociological theory. My present contribution to their evolving paradigm brings back old ideas about the habitus and national character, reflecting challenges besetting postmodern sociology.

Indeed, postmodern sociological schools adopted the "individualist" assumption in social theory—namely the belief that the human psyche is general across cultures and that a universal theory of the mind can explain psychological phenomena across countries (Lukes, 1973). This, however, has led to unresolved empirical conundrums and theoretical dead ends. Indeed, the growing chasm between social theory and social reality began glowing after September 11, 2001. Suicide terrorism, Moslem massacres, and ethnic and national wars in seemingly peace-loving Europe has therefore led social scientists to seek new explanatory schemes for interpreting persistent psychosocial differences across countries and civilisations (Huntington, 2011).

Frustrations about the limitations that universal theories have in explaining national idiosyncrasies were already expressed by perceptive scholars a decade before the grand events of the past two decades. Clifford Geertz (2000) gave early voice to the inability of postmodern theories to explain persistent psychological differences across cultures; Samuel Huntington (1996) provided similar insights about unbridgeable motivations which divide civilisations and set them on colliding tracks; and other scholars have pointed out that even seemingly similar countries—which are otherwise dominated by common individualist modern cultures (Lukes, 1969)—turn out to be highly dissimilar under scrutinised empirical appraisals (e.g., Dundes, 1989; Kron, 2003).

The challenges that general theories face in explaining psychological idiosyncrasies across nations have rekindled interest in the particulars of nations, namely in issues relating to the interplay between culture and national character (Yair, 2015a). These revisions mostly rely on the work of Norbert Elias, who argued long ago that contemporary actions reflect collective "sediments" that cultures habituate in bodies through various means of socialisation—and that scholars should interpret contemporary events holding historical legacies in mind. Recent sociological studies of national habitus rest on Norbert Elias's analysis of the German national habitus, expanding the realm to the American, the English, the Irish, the French, the Israeli, the Austrian, or the Iranian national habitus (Hir, 2014; Hirst, 2007; Mennell, 2007; Yair, 2015a; Yair, 2015b).

Similarly, and extending a Kantian focus on categories of perception, Pierre Bourdieu often described the social manner by which a person's social class "habitus" constitutes "visions and divisions"—tying together social structures and the cognitive psychological senses of dividing and ordering the world (Yair, 2009). Eyes do not see beauty, suggested Bourdieu, unless they are trained to do so by the hard labour of socialisation (Bourdieu & Darbel, 1990). Similarly, men and women can only perceive themselves or act as masculine or feminine to the extent that they were trained to adopt an historically devised and socially accepted gendered habitus (Bourdieu, 2001). Elias—who mainly used the idea of the habitus in explicating the German national habitus—had a similar though less cerebral approach to the idea of habitus (1996). Indeed, in a recent review of Bourdieu and Elias, several scholars suggested that "Both ... sought to emphasize the importance of taken-for-granted ways of perceiving, thinking, and acting on the part of (more or less) competent actors immersed in their everyday practices" (Paulle, van Heerikhuizen, & Emirbayer, 2012, p. 71).

The present chapter advances this evolving sociological field by focusing on the concept of the national habitus while trying to reconnect it with the kindred approach of group analysts. I will suggest that the national habitus concept should play a key role in attempts to bridge between social theory and persisting cultural idiosyncrasies. In the following sections I focus on three theoretical insights about the constituting processes of the national habitus, namely constituting traumatic narratives, chosen traumas that are celebrated through national rituals, and resulting habituated modes of perceiving and conceiving reality (Lomsky-Feder, 2004; Volkan, 2001).

Cultural traumas and constituting national narratives

During the past decade, a group identified with Yale cultural sociology began highlighting the role of cultural trauma in creating particular national habitus or character (Alexander, 2003, 2012; Eyerman, 2001; Giesen, 2000, 2004; Paterson, 2000; Robben & Suarez-Orozco, 2000; Sztompka, 2000). Similar to the idea of "social trauma", those scholars emphasise that suffering, colonisation, massacres, slavery, and brutal violence become anchors of memory for generations, and that cultural traumas remain vital in creating pulsating memories and in driving contemporary perceptions and reactions long after the trauma receded into myth and history. This is not a new idea, indeed. As German historian Oswald Spengler wrote in 1924: "In history, character is wrought more by suffering than by success ... the intense gaiety of some regions, even the laughter of the inns and folk festivals still bears testimony to streams of blood and tears, to countless massacres, heart-breaking disappointments, the sacrifice of whole generations, and repeated failures and defeats."

The evolving study of cultural trauma suggests that it is a critical historical event—or a series of such events—that forms the basis of national culture and collective identity (Giesen, 2000). It is a critical turning point that sets long-term trajectories of national development (Abbott, 2001). The classical statement on this theme was made by Norbert Elias, indeed. His book, *The Germans* (1996), explained Germany's effervescent enlistment into World War II and the horrors it perpetrated during the Holocaust against the background of the catastrophes of the Thirty Years' War and the experience of repeated defeats to foreign powers. As Elias suggested, nations maintain memories of an historical and mythical past, and their collective habitus responds to contemporary events through the echoes of ancient traumas, defeats, and massacres. He argued that cultural trauma is a past that keeps sending expressions through people's thoughts and actions decades and centuries after the historical event took place. Empirical studies have indeed mapped the role of trauma in different countries (Eyerman, Alexander, & Breese, 2011; Kleber, Figley, & Gersons, 1995; Yair & Akbari, 2014) and minority groups (Paterson, 2000). They show that contemporary actions emanate from critical historical events, which continue directing thoughts and actions even generations after the traumatic event has taken place. They also demonstrate that defeats and humiliating collective experiences have long-term effects on national identities (Mock, 2012; Zerubavel, 2002).

Indeed, cultural traumas—slavery in America (Eyerman, 2001; Mennell, 2007), the Ancien Régime in France (Yair, 2009), Islamic wars in the Arab world (Yair & Akbari, 2014), and the Holocaust in Israel (Yair, 2015b)—constitute a national habitus—an embodied amalgam of worldviews and sensations that mould contemporary perceptions and actions (Kalberg, 2004). As Hopper and Weinberg (2011) suggested, cultural traumas are stamped in psyches generations after the traumatic experiences took place, while cultural reworking of the trauma and its persistent memorisation guarantee that it remains vivid even after all the bearers of the personal trauma passed away. In developing Foulkes's ideas about the "foundation matrix", they suggested that societies embed sociocultural aspects in the senses, that is, in directing eyesight and ear-sensitivity (Hopper, 2003a, 2003b). These insights are exemplified in two recent empirical studies. In the first I have shown how the Jewish trauma of exile and persecution constitutes the Israeli Zionist habitus around existential anxieties and fear of annihilation (Yair, 2015b); and the second, indeed, exposes how that traumatised habitus constitutes "eyesight" and "ear-sight"—repeated sensual perceptions of "Nazis" that Israelis experience in encountering contemporary Germany (Nuttman-Shwartz & Weinberg, 2012; Yair, 2015a).

Those studies exposed that the national habitus is constituted by the interplay of four analytic levels: a mythological past; known and verified historical events; contemporary geopolitical risks and challenges; and, a future strewn with risks (Beck, 1992, 2001). The four levels that constitute the national habitus—arranged as a temporal continuum—penetrate and feed each other (Yair, 2015b). People interpret their personal and national challenges while employing all four levels. Indeed, cultural narratives of trauma provide them with ready-made explanations for their personal and national predicament. Those narratives also justify their own and their government's political stances by tying the past, the present, and the future together through traumatic constituting narratives. Crucially, all levels work as a syndrome. Though myth and history precede contemporary risks and future challenges—all levels work in concert, and people pick on those four elements in interpreting or taking action towards immediate events or counterparts. Consequently, hypothetical and elusive risks might be charged by the past so as to create real effects in the present: fear, on the one hand, and aggressiveness, on the other. The root cause is the same: a cultural interpretation of a national trauma as a symptom of an eternal predicament. That cultural traumas direct sense and making-sense stands at the basis of a self-fulfilling prophecy; that people feel or see past victimisation as if it happened to themselves, makes past ghosts relevant on a daily level. People, in that sense, are prisoners of cultural traumas, and their authentic psychological experiences are mere refractions of socially embedded collective memories and predispositions (Hopper & Weinberg, 2011; Volkan, 2001).

Producing the national habitus: ceremonies and rituals

Nation states have found collective traumas to be highly effective in creating collective identities. They often use such traumas in establishing anthems and major national memorials and ceremonies that justify contemporary values and worldviews. Studies have also shown that systems of education often use textbooks and school rituals for inculcating collective memories, feelings, and identities (Lomsky-Feder, 2004). Such national rituals and ceremonies stir emotions and cathex individuals' sentiments while creating common psychological and emotional experiences. They stir and direct emotions by recreating the narrative of trauma in play and drama; they use mournful music and rituals of mourning in order to excite participants' emotions; and they often play out those national dramas in authentic locations that have a "halo", an authentic element to them. Museums, for example, often use such emotive tools to recreate experiences and congeal a sense of sameness—creating in people a shared history, and the sense of having a shared predicament. Visitors to the Communism Museum in Prague, for example, shed tears at the end of the tour—where emotive visuals and musical effects recreate memories of Jan Pallach and the revolt of 1968—allowing visitors to reflect on their national habitus and feel part of a long chain (e.g., the idea of resistance in the Czech context, which starts with Jan Hus in the fourteenth century).

Since national ceremonies and rituals recur yearly, people's emotional experiences slowly become entwined with the cultural trauma that was constituted by cultural inculcation (Demerath, 2002). As they annually participate in those national memorials and events, individuals become emotionally cathexed to national symbols like the anthem and the flag; they also learn to feel sadness during ceremonies of national independence and proud at its climax. Through such cultural tools people become part of the long chain of history, becoming bearers of existential national testaments. One can observe those habitual modes where the national invades the individual psyche and captures it during public performances. For example, athletes often shed a silent tear in hearing their national anthem while standing on a podium; and adolescents often express anger in hearing criticisms against their country. In such instances the national habitus reacts while controlling the individual's psyche—testifying to its embodied nature (Durkheim, 1964, 1973b). My theoretical position—implemented in various studies (Yair, 2015a, 2015b;

Yair & Akbari, 2014)—suggests that individuals feel like agents of free will, but that they are actually captives of their national habitus.

As they grow up, individuals supplant the emotional infrastructure of their national habitus with more intellectual understandings of "their roots", or with more cerebral interpretations of their national predicament and vision. Upon reaching puberty, indeed, individuals have fully become bearers of a national habitus that directs their emotional styles, thought patterns and perceptions. As Kuzmics and Axtmann suggested, indeed, "the 'national character' or 'habitus' must be construed in terms of a relatively permanent imprinting of emotions and affects, or, to be more precise, in terms of the entire 'affective household' of nations" (2007, pp. 5–6).

The affective household of the national habitus is created by collective ceremonies that teach individuals to associate their individual psyche and morality with the cultural trauma of their national group. It is the process by which an indivividual's "ontogenesis" is entwined with his "phylogenesis"—with the collective history and cultural narrative of the national group. Participation in national ceremonies creates pre-reflexive experiences and socialises individuals to embody their national predicament as taken-for-granted perceptions and sensations (Berger & Luckman, 1967). What people perceive as authentic psychological experiences are in that sense predetermined by cultural imprinting. Through participation in national mourning and celebrations people learn a collective story about their past, present, and future identity. In that sense, people's emotional and intellectual experiences reflect predetermined national narratives of trauma. Holiday after holiday, celebration after ceremony—participation in consecutive and thematically coherent events creates meaningful experiences and schemes of perception and interpretation. Those experiences—to the extent that they are staged in original places where the horrors took place and in the presence of relevant documentation of the events—associate personal biographies with national narratives of trauma. Hence, by participating in orchestrated and emotionally charged national ceremonies people become one with their collective identity (Durkheim, 1961, 1973a, 1973b). They also gain significant insights about the interplay between their personal biography and their national identity. Such ceremonies and rituals produce a coherent and consistent worldview that directs people's perceptions, and their cognitive knowledge becomes entwined with emotions while acquiring existentially significant meanings. Ceremonies transform meaningless facts—for example, how many people died in war—into personally meaningful experiences; they turn disconnected pieces of information into an insightful and coherent vision. People can thus tie their personal experience with their compatriots, developing a common national habitus or a collective identity. At the end of the day, such ceremonies guarantee that national legacies of the past become embodied and habituated, thereby perpetuating cultural trauma up to the present.

The national habitus creates a common ground for psychologically diversified individuals. It supplies a foundation matrix in the language of analytic group psychologists—the unconscious visions and predicaments that create similar emotional experiences and cognitive insights in otherwise psychologically diverse people. The national habitus creates a unified psychic tendency to perceive reality and react towards it in culturally predetermined ways. The national habitus thereby connects together individuals and social groups, creating common experiences and interpretations that transcend individuals and groups. It coalesces various social classes and ethnic groups into something that is larger than themselves. Essentially, the national habitus links individuals and groups to the long chain of the generations (even if those generations are imagined (Anderson, 1983)), making them part of a whole, agents in an evolving national trajectory. The national habitus constitutes the mechanism by which the past has consequences for today (Brownlie, 2012).

In that sense, a traumatised national habitus is an effective means for creating solidarity and similarity in diverse societies (Gantt & Hopper, 2008; Hopper, 2009). It guarantees that a person's way of thinking and the logic that he or she employs becomes stylised with his or her compatriots—all expressing a common national habitus. Especially in situations of risk and identity threat, social and psychological processes of "massification" or "aggregation" create sameness around core collective elements. This is why people casually—and often correctly—speak of "the Germans", "the Americans", or "the Israelis". They are correct in making such generalisations because there are common German, American, and Israeli ways to perceive reality and react towards it in culturally determined ways. And those common ways reflect deep cultural traumas.

Admittedly, prior attempts to describe "national character" have been rejected as politically incorrect and scientifically defunct. As Kuipers admitted in analysing the Dutch case, "The notion of 'national character' is not entirely pleasant" (Kuipers, 2011). But as recent scholars proved, the concepts of national habitus and national character are back in vogue (Yair, 2015C). Indeed, Geert Hofstede—a Dutch comparative analyst of business—launched one of the most influential paradigms in the study of culture and national character at the very time that sociologists decided to abandon it. According to Hofstede (1991), cultural values constitute "mental programs" or "software of the mind"—discrete elements which direct family patterns, education systems, legislative codes, and even political systems (see Hofstede, 2001, p. 12). Hofstede's theory uses the concept of habitus like Bourdieu (2000) and Elias (1996) do. He suggests that the "mental software" that cultures constitute is "usually unconscious conditioning which leaves individuals considerable freedom to think, feel, and act but within the constraints of what his or her social environment offers in terms of possible thoughts, feelings, and actions" (1991, p. 235). Similarly, work by comparative psychologists and other professors of business shows that the idea of national character is indeed alive and kicking (see review in Pickel, 2004). For example, Terry Clark (1990) suggested that market analysts should pay close attention to national variations in tastes and preferences; Langlois suggested that corporate codes of ethics reflect national idiosyncrasies (Langlois & Schlegelmilch, 1990); and Peter Smith (2011) suggested that response rates in international surveys should be interpreted through national communication styles. A recent publication in *Science* (2005) has indeed brought the idea of national character into the limelight, inviting corroboration and critique (Fischer, 2006; McCrae & Terracciano, 2006; Robins, 2005; Terracciano & McCrae, 2007; Terracciano et al., 2005).

Cultural trauma, national habitus, and psychological empowerment

The attempt to reconnect sociological and psychological insights about trauma and its effects should not blur the unique path that the former discipline takes. In contrast to the vast psychological literature on personal trauma or PTSD (Goodman & Friedman-Peleg, 2010), sociological studies suggest that cultural traumas actually can and often do empower people. They suggest that cultural traumas form the basis of social institutions while motivating and empowering individuals' perceptions in their attempt to identify hidden patterns in mundane, seemingly unremarkable phenomena (Smelser, 2004). While psychological trauma often cripples individuals (e.g., James, 2004), cultural traumas amplify perceptions and empower actions. And although psychological traumas often lurk unconscious, cultural traumas serve as conscious pedestals of perception and as springboards of action. They come in handy as explanatory narratives, allowing people to rationalise or justify their emotions and actions, or to explain baffling behaviours or contexts. Even what seem to be non-rational reactions become meaningful through the lens of cultural trauma and its resultant national habitus (Löwenheim & Heimann, 2008).

The "positive" psychological effects of the national habitus are profusely apparent. American youngsters, for example, often insist on their personal freedoms at home using the same terminology that adult Americans attach to their right to bear arms. They all justify personal rights and liberties by referring to the trauma of the War of Independence. They defend human rights while justifying their position based on the experiences of generations long gone. Specifically, they draw on the trauma that the Pilgrims, Puritans, and other Dissenters experienced 300 years ago—constituting the New England Protestant tradition. This cultural prototype was later strengthened by recurring historical traumas. The overtly religious objection to monarchical government and religious oppression expressed by the Dissenters was expanded to a more encompassing rejection of unrestrained government power in general. The collective traumas caused by the English military occupation of the American colonies following the French and Indian War (1754–1763) and through the American Revolution (1775–1783) firmly established in the American collective consciousness a fear and resentment of powerful central government. Arbitrary rule by military governors sent from abroad, a lack of political representation, taxes and restrictions imposed against the will of the public, and government violations of property rights—all those fomented a mistrust of the distant government in London which not only led to the American Revolution, but formed the root of the American national habitus.

Similarly, Israelis often perceive themselves as would-be victims in a never ending chain of persecution and annihilation. In responding to its cultural trauma, the Israeli national habitus creates a sense of uniqueness among the nations; and the Zionist element in it charges the Israeli psyche with a sense of potency, invincibility, and *hutzpa* (Gratch, 2014; Nuttman-Shwartz & Weinberg, 2012). Similarly, Germany's national habitus reacts to the horrors of the Holocaust—in becoming ardent pacifists—but also to the ancient battles with Rome and Paris (Kahler, 1985). In case after case sociologists observe the empowering or potentiating effects of cultural traumas; in case after case they see how individuals draw upon cultural reservoirs of collective predicaments that work through psychologically embedded emotions and cognitive schemes to empower their actions. The working through of the trauma with cultural means transforms painful experiences into gainful legacies.

The psychological implications of the interplay between cultural trauma and the national habitus go even "deeper", necessitating reconnecting the severed bonds between macro-sociology and micro-psychology (Mouzelis, 2008). Essentially, their national habitus arms actors with ready-made but culturally particular defence mechanisms. People project, repress, ignore, and omit to observe and record, or shun out of consciousness what seems to trouble them because their culture implanted those psychic mechanisms and capabilities in them—and, most important, provided the rules under what conditions to use them. The national habitus—with the cultural trauma and the pain associated with it—leads people to employ particular defence mechanisms in places and moments that their predecessors found troubling. True, there are universal psychological capacities to repress, evade, and project; but the national habitus determines which mechanism would operate and under what conditions—at least in socially meaningful contexts. Americans, for example, have a hard time recognising the trauma they inflicted on native populations; Turks seem to repress the historical record about the Armenian genocide; and the cultural trauma of the Israeli habitus desensitises Israelis to the suffering of the Palestinians. Those omissions and evasions are triggered by cultural rather than individual defence mechanisms, as they are expressions of cultural trauma that became embodied in a national habitus. This habitus—being socialised and culturally determined—also determines which events or experiences will become conscious or will be relegated to the unconscious.

Individuals are often taken by surprise by their own reactions. They are struck by feelings that erupt uncontrollably and unforeseeably—and at those rare moments the national habitus may be the culprit. Often the cultural trauma lays dormant; on most occasions people act out their individual unique predisposition. But in some contexts it is the national habitus which erupts seemingly out of nowhere—giving voice to the trauma and defending the individual from potential degradations or shaming experiences. It is during those rare moments that people become alive to their socialised habitus; in those contexts they can clarify how intertwined their own life is with their national narratives of trauma. Those moments also invite sociologists and psychologists to reconnect the broken paradigms that set them apart.

There are some particular areas where such reconnections can work out. The sociology of emotions (Scheff, 1994) is one domain where Mouzelis's call (2007, 2008) for reconnection between sociology and group analysis would be fitting. The area of commemoration and difficult pasts (Vinitzky-Seroussi, 2002) is also a candidate for this timely task. In both cases, as well as in other kindred areas, the concept of the national habitus holds great promise for advancing knowledge about individuals in their social and cultural settings. The advent towards bridging across the severed disciplines has begun in various circles, and I hope that the present contribution by a sociologist of culture to the evolving theory of the social unconscious in group analysis provides one more step towards conciliation of the opposites.

References

Abbott, A. (2001). *Time Matters*. Chicago, IL: University of Chicago Press.

Alexander, J. C. (2003). *The Meaning of Social Life: A Cultural Sociology*. New York: Oxford University Press.

Alexander, J. C. (2012). *Trauma: A Social Theory*. Malden, MA: Polity.

Anderson, B. (1983). *Imagined Communities*. London: Verso.

Beck, U. (1992). *Risk Society: Towards a New Modernity*. London: Sage.

Beck, U. (2001). *World Risk Society*. Cambridge: Polity.

Benedict, R. (1947). *The Chrysanthemum and the Sword: Patterns of Japanese Culture*. London: Secker & Warburg.

Berger, P., & Luckman, T. (1967). *The Social Construction of Reality*. London: Allen Lane.

Bourdieu, P. (2000). *Pascalian Meditations*. Stanford, CA: Stanford University Press.

Bourdieu, P. (2001). *Masculine Domination*. Stanford, CA: Stanford University Press.

Bourdieu, P., & Darbel, A. (1990). *The Love of Art: European Art Museums and their Public*. Stanford, CA: Stanford University Press.

Brownlie, S. (2012). Does memory of the distant past matter? Remediating the Norman Conquest. *Memory Studies, 5*(4): 360–377.

Clark, T. (1990). International marketing and national character: A review and proposal for an integrative theory. *Journal of Marketing, 54*(4): 66–79.

Demerath, L. (2002). Epistemological culture theory: a micro yheory of the origin and maintenance of culture. *Sociological Theory, 20*(2): 208–226.

DeVos, G. A. (1968). National character. In: *International Encyclopedia of the Social Sciences.*

Dundes, A. (1989). *Life Is Like a Chicken Coop Ladder: A Study of German National Character through Folklore.* Detroit, MI: Wayne State University Press.

Durkheim, E. (1951). *Suicide: A Study in Sociology.* New York: Free Press.

Durkheim, E. (1961). *The Elementary Forms of the Religious Life.* New York: Collier.

Durkheim, E. (Ed.) (1964). *Essays on Sociology & Philosophy.* New York: Harper Torchbooks.

Durkheim, E. (1973a). *Moral Education.* New York: Free Press.

Durkheim, E. (1973b). *On Morality and Society.* Chicago, IL: University of Chicago Press.

Elias, N. (1996). *The Germans: Power Struggles and the Development of Habitus in the Nineteenth and Twentieth Centuries.* Cambridge: Polity Press.

Eyerman, R. (2001). *Cultural Trauma: Slavery and the Formation of African American Identity.* Cambridge: Cambridge University Press.

Eyerman, R., Alexander, J. C., & Breese, E. B. (Eds.) (2011). *Narrating Trauma: On the Impact of Collective Suffering.* Boulder, CO: Paradigm.

Fischer, R. (2006). Congruence and functions of personal and cultural values: Do my values reflect my culture's values? *Personality and Social Psychology Bulletin, 32*(11): 1419–1431.

Freud, S. (1930a). *Civilization and Its Discontents.* New York: W. W. Norton, 1961.

Fromm, E. (1963). *Beyond the Chains of Illusion: My Encounter with Marx and Freud.* New York: Pocket Books.

Gantt, S. P., & Hopper, E. (2008). Two perspectives on a trauma in a training group: the systems-centred approach and the theory of incohesion: Part I. *Group Analysis, 41*(1): 98–112.

Geertz, C. (2000). *Available Light.* Princeton, NJ: Princeton University Press.

Giesen, B. (2000). National identity as trauma: the case of Germany. In: B. Stråth (Ed.), *Myth and Memory in the Construction of Community: Historical Patterns in Europe and Beyond* (pp. 227–248). Brussels: Peter Lang.

Giesen, B. (2004). The Holocaust as the traumatic reference of German national identity. In: J. C. Alexander, R. Eyerman, B. Giesen, N. Smelser, & P. Sztompka (Eds.), *Cultural Trauma and Collective Identity* (pp. 113–139). Berkeley, CA: University of California Press.

Goodman, Y., & Friedman-Peleg, K. (2010). From post-trauma intervention to immunizing the social body: Pragmatics and politics of a resilience program in Israel. *Culture, Medicine and Psychiatry, 34*(3): 421–442.

Gorer, G. (1949). *The People of Great Russia: A Psychological Study*. London: Cresset.

Gratch, A. (2014). *The Israeli Mind*. Or Yehuda, Israel: Kinneret, Zmora-Bitan, Dvir (in Hebrew).

Hir, M. -P., & Le. (2014). *The National Habitus: Ways of Feeling French, 1789–1870*. Berlin: De Gruyter.

Hirst, J. (2007). *The Australians: Insiders and Outsiders on the National Character since 1770*. Melbourne, Australia: Penguin Australia.

Hoebel, E. A. (1967). Anthropological perspectives on national character. *Annals of the American Academy of Political and Social Science, 370*: 1–7.

Hofstede, G. (1991). *Cultures and Organizations: Software of the Mind*. London: McGraw-Hill.

Hofstede, G. (2001). *Culture's Consequences: Comparing Values, Behaviors, Institutions, and Organizations Across Nations*. Thousand Oaks, CA: Sage.

Hopper, E. (2003a). *The Social Unconscious: Selected Papers*. London: Jessica Kingsley.

Hopper, E. (2003b). *Traumatic Experience in the Unconscious Life of Groups*. London: Jessica Kingsley.

Hopper, E. (2009). The theory of the basic assumption of incohesion: aggregation/massification or (BA) I:A/M. *British Journal of Psychotherapy, 25*(2): 214–229.

Hopper, E., & Weinberg, H. (Eds.) (2011). *The Social Unconscious in Persons, Groups and Societies: Volume 1: Mainly Theory*. London: Karnac.

Huntington, S. P. (1996). *The Clash of Civilizations and the Remaking of World Order*. New York: Simon & Schuster.

Huntington, S. P. (2011). *The Clash of Civilizations and the Remaking of World Order*. New York: Simon & Schuster.

Inkeles, A., & Levinson, D. J. (1997). *National Character: A Psycho-Social Perspective*. New Brunswick, NJ: Transaction.

James, E. C. (2004). The political economy of "trauma" in Haiti in the democratic era of insecurity. *Culture, Medicine and Psychiatry, 28*(2): 127–149.

Kahler, E. (1985). *The Germans*. Boulder, CO: Westview.

Kalberg, S. (2004). The past and present influence of world views: Max Weber on a neglected sociological concept. *Journal of Classical Sociology, 4*(2): 139–163.

Kleber, R. J., Figley, C. R., & Gersons, B. P. R. (Eds.) (1995). *Beyond Trauma: Cultural and Social Dynamics*. New York: Plenum.

Kron, T. (2003). The specific way of individualization in Germany: A culture-theoretical comparison to the USA. *International Journal of Contemporary Sociology, 40*(2): 219–238.

Kuipers, G. (2011). Her Majesty's bicycle: on national habitus and sociological comparison. *Figurations, 34*: 1–14.

Kuzmics, H., & Axtmann, R. (2007). *Authority, State and National Character: The Civilizing Process in Austria and England, 1700–1900*. Farnham, UK: Ashgate.

Langlois, C. C., & Schlegelmilch, B. B. (1990). Do corporate codes of ethics reflect national character? Evidence from Europe and the United States. *Journal of International Business Studies, 21*(4): 519–539.

Lomsky-Feder, E. (2004). The memorial ceremony in Israeli schools: between the State and civil society. *British Journal of Sociology of Education, 25*(3): 291–305.

Löwenheim, O., & Heimann, G. (2008). Revenge in international politics. *Security Studies, 17*(4): 685–724.

Lukes, S. (1969). Durkheim's "Individualism and the Intellectuals". *Political Studies, 17*(1): 14–30.

Lukes, S. (1973). *Individualism*. Oxford: Basil Blackwell.

Martindale, D. (1967). The sociology of national character. *Annals of the American Academy of Political and Social Science, 370*: 30–35.

McCrae, R. R., & Terracciano, A. (2006). National character and personality. *Current Directions in Psychological Science, 15*(4): 156–161.

Mead, M. (1965). *And Keep Your Powder Dry: An Anthropologist Looks at America*. New York: W. Morrow.

Mennell, S. (2007). *The American Civilizing Process*. Cambridge: Polity.

Mock, S. J. (2012). *Symbols of Defeat in the Construction of National Identity* Cambridge: Cambridge University Press.

Mouzelis, N. P. (2007). Habitus and reflexivity: Restructuring Bourdieu's theory of practice. *Sociological Research Online, 12*(6): 9.

Mouzelis, N. P. (2008). *Modern and Postmodern Social Theorizing*. Cambridge: Cambridge University Press.

Nuttman-Shwartz, O., & Weinberg, H. (2012). Organizations in traumatized societies: the Israeli case. In: E. Hopper (Ed.), *Trauma and Organizations* (pp. 215–231). London: Karnac.

Parsons, T. (1964). *Social Structure and Personality*. New York: Free Press of Glencoe.

Paterson, O. (2000). Taking culture seriously: A framework and an Afro-American illustration. In: L. E. Harrison & S. P. Huntington (Eds.), *Culture Matters: How Values Shape Human Progress* (pp. 202–218). New York: Basic Books.

Paulle, B., van Heerikhuizen, B., & Emirbayer, M. (2012). Elias and Bourdieu. *Journal of Classical Sociology, 12*(1): 69–93.

Pickel, A. (2004). Homo nationis: The psycho-social infrastructure of the nation-state order. *Global Society, 18*(4): 325–346.

Reich, W. (1970). *The Mass Psychology of Fascism*. New York: Farrar, Straus & Giroux.

Robben, A. C. G. M., & Suarez-Orozco, M. M. (Eds.) (2000). *Cultures under Siege: Collective Violence and Trauma*. Cambridge: Cambridge University Press.

Robins, R. W. (2005). The nature of personality: genes, culture, and national character. *Science, 310*(5745): 62–63.

Scheff, T. J. (1994). *Bloody Revenge. Emotions, Nationalism and War*. Boulder, CO: Westview.

Smelser, N. J. (2004). Psychological trauma and cultural trauma. pp. 31–59 In: J. C. Alexander, R. Eyerman, B. Giesen, N. J. Smelser, & P. Sztompka (Eds.), *Cultural Trauma and Collective Identity* (pp. 31–59). Berkeley, CA: University of California Press.

Smith, P. B. (2011). Communication styles as dimensions of national culture. *Journal of Cross-Cultural Psychology, 42*(2): 216–233.

Spengler, O. (1924). On the German national character. *Deutsches Adelsblatt, XLII.*

Sztompka, P. (2000). Cultural trauma: The other face of social change. *European Journal of Social Theory, 3*(4): 449–466.

Terracciano, A., & McCrae, R. R. (2007). Perceptions of Americans and the Iraq invasion: Implications for understanding national character stereotypes." *Journal of Cross-Cultural Psychology, 38*(6): 695–710.

Terracciano, A., et al. (2005). National character does not reflect mean personality trait levels in 49 cultures. *Science, 310*(5745): 96–100.

Vinitzky-Seroussi, V. (2002). Commemorating a difficult past: Yitzhak Rabin's memorials. *American Sociological Review, 67*(1): 30–51.

Volkan, V. D. (2001). Transgenerational transmissions and chosen traumas: an aspect of large-group identity. *Group Analysis, 34*(1): 79–97.

Yair, G. (2009). *Pierre Bourdieu: The Last Musketeer of the French Revolution*. Lanham, MD: Lexington.

Yair, G. (2015a). National character. In: J. Stone, R. M. Dennis, P. S. Rizova, & A. D. Smith (Eds.), *The Wiley-Blackwell Encyclopedia of Race, Ethnicity and Nationalism*. New York: Wiley-Blackwell. http://eu.wiley.com/WileyCDA/WileyTitle/productCd-1405189789.html.

Yair, G. (2015b). The Germans: Cultural trauma and the Israeli habitus. *American Journal of Cultural Sociology, 3*: 254–279.

Yair, G. (2015c). The Israeli existential anxiety: cultural trauma and the constitution of national character. *Social Identities, 20*(4–5): 346–362.

Yair, G., & Akbari, B. (2014). From cultural trauma to nuclear war? Interpreting the Iranian-Israeli conflict. *Human Figurations, 3*(2). http://hdl.handle.net/2027/spo.11217607.0003.204.

Zerubavel, Y. (2002). The "mythological Sabra" and Jewish past: Trauma, memory, and contested identities. *Israel Studies, 7*(2):115–144.

CHAPTER FOUR

The inner organisation of the matrix

Juan Tubert-Oklander

The metapsychology of the matrix

Freud introduced the concept of metapsychology as a deeper level of reality that underlay the psychological level of experience, behaviour, and relationship. This he conceived to be the "material" basis of psychology, and hence necessarily biological. His speculative theory-building in this area has been the object of much criticism, on account of its high level of abstraction, which seems far apart from the actual human experience of an analytic treatment, and also its mechanistic and pseudo-positivistic language. The first objection is to every imaginable metapsychology, while the second is only to that particular type of metapsychology that Freud developed ever since his "Project" (1950a). It seems to me that the latter is truly inimical to the understanding and development of the sort of knowledge derived from the analytic experience, but that analysis—and by this I mean *psycho*-analysis, *group* analysis, and *socio*-analysis alike—*needs* something like a metapsychology.[1] This is so because any psychological analysis is founded on a whole set of assumptions on the general nature of mind and its functioning. These are, more often than not, kept tacit, and even unconscious, so they require a thorough work of interpretation and reconstruction to come to the fore. Freud's great accomplishment was that he spelt out his assumptions, thus laying them open to criticism. Other authors have not done it, thus leaving the task to their critics.

Foulkes introduced for us the beginning of a metapsychology of group processes and the person-group relationship, with his concept of the *matrix*. He also suggested that in this dynamic network there are several levels of communication and relationship, which operate simultaneously, although one of them predominates over the others at any given moment. The four levels are: i) *the current level*, in which the group represents the community and the conductor as a leader or authority; ii) *the transference level*, corresponding to mature object relations, in which the group represents the family, the conductor father or mother, and the other members siblings; iii) *the level of bodily and mental images (projective level)*, corresponding to primitive, narcissistic "inner" object relations, and the individual members represent parts of the self and the group often appears as the mother image; and iv) *the primordial level*, which corresponds to Freud's primordial fantasies and Jung's archetypes of a collective unconscious (Foulkes, 1957, pp. 114–115).

Obviously, with this schema Foulkes was trying to formulate an ecumenical theoretical framework, one that included the contributions of the social sciences, Freud, Klein, and Jung, but he left open the question of how this descriptive analysis of group processes might relate to a general theory of mind. This is what I shall try to do now, on the basis of a development in object relations theory that has taken place in Latin America, stemming from the work of Enrique Pichon-Rivière and some of his disciples and continuators, including myself. In this, my exposition must be necessarily sketchy, on account of space limitations. Nonetheless, it represents an attempt to transcend this theoretical framework and descriptive analysis, in order to develop a model for analysing the foundation matrix of any particular social system, as well as the dynamic matrix of its component groups of variable size and complexity.[2] Hence, the use of the term "paradigm" to describe such a schema.

The syncretic paradigm

Enrique Pichon-Riviere, pioneer of psychoanalysis and group analysis in Argentina, always insisted, like Foulkes, on the essential identity of individual, group, and society (Tubert-Oklander, 2011b; Tubert-Oklander & Hernández-Tubert, 2004, 2014a). However, this demanded some explanation of how did this work within the general functioning of mind, and this problem was tackled by his former analysand, student, and colleague José Bleger (1967), who made a thorough study of the deeper undifferentiated levels of mind, in which there is a fully indiscriminate primary fusion between subject and object, mind and body, self and environment, which he called "syncretism".

This kind of symbiosis is not established by projective identification, because there is no subject-object boundary to be violated by this defence mechanism; hence, we are talking of *fusion*, not *confusion*. The flow between the person and the others takes place as a passive flow, and not as an active process, since there is a deep continuity between them and the collective bodies to which they belong. The human group is conceived as a single and continuous mass in which are contained the nuclei of individual identifications and experiences that correspond to the various subjects.[3]

This kind of minding cannot be conceived only as an early phase of development, which should be surpassed, but also as a permanent organisation of mind that coexists and alternates in predominance with the other two (Tubert-Oklander, 2011a, 2014). This would be the very basis of collective existence—relational, group, institutional, and social—as, although human groups are apparently made up of individuals, in the syncretic mode they live as if they were interconnected, like communicating vessels.[4]

This theoretical perspective, which I call the "syncretic paradigm", was further developed by the Argentine psychoanalyst Blanca Montevechio (1999, 2002) and myself, among others who have also been influenced by Bleger's thought.[5] Montevechio developed a schema of three different organisations of experience, which I prefer to call "models", that could either be thought of as a developmental sequence or as simultaneous phases in a dialectic equilibrium; these she identified in terms of three iconic figures from the Greek mythology: Dionysus, Narcissus, and Oedipus.

The Dionysian dimension is that of primeval fusion, syncretism, ambiguity, and bodily existence. It is the source of passion and creativity, of collective life, of compassion and ruthlessness. The narcissistic one is a world of images and dreams, reflections and echoes, reversible relationships, idealisation and appearance; it is the realm of primitive fantasy that Melanie Klein explored. The oedipal is the world of difference and contrast, of language, enquiry, and individual existence, of interpersonal relationships, conflicts, and negotiations, law and order, sin and virtue.

My further addition to this model was a fourth organisation, one that emerges from the dialectical interchange between the three previous ones (Tubert-Oklander, 2004). This allows the rational and frequently dogmatic and unilateral view of the world that characterises the oedipal organisation, to recover and include the richness of the narcissistic fantasy and imagination, and the impetus, depth of feeling, creativity, and participatory identification of the Dionysian way of existence, which had been previously repressed.

If we see this diachronically, in terms of a maturational process, such emerging organisation could be called "post-oedipal" or "late oedipal", since it may be depicted by the evolution from Young Oedipus to Old Man Oedipus; that is, from the arrogant riddle-solver, king, and enquirer of fateful crimes, who nonetheless completely missed the need for self-knowledge and violently rejected it when it came unbidden, of Sophocles's *Oedipus Tyrannus*, to the withered and mellowed blind old man of *Oedipus at Colonus*, who had transcended mere cleverness and knowledge, to finally attain the wisdom that allowed him to accept Death, when the thunder of Zeus bid him to go. But, if looked at from the synchronic perspective of a tripartite system that is kept in a dynamic equilibrium in order to attain and maintain both the identity and the unity of the three forms of a single being, I have found no Greek myth to represent it. Perhaps the only such myth that might give us an inkling of this form of existence is the Christian concept of the Holy Trinity, the triune God, which is always three and one at the same time, thus becoming a most suitable metaphor to describe three mental organisations that interact to become one single encompassing self, without losing their specificity (Tubert-Oklander, 2004, 2008, 2011b).

The concept of "levels"

Now, when this theoretical schema of the functioning of the mind is articulated with Foulkes's description of the various levels of group functioning, it becomes apparent that there is a striking similarity between them. Thus, the group's *current* and *transference levels*, which refer to the structural and dynamic functioning of social systems, and to mature object relations, in interpersonal terms, between group members, corresponds to the *oedipal model*; the *projective level of bodily and mental images*, which is that of fantasy, play, and dream, to the *narcissistic model*;

and finally, the *primordial level*, which Jungians would call "archetypal", represents the *Dionysian model* (Tubert-Oklander, 2011b, 2014).

This articulation has proved to be fruitful, but I now want to take it one step further, in order to construct a description of what I originally conceived as a "stratification of the matrix", based both on Foulkes's group analytic theory and on the metapsychological schema of the functioning of the mind outlined above. There is, however, a caveat: the very concepts of "stratification" and "levels" imply a hierarchical structure of the mind, based on a developmental sequence, and this has two connotations that are alien and even inimical to what I am trying to convey. First, there is the suggestion of a time sequence represented by successive layers that are deposited one on top of the other; then, there is the idea of a hierarchy of sophistication and prestige. In our culture, verbal, rational, secondary process thinking is considered to be intrinsically superior to other forms of thought and experience, which are deemed to be more primitive and *a priori* inadequate, and are consequently split-off and repressed, to the impoverishment of the personality. Even though this is precisely one of the distortions one would expect an analytical treatment to solve, such value judgement impregnates the whole of Freudian theory and much of contemporary psychoanalysis.

So, we should do well to keep a vigilant eye to avoid falling into this widespread prejudice—which was certainly Freud's—that values conscious, verbal, and rational thought over iconic thinking and other more carnal modes of functioning, especially since there is reason to believe that the latter more primitive and basic levels of mental and group functioning are essential for liveliness, creativity, mature relating, and social participation. In Britain, some authors belonging to the Independent Group, such as Donald Winnicott (1971), Marion Milner (1987) and Charles Rycroft (1968), emphasised, many years ago, the essential complementarity of the primary and the secondary processes, linked by the imaginative mental function. In a similar vein, the following description will underscore the complementarity and integration of the various levels of group functioning. This is why I opted for the title "The inner organisation of the matrix", instead of "The stratification of the matrix".

Nonetheless, it seems that we cannot completely escape from the idea of "levels", since it is quite handy in presenting the various models—six in the description that follows—in a sequence that goes from the more basic to the more sophisticated one. Hence, I shall alternate between the term *levels*, when I want to emphasise the degree of complexity of their respective organisations, and *models*, when describing mental functioning as a system of mutual resonance between the various forms of minding. I shall therefore present the six levels or models of experience and mental functioning in the group that I have found useful to think-through the articulation of individual and collective life.

It must be emphasised that this description, which stems from certain developments in psychoanalytic theory, is conceived from the perspective of subjective experience. Now, we know much more about the individual interpersonal experiences than about collective experience, as we do have devices for exploring the former—psychoanalysis and small group analysis—and still lack a similar instrument for the inquiry of collective experience in institutions, communities, nations, and international relations. Indeed, even the very existence of something that might give a meaning to the concept of a "collective experience" is a moot question. The social sciences have traditionally adopted the perspective of an external observer, which eschews the subjective dimension, with the notable exception of Max Weber's (1968) "interpretative sociology" (*verstehende Soziologie*) and Talcott Parsons's (1937) later development of his ideas. Another such contribution was that of the original members of the Frankfurt School, such as Max Horkheimer (1968) and Theodore Adorno (Horkheimer & Adorno, 1944), and, more recently, Jürgen Habermas (1981), on its philosophical branch. Also, on the sociological one, there is the work of Karl Mannheim (1936) and Norbert Elias (1939), and, in a socio-psychoanalytical vein, Erich Fromm (1941). All of them, especially Mannheim and Elias, had an impact on Foulkes's thought and on the later development of group analysis. Nonetheless, it is a fact that mainstream contemporary sociology has left aside the study of subjectivity. In this, I believe that group analysis and psychoanalysis have much to offer to the inquiry and understanding of society.

Six models or levels of group minding

First: the level of being

This corresponds to the Dionysian model, in which experience is syncretic and ambiguous, communication is immediate, relationship is fusional, sociability is syncytial and participative (see endnote 3), and mental processes are non-representational, but simply experiential. Bodily existence is the fountain of passion, both creative (Eros) and destructive (Thanatos). There is a primeval function of everything that is, including the other group members, the frame, and the institutional, social, cultural, and political contexts. In the members' mutual relationship, this is the basis for concern, empathy, compassion, solidarity, and resonance. Such a way of existence has been described by John Donne (1624), in his "Meditation XVII", when he wrote: "No man is an island, entire of itself; every man is a piece of the continent, a part of the main." But, when there is a hazardous situation, the members of the group are carried away by an overpowering impersonal current that emerges at the service of survival—what Ferenczi (1985) called the "*Orpha*". The mental process that rules all these happenings is what we may call the *primordial process*, which puts experience into form and action, without representing it. Hence, the impersonal nature of the experiences that ensue when this level of functioning comes to the fore. This corresponds to Foulkes's (1957) *primordial level*. The myth that best represents this level of mental and group functioning is, of course, that of Dionysus, on account of this god's particular characteristics: he was the only one to have been born of a mortal woman, did not reside in Olympus, and he was a god who suffered, in sharp contrast to the imperviousness of the other gods. But his main characteristic was that he was a god of contradictions: he came from fire and rain, and his cult represented liveliness and creativity, on the one hand, and ruthless destructiveness, on the other (Hamilton, 1942).

This is the way in which this aspect of the mind works, since it contains liveliness, both in its loving and caring aspect, and in its more sombre one, which brings about violence and destruction. It also determines the person's social nature, as a full member of the community, in a true continuity with others and with the whole non-human environment (Searles, 1960). This contrasts with and complements the experience of the self as an autonomous entity, which is an oedipal trait.

When seen from the social perspective, this dimension of mental functioning in collective entities would explain the fact that, in certain circumstances, the members of a group, particularly in the case of a large one, will show a remarkable uniformity in their feeling, thought, and action. This can be found even in the case of collective entities so large that they cannot be properly called "groups", since they have such an extension in space and time that an observer would not be able to perceive directly any concrete interactions among its members. This is the case of institutions, communities, nations, and the international system.

This was, of course, Freud's point of departure (1921c) in *Group Psychology and the Analysis of the Ego*, in discussing what he termed "mass psychology" (*Massenpsychologie*). The problem is that he based it on Gustave Le Bon's (1895) ideological version of collective behaviour in mobs (*foules*), which he implicitly endorsed, upholding the bourgeois unquestioned belief that the populace is incapable of thinking and that higher mentation is necessarily reserved for the isolated individual and the elite.

On the contrary, the idea of an indiscriminate unity of all people and their surroundings is not dependent on the quality of the persons involved, and poses the thesis that large groups, in which the members are intimately fused, have the potential both for violent, impulsive, and disorderly conduct, and for empathy, solidarity, compassion, and creativity.

This has usually been conceived in terms of "regression", but this is surely unsatisfactory, since it brings us back to the notion—upheld by both Freud (1921c) and Bion (1961)—that the kind of unity which emerges in groups is necessarily a primitive phenomenon that implies a loss of the more sophisticated mental functions. This point of view may be a consequence of the fact that this was initially studied in the case of regression in traumatised groups, since the healthy fusional level of relation that underlays group cooperation, solidarity, and understanding is usually mute, in sharp contrast to the loud products of systemic regression.

Earl Hopper (2003b) has studied extensively the processes of aggregation and massification that emerge when groups respond to massive trauma with a systemic regression. These are the pathological forms of what I am trying to describe as an essential dynamic of collective life. Massive trauma is what happens when human groups and individuals are overwhelmed by a noxious situation that surpasses their normal resources and forces them to turn to the heroic remedy of regression, in order to survive.[6]

Second: the level of dream, play, and myth

This corresponds to the narcissistic model, in which experience is imaginary—in its archaic sense of "something of the nature of an image", which has been revived by Lacan's (1966) use of the term—an appearance without substance, like a shadow on the wall or the reflection in a mirror; communication is mediated by semblance, gesture, and dance; relationship is mirror-like and reversible, and tinted by the pair admiration/denigration and by the need for survival through the Other (I am the Other, and the Other is me); sociability is ludic and imaginative, and mental processes are based on the iconic representations of fantasy. Here everything is based on identity or resemblance, and the members' mutual relationship is framed in terms of mutual projection; this is why their respective positions are always reversible. This is also the level that sustains the feeling of identity with one's group, race, or nation. The mental process that underlies all this is what Freud (1900a) called the *primary process*, which represents the already formed experience by means of iconic signs, images that reproduce some resemblance to the original sensory or bodily experience, hence putting it into image. The logic of this process is *symmetric* and *reversible*, as shown by Matte-Blanco (1988), hence, there is no quantitative space or time, causality, or negation. This is equivalent to Foulkes's (1957) *projective level*. The Greek myth that depicts this way of functioning is that of Narcissus and Echo (Pines, 1982, 2011).

A great part of social living is framed according to this model. National and religious symbols and rituals, propaganda, advertising, myths, and rumours all thrive on the use of iconic signs corresponding to the imaginary dimension of existence. In situations of crisis, such as natural disaster, war, revolution, economic collapse, or death of idealised leaders, the turbulence experienced on the Dionysian level is usually processed in terms of the narcissistic model, generating all sorts of collective fantasies that are taken as unquestionable facts. The idealisation of one's social group and the denigration of others sustain the belief in the imaginary sameness of all the members of the group.

Third: the level of language, shared reality, and common sense

This is the oedipal model, based on *discrimination* (between self and other, the sexes, the generations, and the families or clans). Experience is now shaped by language, which brings with it a conventional classification of it and a sociocultural perspective of reality and relationships (Whorf, 1956). It is therefore verbal, rational, and discriminate; there is space and time, discrete objects, causality, and negation (the affirmation of an absence). Here mental processes are based on the verbal sign system—what Lacan (1966) called "the symbolic". All this is what Freud (1900a) called the *secondary process*, whose logic is *asymmetric* and *irreversible* (Matte-Blanco, 1988), and whose task is putting experience and fantasy into words. The subject is now smart and knowledgeable, but not wise, a riddle-solver, like Young Oedipus and our present scientific-technological civilisation. Discrimination brings about a subdivision of space in inner and outer, of relationships into self and others, all inhabiting a containing space that is limited, just as are its resources; this brings about the individualism, competition, ruthlessness, territoriality, and greed that characterise our present society. The emphasis is on difference, not on similarity or identity. Sociability is interpersonal, interactive, and competitive, hence, inherently conflictual and hierarchic. The corresponding Greek myth is the tragedy of Oedipus, as presented in *Oedipus Tyrannus*.

Fourth: the level of integration

This fourth level, which I have added in my own work (Tubert-Oklander, 2004, 2008, 2011a, 2011b), can be conceived, as I have already discussed, in developmental terms as a fourth, post-oedipal or late oedipal stage, consisting of the dialectic interaction of the three previous organisations, which gives birth to the mature human subject. Each of these organisations, and the corresponding levels of group functioning, is characterised by a specific kind of experience—fusional, passional, and organic in the Dionysian; visual, specular, and reversible in the narcissistic, and discriminate, oppositional, and rational in the oedipal.

Consequently, the late oedipal organisation implies transcending the clear, oppositional, and dogmatic distinctions of the secondary process thinking of the oedipal organisation, which are a necessary consequence of the rational structure of language. Primary process and secondary process thinking are complementary (Rycroft, 1968), as each gives only a partial rendering of the complexity of experience. Hence, the more comprehensive and subtle access to knowledge should come from the confluence of the primary and the secondary processes, which thus achieves an analogical balance between imagination and rigour. But, from the point of view that I have been advancing, such integration also requires the participation of the primeval indiscriminate experience of the primordial process, in order to add liveliness, depth, and substance to this concoction. As I suggested before, the myths that give us an analogical indication of this evolution are those of the Old Man Oedipus, who attains wisdom, accepts Death, and finally departs without leaving behind corpse or tomb, metamorphosing into a god that is to watch over Athens from then on, and that of the Holy Trinity, in which the three forms of God are really one, without ever losing their individuality. In a group, this takes the form of a fluid interchange among the members, one that includes the body, the emotions, fantasy, play, and thought, finally turning into a verbal rendering, in poetic language, of their shared experience. In society, this corresponds to those moments in which the members of a community are able to cooperate and develop a common project, without having to depend on a common enemy or an all-powerful leader.[7]

Fifth: the level of law and the Weltanschauung

This level is not a part of my previous schema of the levels of relationship and experience, nor of Foulkes's (1957) description of the levels of group functioning, although it is somewhat related to his *current level*. This is so because it is a normative way of functioning that is not readily observable in the dynamic stranger groups that Foulkes conducted. It is, nonetheless, essential for understanding enduring groups, made of people who live and work together, before, during, and after the conductor's intervention, such as families, work groups, institutions, intergroup relations, and communities. The technical device that projects this problematic into the fore is, of course, the large group (de Maré, Piper & Thompson, 1991; Hopper, 2003a, 2003b; Kreeger, 1975; Schneider & Weinberg, 2003; Tubert-Oklander & Hernández-Tubert, 2014b, 2014c). This is a level of maximum abstraction, since it consists of a set of regulatory principles for action and general assumptions for experience, thought, and communication, which are independent from any individual human actors. It contains the basic set of moral principles (like the Ten Commandments) and of beliefs about the nature of reality and how it came about (like the biblical *Genesis*), as well as the nature, aim, and meaning of human existence. It is therefore a combination of the *Weltanschauung* (conception of the world), *Lebensanschauung* (conception of life), and the Law (Hernández-Tubert, 2009). It comprises institutions, traditions, codes, ethics, arts, mores, politics, philosophy, religion, science, technology, and patterns and rules for kinship; in a word, culture, or what Karl Richard Popper (1972) called the "third world" of symbolic systems and objective knowledge. This level may be seen as the collective form of the oedipal level, but it is worth differentiating it, since it is not usually addressed in our everyday group practice.

As this is the very stuff of the foundation matrix, which is shared by the conductor and the members of the group, it usually remains unseen. It is only when there is some striking difference in the origins of the various members of the group (for instance, a meeting of Israelis and Palestinians, as in Friedman, 2010) or when there are sudden changes in the social or physical environment (natural disasters, death of public figures, war, terrorism, national elections, etc.), that this level suddenly becomes visible and a subject for the analytic inquiry. In every other instance, it takes a special interpretative effort by the conductor to pose the need to take this into account, and this usually meets with stubborn resistances. The problem is that this assumptive level, which is mainly unconscious, determines a foundation for rational thinking, on a non-rational basis of shared belief. Hence, any attempt to analyse it is experienced as a vicious attack on the very possibility of rationality and on reality itself.

This normative mental process, which we may consider related to the Freudian concept of *Kulturarbeit* (the work of culture),[8] has the task of developing the collective basis for shared thinking and experience in a social group, and this is what we call "culture" (Hernández-Tubert, 2012; Smadja, 2012). Since it seems to me that the myth which captures this best is that of Moses coming down from Mount Sinai with the Law carved on two tablets of stone, I shall call this the *Mosaic level*. This ordering principle of social life has been studied mainly by the social sciences and the humanities, and still represents a major lack in psychoanalytic theory and thinking, although not in group analysis, as conceived by Foulkes, or in Pichon-Rivière's social psychology.

Sixth: the level of negotiation, reflection, and dialogue

This is more a work in progress than a level. It represents the effort to oscillate between and achieve a dialectic synthesis—although always partial and temporary—of the five previous levels. It requires a kaleidoscopic ongoing change in perspective, in order to preserve an awareness of the enormous complexity of human experience, both individual and collective, and salvage those facets of experience that have been lost by splitting, denial, or repression, usually in the aftermath of traumatic experience (Hopper, 2003b). This is the *analytic experience*. The result is a more comprehensive state of the personality and relationship, one in which there is no supremacy among the various levels of experience and group process, but a coexistence that generates a continuing tension between them. But this tension and its ongoing negotiation *is* human life, and the result of this—what Pichon-Rivière (1971) called the *spiral dialectic process*—is attaining a true human functioning, in which there is an increasing development of the potentialities of those who partake in the experience.

The *via regia* for such development is through *dialogue* and its basic principle is that everything that is, is: reality is the only truth, but reality is not equivalent to any human concept of it. Reality is not just bodily existence and emotion, fantasy and dream, rationality and discourse, or the Law, although it includes them all. Thinking and dialogue are always partial, temporary, and humble attempts to depict and encompass *some* part of the hyper-complex, multiform, and ever-changing flow of human existence, and that is the only knowledge that is available to us human beings (Beuchot, 1997; Tubert-Oklander & Beuchot Puente, 2008).

The Greek myth that best reflects this multifarious process is that of Proteus, whom Homer calls "the Old Man of the Sea", a seagod, whose ever-changing and fluid nature reminds us of water and watercourses. He was the herdsman of Poseidon's seals. Proteus knew all things about the past, the present, and the future, but actively resisted giving this knowledge to anyone. The only way to force him to do so was to seize and capture him, while he had his daily nap among the heard of seals—that is, a group—and hold him fast while he changed form over and over again, in order to escape. Then, he would return to his proper shape, reveal the truth, and plunge back into the sea.

This is a depiction of the group analytic process. When this dialogical process (which is both internal and external, individual and collective) is installed, the result is a transfiguration of the experience of I, thou, we, us, and them, and this is the access to a true human subject. Such transformation cannot be effected by a single person in isolation (if this be possible), since it requires a relation and a dialogue that open the closed system of the individual construction of the oedipal self. In this, two is better than one, but several is even better. Hence, the need for the group.

In an analytic group, this occurs at some privileged moments in which mutual understanding and cooperation lead to a shared awareness of what it means to be human. It is difficult to imagine how this might take place in larger social units, such as institutions, communities, and society as a whole, since it would require a major change in human living, such as that proposed by the various religions. But it is conceivable that the kind of work we do with those smaller units that are accessible to our professional interventions might have some effect on those larger ones of which they are a part.

A caveat

One brief comment about the schema that I have just presented ... It must have become quite clear to the reader that these six levels are in no way equivalent, and that this enumeration is not really a classification of the mental processes that take place in the group, but that was never my intention. It is true that the first three levels—the Dionysian, the narcissistic, and the oedipal—may be construed as a sequence of developmental stages, and the fourth, the late-oedipal one would then occupy the place of a maturational ideal, such as genitality or the depressive position in other theoretical systems. This would imply maintaining the developmental individual models of psychoanalysis in the description of group processes. But if we understand them as three alternate and oscillating phases—like the phases of the moon—of the relational and dialogical matrix, and the fourth one as their dialectic synthesis, then the schema becomes viable for both individual and group processes.

Now, the fifth, Mosaic level is not one of the actors of the previously described dialectics, but the context in which it takes place, its very basement, and the rules and procedures from which all these configurations are made, out of the clay of human experience. As such, it cannot be compared with the other previous levels, and it is ever-present, before the group even meets, since it is an essential part of the very being of its members, and the scene in which they dwell and relate. But it is also a theme in the analysis, which frequently comes to the fore and becomes figure, where it had been hiding in the ground. It may therefore be conceived as a main aspect of Foulkes's concept of the foundation matrix.

Finally, the sixth, Protean level is so wide and encompassing that it can be equated with human existence—or, at least, to a certain possible evolution of such existence, which we deem to be desirable, something to work for. There is, of course, a similarity between this level and the late-oedipal or Trinitarian, since both are characterised by an effort in dialectic synthesis. One may even consider the fourth level to be a partial and incomplete version of the sixth. My description, however, is not intended to offer a systematic classification, but only an evocative depiction of what actually happens in human groups.

Some conclusions

S. H. Foulkes's and Enrique Pichon-Rivière's main contribution to our study of human existence is that they showed, each of them in his own way, that such study is an inquiry of processes, and not of individuals or things. And these processes are mental by definition, even though they are not limited—as Foulkes pointed out—to the realm of the intra-dermic or to the functioning of any given brain.

Foulkes was quite explicit about this. In his book with Anthony (Foulkes & Anthony, 1965), he wrote, "to us intra-psychic does *not* convey ... 'intradermic', and we look upon the dynamic processes in their interaction" (p. 21). A few years later, he added,

> What is mind? ... I do not think that the mind is basically inside the person as an individual. I think our type of group clearly shows that. The mind that is usually called intrapsychic is a property of the group, and the processes that take place are due to the dynamic interactions in this communicational matrix. Correspondingly, we cannot make the conventional sharp differentiation between inside and outside, or between phantasy and reality. What is inside is also always outside, what is outside is inside as well. (1974, pp. 277–278)

And also:

> To me it does not seem difficult to accept that communication, verbal or otherwise, can take place, from one mind to the other with complete disregard of whether the brain substance is located in one or other skull of the participants. (1967, p. 18)

Such collective mental process is what Foulkes wished to refer to with his concept of the *matrix*. The *dynamic matrix* is everything that happens unconsciously in the group. The *individual matrix* is what each of the members, including the conductor, brings to the encounter, this being, of course, also a reflection and an expression of their participation in other groups or collective entities—past, present, or wished-for. The *foundation matrix* is the complex mental continent to which all of them belong. It is therefore invisible, since it has always been and always shall be there (it is said that a fish would be the last living being to discover water), unless its inherent contradictions or the fact that the various members have come from different collective contexts throw it into a sharp relief, turning it from ground to figure. But this is precisely what is clearly avoided when the selection of the members of a group is based, as Foulkes and Anthony (1965) suggested, on

> ... patients ... talking the same language against the same background of national feeling and participating in all the imponderables that go to make a pattern of culture ... [and] *other shared conditions, such as age, sex, religion, social background, intelligence, education, profession, marital status.* (p. 65, italics added)

In such a homogeneous group,[9] social and political issues are not likely to come to the fore, and the focus of the discussion will most probably centre on personal, emotional, and interpersonal conflicts, which is, after all, what is expected to happen in a therapy group, even though it leaves out a large portion of what is actually happening. Perception comes from difference, and hence I believe that our groups should be as heterogeneous as can be tolerated by the members, the conductors, and the institutional setting (Hernandez-Tubert, 2011; Tubert-Oklander, 2010). This is what Pichon-Rivière (1971) conceived as one of the basic laws of his technique: "The greater heterogeneity in the members and the greater homogeneity in the task brings about a greater productivity" (p. 151, translated for this edition).

This making visible some invisible aspects of the foundation matrix is more likely to happen in large groups than in small groups or in bipersonal psychoanalysis. It may, however, occur if the analyst is aware and actively looks for them. This also happens when there is a rupture, commotion, or catastrophe in the socio-political context that both analyst and group members or patients share, determining what Puget and Wender (1982; Puget, 1988) have called the "phenomenon of the overlapping worlds"—meaning a situation in which the members and the conductor are "together in the same boat", under the impact of a shared social trauma, and must also work it through together (unless, of course, they associate in a common denial of the present traumatic reality, as shown by Hopper, 1996).

Another way of analysing the foundation matrix is by means of applied group analysis, which uses a combination of multiple methods—historical evidence, political analysis, clinical evidence, the hermeneutical inquiry of culture, literary analysis, and the study of rumours, jokes, political cartoons, jokes, songs, and other popular expressions—in order to develop an analytic understanding of the particular foundation matrix of the various countries and cultures, as can be seen in the contributions to Part II of this book, dedicated to the specific foundation matrices of particular countries, cultures, and/or peoples.

Notes

1. I have developed this argument in Chapter 2, "The syncretic paradigm", of my book *The One and the Many* (Tubert-Oklander, 2014), in which I introduce an approach to a metapsychology of individuals and groups.
2. This implication of my theoretical model of individual and collective mental processes was pointed out to me by Earl Hopper (2014).
3. Bleger compares this organisation to a syncytium, which is "a multinucleate mass of protoplasm that is not differentiated in cells", hence, a *syncytial structure*.
4. This was remarked by Foulkes (1948), in the following terms: "Each individual—itself an artificial, though plausible, abstraction—is basically and centrally determined, inevitably, by the world in which he lives, by the community, the group, of which he forms a part" (p. 10). Pichon-Rivière (1979) was even more forceful, when he wrote: "One cannot think in terms of a distinction between the individual and society. It is an abstraction, a reductionism that we cannot accept" (p. 57, translated for this edition).
5. See Chapter 2 of Tubert-Oklander (2014) for an extensive treatment of this theoretical model and its antecedents in the contributions of Ferenczi, Freud, Hans Loewald, Margaret Mahler, Marion Milner, Margaret Little, and Donald Winnicott.
6. It was Hopper (2014) himself who pointed out to me that "... aggregation and massification ... are 'abnormal' forms of what you are describing as the dynamics of 'normal' forms".
7. This is akin to Bion's (1961) concept of the "work group".
8. Strachey translates this Freudian term as "the work of civilization" (Freud, 1930a).
9. Homogeneous in social, cultural, and political terms, since they may be, and usually are, heterogeneous in terms of gender, occupation, diagnosis, personal experience, and frequently also age. Hence, all groups are simultaneously both homogeneous and heterogeneous (Hopper, 2014). But this always sets a limit to what aspects of human experience may be explored in the group.

References

Beuchot, M. (1997). *Tratado de hermenéutica analógica* [Treatise of analogical hermeneutics], *fourth edition*. Mexico City: National Autonomous University of Mexico/Itaca, 2009.

Bion, W. R. (1961). *Experiences in Groups*. London: Tavistock.

Bleger, J. (1967). *Symbiosis and Ambiguity: A Psychoanalytic Study*. J. Churcher & L. Bleger (Eds.). London: Routledge, 2013.

de Maré, P., Piper, R., & Thompson, S. (1991). *Koinonia: From Hate, through Dialogue, to Culture in the Large Group*. London: Karnac.

Donne, J. (1624). Meditation XVII. In: *The Literature Network* web page (visited 16 October 2011) <http://www.online-literature.com/donne/409>.

Elias, N. (1939). *The Civilizing Process, revised edition*. E. Dunning, J. Goudsblom, & S. Mennell (Eds.). London: Blackwell, 2000.

Ferenczi, S. (1985). *The Clinical Diary of Sándor Ferenczi*. J. Dupont (Ed.), M. Balint, & N. Z. Jackson (Trans.). Cambridge, MA: Harvard, 1988.

Foulkes, S. H. (1948). *Introduction to Group-Analytic Psychotherapy*. London: Maresfield, 1984.

Foulkes, S. H. (1957). Psychodynamic processes in the light of psychoanalysis and group analysis. In: *Therapeutic Group Analysis* (pp. 108–119). London: Maresfield, 1984.

Foulkes, S. H. (Ed.) (1967). *Group Analysis International Panel and Correspondence*. Preliminary number. London: Group Analytic Society.

Foulkes, S. H. (1974). My philosophy in psychotherapy. In: *Selected Papers: Psychoanalysis and Group Analysis* (pp. 271–280). London: Karnac, 1990.

Foulkes, S. H., & Anthony, E. J. (1965). *Group Psychotherapy: The Psychoanalytic Approach, second edition*. London: Maresfield, 1984.

Freud, S. (1900a). *The Interpretation of Dreams. S. E., 4–5*. London: Hogarth.

Freud, S. (1921c). *Group Psychology and the Analysis of the Ego. S. E., 18*: 65–144. London: Hogarth.

Freud, S. (1930a). *Civilization and Its Discontents. S. E., 21*: 57–146. London: Hogarth.

Freud, S. (1950a). A project for a scientific psychology. *S. E., 1*: 281–391. London: Hogarth. (Originally written in 1895.)

Friedman, R. (2010). The group and the individual in conflict and war. *Group Analysis, 43*: 281–300.

Fromm, E. (1941). *Escape from Freedom*. New York: Holt, 1994.

Habermas, J. (1981). *The Theory of Communicative Action, in two volumes*. T. McCarthy (Trans.). Boston, MA: Beacon, 1984–1987.

Hamilton, E. (1942). *Mythology: Timeless Tales of Gods and Heroes*. New York: Warner, 1999.

Hernández-Tubert, R. (2009). Inconsciente y concepción del mundo. Implicaciones filosóficas y psicoanalíticas [The unconscious and the Weltanschauung: Philosophic and psychoanalytic implications]. In: R. Blanco Beledo (Ed.), *Filosofía ¿y? Psicoanálisis* [Philosophy and? psychoanalysis] (pp. 79–103). Mexico City: National Autonomous University of Mexico.

Hernández-Tubert, R. (2011). The politics of despair: from despair to dialogue and hope. *Group Analysis, 44*: 27–39.

Hernández-Tubert, R. (2012). Commentary on Erik Smadja's paper "The notion of *Kulturarbeit* (the work of culture) in Freud's writings". Read at the Mexican Psychoanalytic Association, Mexico City, February.

Hopper, E. (1996). The social unconscious in clinical work. In: *The Social Unconscious* (pp. 126–161). London: Jessica Kingsley, 2003.

Hopper, E. (2003a). *The Social Unconscious*. London: Jessica Kingsley.

Hopper, E. (2003b). *Traumatic Experience in the Unconscious Life of Groups*. London: Jessica Kingsley.

Hopper, E. (2014). Personal communication.

Horkheimer, M. (1968). *Critical Theory*. New York: Continuum, 2002.

Horkheimer, M., & Adorno, T. (1944). *Dialectic of Enlightenment*. London: Verso, 1997.

Kreeger, L. (Ed.) (1975). *The Large Group: Dynamics and Therapy*. London: Karnac.

Lacan, J. (1966). *Ecrits: The First Complete Edition in English*. B. Fink (Trans.). New York: W. W. Norton, 2006.

Le Bon, G. (1895). *Psychologie des foules*. Paris: Alcan. [English translation: *The Crowd: A Study of the Popular Mind*. Mineola, NY: Dover, 2002.]

Mannheim, K. (1936). *Ideology and Utopia*. London: Routledge, 2000.

Matte-Blanco, I. (1988). *Thinking, Feeling, and Being*. London: Routledge.

Milner, M. (1987). *The Suppressed Madness of Sane Men*. London: Tavistock.

Montevechio, B. (1999). *Las nuevas fronteras del psicoanálisis. Dionisio, Narciso, Edipo* [The new frontiers of psychoanalysis: Dionysus, Narcissus, Oedipus]. Buenos Aires: Lumen.

Montevechio, B. (2002). *Más allá de Narciso. La problemática de las identidades* [Beyond Narcissus: The problematics of identities]. Buenos Aires: Lumen.

Parsons, T. (1937). *The Structure of Social Action (in two volumes)*. New York: Free Press, 1968.

Pichon-Rivière, E. (1971). *El proceso grupal. Del psicoanálisis a la psicología social (1)* [The group process: From psychoanalysis to social psychology (1)]. Buenos Aires: Nueva Visión.

Pichon-Rivière, E. (1979). *Teoría del vínculo* [Theory of the bond]. Buenos Aires: Nueva Visión.

Pines, M. (1982). Reflections on mirroring. In: *Circular Reflections* (pp. 17–37). London: Jessica Kingsley, 1998.

Pines, M. (2011). Desire leading to death: The myth of Echo and Narcissus. In: L. Navaro, R. Friedman, & S. L. Schartzberg (Eds.), *Desire, Passion and Gender: Clinical Implications* (pp. 65–79). New York: Nova.

Popper, K. R. (1972). *Objective Knowledge, revised edition*. Oxford: Oxford University Press, 1979.

Puget, J. (1988). Social violence and psychoanalysis in Argentina. *Free Associations, 1*: 84–140.

Puget, J., & Wender, L. (1982). Analista y paciente en mundos superpuestos [Analyst and patient in overlapping worlds]. *Psicoanálisis, 4*: 503–536. [This includes the comments of M. I. Siquier and R. Serebriany, as well as the authors' response.]

Rycroft, C. (1968). *Imagination and Reality*. New York: International Universities Press.

Schneider, S., & Weinberg, H. (Eds.) (2003). *The Large Group Revisited*. London: Jessica Kingsley.

Searles, H. F. (1960). *The Nonhuman Environment*. New York: International Universities Press.

Smadja, E. (2012). The notion of *Kulturarbeit* (the work of culture) in Freud's writings. Read at the Mexican Psychoanalytic Association, Mexico City, February.

Tubert-Oklander, J. (2004). Dionisio y Narciso. La contribución de Blanca Montevechio al estudio del sincretismo [Dionysus and Narcissus: The contribution of Blanca Montevechio to the study of syncretism]. Read at the 43rd International Congress of Psychoanalysis, New Orleans, LA, March.

Tubert-Oklander, J. (2008). An inquiry into the alpha function. *Canadian Journal of Psychoanalysis, 16*: 224–245.

Tubert-Oklander, J. (2010). The matrix of despair: from despair to desire through dialogue. *Group Analysis, 43*: 127–140.

Tubert-Oklander, J. (2011a). Lost in translation: A contribution to intercultural understanding. *Canadian Journal of Psychoanalysis, 19*: 144–168.

Tubert-Oklander, J. (2011b). Enrique Pichon-Rivière: the social unconscious in the Latin-American tradition of group analysis. In: Hopper, E. & Weinberg, H. (Eds.), *The Social Unconscious in Persons, Groups, and Societies: Volume I: Mainly Theory* (pp. 45–67). London: Karnac.

Tubert-Oklander, J. (2014). *The One and the Many: Relational Psychoanalysis and Group Analysis*. London: Karnac.

Tubert-Oklander, J., & Beuchot Puente, M. (2008). *Ciencia mestiza. Psicoanálisis y hermenéutica analógica* [Hybrid science: Psychoanalysis and analogical hermeneutics]. Mexico City: Torres.

Tubert-Oklander, J., & Hernández de Tubert, R. (2004). *Operative Groups: The Latin-American Approach to Psychoanalysis*. London: Jessica Kingsley.
Tubert-Oklander, J., & Hernández-Tubert, R. (2014a). The social unconscious and the large group—Part I: the British and the Latin-American traditions. *Group Analysis, 47*(2): 99–112.
Tubert-Oklander, J., & Hernández-Tubert, R. (2014b). The social unconscious and the large group—Part II: a context that becomes text. *Group Analysis, 47*(3): 329–344.
Tubert-Oklander, J., & Hernández-Tubert, R. (2014c). The social unconscious and the large group—Part III: listening to the voices in the wind. *Group Analysis, 47*(4): 420–435.
Weber, M. (1968). *Economy and Society: An Outline of Interpretive Sociology*. G. Roth & C. Wittich (Eds.). Berkeley, CA: University of California Press, 1978.
Whorf, B. J. (1956). *Language, Thought, and Reality*, J. B. Carroll (Ed.). Cambridge, MA: M. I. T. Press, 1967.
Winnicott, D. W. (1971). *Playing and Reality*. London: Routledge, 1999.

PART II

NON-VERBAL COMMUNICATION

CHAPTER FIVE

The unbearable appeal of totalitarianism and the collective self: an inquiry into the social nature of non-verbal communication

Helena Klímová

How has it come about that so many people can identify with totalitarianism? Here are some images from the last century:

- thousands of peasants dying of hunger in the fertile Ukraine during the "class enemy struggle"
- thousands of living skeletons found in the Nazi concentration camps
- thousands of people saluting god-like leaders as they march through the main squares of Moscow, Berlin, Peking, Prague, Pyonyang ...
- the phenomenon of the "double culture", when the official media use "newspeak", purged of information and meaning, while meaningful communication exists only underground and under punishment ...

Some of these social catastrophes were born in the context of enthusiastic social movements. Only later was the fanaticism recognised. What made the masses succumb to totalitarian patterns and leaders?

How did democratic values, institutions, and practices re-emerge?

Some hypothetical answers to these questions can be formulated in terms of conceptualisations of the social unconscious, sociocultural regression, communitas, the fourth basic assumption, the role of non-verbal communication within the foundation matrix, rituals, and true and false collective selves.

The true collective self as the driving energy of history

The individual self of an infant (Winnicott, 1960) may develop in two ways: the true self emerges when the natural needs of the child are recognised by the "good-enough mother"; but a false self is likely to develop when the primary caregiver is not a "good-enough mother".

According to group analytic theory, the group creates its own subjectivity, which suggests the possibility of the formation of a group-self or a collective self (Pines, 1966, p. 183; Stone, 2009). The collective self might be either true or false, based on a true-we or a false-we (Klímová, 2011, pp. 187–208).

The developmental pattern of the collective false self is comparable to that of the individual false self, where:

- the needs, qualities, uniqueness, and boundaries of the subject (here, of the group) were suppressed, not verbalised in dialogue
- instead, ideology was substituted, then identified with, by group members
- although the process was enforced, it was experienced as the genuine wish of the subject because the subject had identified with the aggressor (ibid., p. 198).

Neither the individual false self nor the collective false self has to begin as a conscious pretence or lie; in each case, the false identities begin in genuine identification. Under normal conditions, groups are likely to develop communitas (Turner, 1969): to proceed to a new state of development, a human group regresses from its everyday structure and function and immerses itself in a state of undifferentiatedness, of liminality. The threshold or limen marks a rite of passage. This is a time of transition. The primal state of communitas is experienced as follows:

> It is as though there are here two major "models" for human interrelatedness ... The first is of society as a structured, differentiated, and often hierarchical system of politico-legal-economic positions with many types of evaluation, separating men in terms of "more" or "less". The second ... is of society as an unstructured or rudimentarily

> structured and relatively undifferentiated … communion of equal individuals who submit together to the general authority of the ritual elders …. Communitas is of the now; structure is rooted in the past and extends into the future through language, law, and custom … communitas and structure are to be found at all stages and levels of culture and society. (ibid., pp. 82–100)

Communitas corresponds in various ways with millenarian movements: homogeneity, equality, absence of property, reduction of everybody to the same status, sexual continence or sexual community (both liquidate the structural status of the family), minimisation of sex distinctions, abolition of rank, disregard for personal appearance, total obedience to the prophet or leader, acceptance of pain and suffering … Everyone is a "sibling" or "comrade" and independent positions and individual boundaries are reduced; everyone identifies with everyone else, with nature, with the universe … there is a longing for transcendence.

Communitas is, however, a transitional phenomenon. It resembles lightning through which energy flashes, connecting the highest with the lowest, heaven with earth, killing and creating. It connects body and soul. It can be experienced by participants as social and spiritual intercourse that gives birth to new life in the group. This is the time when values and rules emerge that will be fundamental and sacred for the new social structure.

The birth of the false collective self

The need to create communitas can be noticed in all human societies and cultures as a result of the group tendency to structure societal time and to keep the group alive, prosperous, and attractive, worth identifying with; but the existential need of the group members for the experience of the social and spiritual energy of communitas may be misled and misused politically. Any group or any organisation, a religious community, political party, sect, or social movement may try to use the elements of communitas—totality, equality, absence of property, absence of status and rank, total obedience, disregard for individual personality—in the service of social engineering:

> In practice, of course, the impetus soon becomes exhausted, and the "movement" soon becomes itself an institution among other

> institutions—often one more fanatical and militant then the rest, for the reason that it feels itself to be the unique bearer of the universal-human truth .... (ibid., p. 98)

In this way the totalitarianism may be introduced, quite willingly and enthusiastically, when the regressed masses identify with smuggled-in values and patterns. These smuggled objects are then accepted as part of the collective self which, thereby, becomes a false collective self.

In response to traumatic event(s), groups are likely to regress, and in extreme forms they are likely to regress to states of incohesion as Hopper (2003; Hopper & Weinberg, 2011) explained in a theory of incohesion:

> People who have experienced the fear of annihilation ... are likely to form groups that are characterised by general processes of incohesion. These processes of incohesion are likely to be characterised by "aggregation", in response to fission and fragmentation and, then, by "massification" in response to fusion and confusion and, in turn, by oscillations between massification and aggregation. In other words, primary and secondary aggregation and primary and secondary massification comprise the bi-polar forms of incohesion. Thus, I call this fourth basic assumption "Incohesion:Aggregation/Massification" or (ba)I: A/M. (Hopper, 2003, p. 66)

The liminal time of the group, even during ordinary developmental transformation, is characterised by totality, homogeneity, equality, anonymity, and total unity. As the members' individual boundaries are temporarily suspended, their united energy is invested outward: to build outer boundaries against the enemy. This may be experienced by group members as a negative attitude towards anything or anybody that differs—outside the group as well as inside. Such experience may lead to behaviour which is marked by scapegoating and/or purification—and this behaviour may prevail especially when the group feels endangered.

Scapegoating and purification are associated with the total uniformity of beliefs, enchantment, homogeneity, anonymisation, fundamentalism, hate masquerading as love, shunning ... which characterises the social system in a state of massification (ibid., pp. 71–81).

The false collective self is a totalitarian phenomenon

It may be introduced into society by a totalitarian movement or—vice versa—a group's false collective identity may stabilise a totalitarian system. On the other hand, when more groups are able to experience and express their true collective selves, then the totalitarian system begins to lose its charisma and power.

This development took place in central Europe from the middle of the last century.

Vignette

The Czechs, Slovaks, Poles, Hungarians, eastern Germans ... having been deeply traumatised by the Second World War, fell prey to Communist totalitarianism imported from the former Soviet Union, one of the WWII victors. In the former Czechoslovakia the Communist Party, presented as a part of the liberating force, even won the free elections in 1946. Later this victory was recognised as erroneous, a result of fascination with a social predator, as identification with the aggressor. The subject—both the creator and the child of this faulty decision-making—was the false collective self.

Leaving aside deficiencies in rational political analysis and the lack of historical experience with totalitarian regimes in their various masks and potentialities, what was the social mechanism that enabled the collective self to influence history this way?

The non-verbal dimension of the foundation matrix as a social tool

Throughout history, non-verbal communication has been a substantial and important element of social evolution: symbols, rituals, dance, music ... have been a strong archaic instrument of existential maturation.

Ritual behaviour is a phylogenic invention to create social structure and culture. In the course of evolution a species started to use one of its functions in a new way—as a way of communication. The function is, in its performance, transformed for the purpose of symbolic behaviour to be distinguished from its ordinary existence. According to Konrad Lorenz (1992, p. 60) a number of animals use various functions: deer use their running ability to make threatening steps; some birds transform their walk into an attractive dance; bees announce a new destination by a dancing flight; predators create their social structure through their eating order; dogs fence their territory by leaving odour; certain birds and all humans transform their breathing into singing and speaking …

Human language in phylogeny is likely to have started in the same way as in ontogeny—when the ability to vocalise (the transformed breathing function) was used for relation-sharing between mother and child. The ritually transformed function is nourished by libido; thus the vitally important message also brings pleasure. Language is "maternal"; communication is the function mainly of the mother (as compared with territory, which seems to belong to the father—"Vaterland", "otčina").

It is through language that we develop our brain capacity. However, the more that we have been concentrating on rational meaning, the more our language has been losing its ritual properties. Nowadays, the language of information does not allow any sign of ritual (e.g., repetition, gradation, melody); then its messages are accepted generally, regardless of any cultural differences (Hopper & Weinberg, 2011; Cassirer, 1946).

In contrast, singing, a sibling to language, has kept its full ritual quality: music in general functions as the most universal and powerful way to communicate emotions. These are mainly repetition, gradation, melody, and rhythm—the way time is dealt with—that distinguishes ritual behaviour from non-ritual.

Different ritual behaviour distinguishes the different species and subspecies—and different human cultures

In the plan and functioning of the body and its organs, the human species does not differ basically from some other species. We differ much more through different behaviour. We differ in culture, whose origin is ritual. Rituals and symbols form the organising principle that introduces social order: boundaries and ties, values, identity, roles, belongingness and alienation …

> Powerful drives and emotions associated with human physiology, especially with the physiology of reproduction, are divested in the ritual process of their antisocial quality and attached to components of the normative order, energizing the latter with a borrowed vitality …. Symbols are both the resultants and the instigators of this process, and encapsulate its properties. (Turner, 1969, p. 49)

Specific rituals divide or unite people. It is through them that human beings form their relations with each other in dyads, groups, and societies—and with God. Rituals involve, create, and express a very important message and experience about the nature of the collective self, about the identity of the group. This archaic behaviour powerfully influences the self-perception of the group as a whole, as well as what is perceived as the most truthful and genuine—the sacred.

The origin of ritual is pre-human. It is expressed with the help of body language and perceived by the body as a whole; rituals are lived by the total being. The message may be non-verbal or preverbal, pre-rational; a more proper mediator than verbal language is music. Music is a way to structure and aestheticise time.

Even in modern times, music has strongly influenced the political and social development of groups. Singing-chanting is a powerful tool; it is even possible to chant oneself into somebody else's mind and wishes.

Vignette (cont.)

This was the case of the Czechs after WWII. Alongside major post-war changes in politics and the economy, culture also proved its soft power. Everything was imported from the Soviet Union—political patterns, economic rules, cultural symbols, songs. Yet, contrary to the rest of that import, most melodies were enchanting. Russian songs possessed that ability to enchant and to transform. The pathos and beauty of Russian vocal music was rooted in the historical tradition of the non-instrumental male polyphony of the Russian Orthodox Church. Those chorales expressed the deep spiritual longing of suffering people who were praying for redemption. The tradition of powerful ritual regression was later used and filled with new meaning—accepted with the Soviet totalitarian ideology as a new spirituality.

The hero of the songs was an archetypal figure, gifted with superhuman abilities for fighting, building—and suffering, which is a very important part of the rite of passage. The heroic martyr was the exact embodiment of the messianic sadomasochistic temptation of the revolution. The suffering proletarian hero was a good trigger for more massification.

In addition, a combination of pastoral poetry and political propaganda was written in the USSR during and after the era of famine, monstrous political trials, gulags, the forced transportation of whole nations—and under severe censorship.

Such was the unspoken content beneath the powerful melodies that flooded the mute space of post-war central Europe. The collective false self was born under a "spell"!

The non-verbal part of the foundation matrix has a powerful creative function

Many people enjoyed not only singing together but also moving together. This too contributes to massification:

> *Vignette (cont.)*
>
> Big military parades were organised in the main squares, and mass physical exercise displays (Spartakiades) took place in large sports stadiums. Masses of people dressed alike, looking in the same direction (towards the leaders), marched in rows in rhythm, in an unnatural, numb way. Stiff exaggerated steps recalled the threatening ritual walk of some animals.

Body synchronisation is usually felt as very pleasurable; it helps an individual to regress, to feel united with others. While dancing together, people are harmonising their body rhythms according to their partner or circle. Pilgrimage has been used, in many ancient and contemporary rituals, to symbolise the spiritual transformation of the group. Body synchrony transforms the enchantment of the group into social order, it turns communitas into structure. This basic all-human ritual, too, was misused for political purposes.

> Communist rituals, especially those of the Spartakiada, represent the most radical way of manipulation with the human body. (Roubal, 2009)

In a time of rituals, of communitas, the very concept of time is suspended. People feel immersed in regression, overcome by eternality, timelessness.

The concept of "time collapse" coined by Vamik Volkan and discussed further by Regine Scholz (2012a) should be recalled: the experience of communitas may be artificially brought to life when an old collective trauma is awakened which was not mourned or forgotten, which then grew inside the group identity and now gives meaning to contemporary movements of the group. Old collective heroes, especially tragic ones, are recalled. This reawakened "chosen trauma" may bring communitas to life and the masses may be manipulated by social engineers.

Totalitarian ideology is based on a wrong assumption that the transitory state of communitas (when masses may be easily manipulated) can be maintained forever as a social system. However, the phenomenon of communitas tends to appear periodically, brought to life by the social need of the group, and then vanishes.

The organising principle of the group life is the rhythmisation of societal time, mostly by non-verbal means.

Various cultures prescribe complementary sorts of time: a time for eating or fasting, wandering or homemaking, working or celebrating … This shifting between a time of structure and a time of liminality happens more easily in simple and free societies and contributes to their natural regeneration.

The rhythmisation of societal time is comparable to the biblical principle for individuals: to work for six days (to live in a social structure) and to enjoy the rituals of freedom, family relations, unity with God, on the seventh day. The rhythmisation of time contributes to the sanity of the individual and of society at large. The time of celebration, of prayer, of communitas, cannot last; it must be exchanged for a time of structure, work, rationality, and reality testing. And vice versa—work has to be inspired by the existential meaning born in the time of ritual.

By organising time rhythmically the non-verbal communication supplies the group with energy and existential meaning. It is through rituals that the group realises its need to survive and multiply as a property of nature.

The urge to survive and multiply lacks morals. This vitally necessary requirement is ethically blind. It is culture that has to be developed as an expression of humanity, has to supply morals and ethical values. This is the way the group collective self is cultivated.

Should it happen that the collective self is misled by identification with the aggressor, needs and tendencies alien to the group—false needs—may be involved. Only thanks to the process of reality testing may the true collective self then develop, being both the subject and the child of this process.

Enchantment is replaced by sober truth thanks to the reality principle

This was the case of Central European history during the 1960s.

Vignette (cont.)

All the Eastern imports, the imported economic, political, social, and cultural patterns, were critically evaluated in the search for the true collective self. A movement for freedom and independence grew through the 1960s in Czechoslovakia towards what was called "socialism with a human face" and was labelled the "Prague Spring".

However, in August 1968 the Soviet bloc armies invaded Czechoslovakia. The Prague Spring was defeated, state sovereignty destroyed, and a time of purges arrived. Czechoslovak citizens were forced one by one to sign their agreement with the occupation.

Then the false collective self was totally gone—what dominated the public sphere was the proclaimed conscious lie. (This atmosphere was very well illustrated, much later, by the Oscar-winning film *Kolya*). Splitting one's personality became the main dynamic way of coping—for the individual as for society. A shadow economy and corruption grew side by side with the dysfunctional state economy; the authorities forced on the nation were obeyed formally, while those who had been suppressed were, sometimes, secretly respected as genuine.

The true feelings of the suppressed nation were expressed in underground art. Intellectuals dismissed from their social positions used to meet at home in secret to read aloud their banned publications. The banned literature was typewritten and then distributed underground by self-help. These handmade books represented the new cultural phenomenon—*samizdat*.[1]

Literature and music underwent a parallel process. A strange phenomenon appeared—censored music, thus the magical power of music was proved as a force to be fought against.

Vignette (cont.)

Only some music was officially approved; that which openly supported the system, classical music and sterilised folklore. Music from the West was forbidden, with the exception of spirituals—the black man's songs—seen as a protest against imperialism. While the public media displayed emptied music, people started to search for new artistic expression:loud music full of wrath was an answer to a world full of lies and violence. It was also its complementary part: both consciously and unconsciously, some underground

> musicians invited the primitive political terror to be used against them. By being brutally persecuted, they proved the violent nature of the system … Protest singers—modern minstrels—appeared. They travelled from place to place, into private homes, onto small stages; equipped with mouth harmonica and guitar they sang to people face to face. Many of them turned for inspiration to ancient folklore, some to the forbidden resource—the Bible. All sang their own "handmade" songs, their everyday little stories and individual feelings. They reintroduced daily life, with anger and humour, in truth. One much-loved song praised the "truth-speaking word" (the song created by Jaroslav Hutka).

The protest singers' songs, together with samizdat, both "handmade art production", represented a special cultural phenomenon that spread through Central Europe and played a decisive role later, in the final defeat of totalitarianism. The singers and their audience, while singing often together, face to face, created a special group situation; they undertook together a symbolic journey of mind, a transformative experience. It was the exact opposite to the previous totalitarian mass enchantment, when ego dissolution originally felt pleasurable, but later no longer authentic. Now every person in the audience, suffocated and suppressed by history, was starting to feel human individuality anew, as precious and in truth.

It used to happen in small groups where people were aware of each other through their body senses, that body language participation represented by singing was experienced repeatedly—it was a ritual transformation. A true identity was emerging at both the individual and the group level. A new collective self was being born. Art thus returned to its primordial roots as the voice of a tribe.

The non-verbal language of music was simply expressing and shaping the experience of the group collective self in the best way—as, here and now, we are together in truth. No major religious or ideological concepts were there to mislead into totalitarianism, just the we-feeling and the truth-feeling. Thus those basic values were rediscovered, the values that echoed ancient collective wisdom, historical group tradition; without religion, teaching, or ideology—just the search for truth based on continuous reality testing, on the continuous experience of body and mind. The search for truth as imprinted in the foundation matrix of the group.

Vignette (cont.)

The Czech Republic was established and has been persisting as the most agnostic and least religious country in the whole of Europe.

The independent way of thinking was inspired by Jan Hus: priest, rector of Charles University in Prague, and heretic, who in 1415 was burnt alive by the Church in Constance. He reintroduced the principle of truth into the teaching of the Church: "... search for the truth, hear the truth, learn the truth, love the truth, speak the truth, hold the truth, defend the truth till death: the truth will deliver you from ... the death of your soul ..." (Hus, 1412). Hus's thoughts started the reformation movement in the Bohemian Lands (a hundred years before Luther) until its defeat by the Habsburg monarchy (1620).

After centuries this search for truth was revived by Tomáš Garrigue Masaryk, the first president (1918) of Czechoslovakia; the Czech president's flag bears the device "Truth Prevails" (Veritas Vincit).

Many decades later, under the demoralising and depressing Communist totalitarianism, it was again the idea of the "life in truth" (coined by Václav Havel) that appeared as a saving grace.

The Czechs see themselves—and are known—as non-believers, prone to scepticism; instead of searching for a "true God" or a "true ideology" the spiritual longing of the group traditionally and eventually turns to a search for truth itself. The search for truth is internalised as a struggle between the false and the true collective self.

The true collective self could not be brought into existence without painful decision-making on the individual level

Vignette (cont.)

After the defeat of the Prague Spring in 1968, Soviet hegemony was proclaimed to stay forever. Many hopeless people accepted survival strategies ("We shall submit ostensibly, we shall live in a dual morality") which resembled the learned helplessness syndrome. Lives were dominated by lack of truth and lack of honesty.

Facing persecution, the new elite, consisting of the samizdat producers and the protest folk-singers, slowly rose from the underground. It spoke up publicly in 1977 with the Charter 77 manifesto. Its main demand was expressed by Václav Havel's "life in truth".

> The demand of "life in truth" did not consist of asking people to become heroic martyrs; instead, it suggested a change in everyday morals: to lose degrading habits, like stealing petty things at workplaces (as a small revenge on the system), to stop pretending and lying for political profit ... "Life in truth" meant that in everyday social contact a person honestly found and spoke the truth. The demand brought an unexpected existential discovery: a regained self-respect. There was still no hope for the future, but life in the present was rewarding again. The truth was healing narcissistic injuries. The banned culture gave truth its symbols, rituals, and language. Nevertheless, it took more than a decade for totalitarianism in Central Europe to come to an end.
>
> Then the 1989 revolution in Prague was labelled "velvet"; there was no violence because "We are not like them".

There were no ready-made rituals; neither Church nor ideology was felt to be dominating people's minds. The need for liminal transformation, the atmosphere of communitas, found its own way of expression; people marched, gathered and stayed together spontaneously, and spontaneously they invented a simple ritual of key-ringing (as there were no bells to announce the end), they greeted Václav Havel and other dissidents, and they spontaneously sang the beloved song about the "truth-speaking word" which had been sung as a tribal prayer in small groups many times before ... it was a precious time when the true collective self was present and experienced as living.

The repeated struggle between the false and the true collective self seems to express an important part of the foundation matrix of Czech history.

Even though this developmental struggle is a general phenomenon, it may be considered as a significant component of a particular foundation matrix.

> I prefer the notion of the foundation matrix, a communicational (including body, music, symbols etc. as media) understanding of (un)conscious processes. And if you visualize different densities of communicational acts, you get maps, clusters, patterns—horizontal in space, vertical in time. Those matrices can be seen as [a] pattern that generates patterns. (Scholz, 2012a, p. 27) (See Chapter Two in this volume).

The repeated struggle for the true collective self in the Bohemian Lands started centuries ago as a part of religious dialogue. Later it used the framework of national emancipation … finally, the contemporary search for truth, the struggle for the true collective self, was expressed as a moral demand vis-à-vis the general demoralisation.

In its deep longing, this search may acquire a spiritual quality.

The human group longs to emerge in truth and be gifted with meaning, as a meaningful collective being of its own

The path from nature to culture as the birth of humanity is experienced by group members as a passion: the group is longing to express its special unique meaning, its mission, its identity in the deep truth—the group is longing to live its true collective self.

However, as soon as the group collective self-identifies and verbalises its true meaning—under free conditions—the search continues: for new self-discoveries, which aim to correct the previous one, discoveries of any self-cheating, false enchantment, any outworn, overcome, emptied likeness.

> Culture, language etc. are slow moving entities, but definitely moving … if we are not clear about the fact that we are not dealing with eternal (inherited) but with time bound material … we are not so far from (unwanted) proximities to new right wing thinking, in which culture meanwhile has replaced the notion of race … Identities are consistently under construction … we should be careful not to replicate these idealised entities that can soon take on the character of something sacred … then the next holy war might be not far away. (ibid., pp. 27–28)

Truth is not to be held or possessed, it is to be constantly sought for, discovered, and tested. It is a rule of time rhythmisation that allows the group to prevent its decay, to create its truthful identity anew. In the mass societies of today, with their enormous and multicultural memberships, it is only freedom and free expression that allow unconscious social needs to come to the surface. The group members need to test the established truth and to formulate new findings. This collective need awakes the phenomena of liminality, of communitas. Group members then may participate in spontaneously invented rituals that are experienced as the deepest truth, fitting the best to the time and the participants. The collective self is then experienced as newly born and truthful, perhaps as "reborn".

The need for liminal transformation may also appear in the case of an unexpected touching event.

Death of a "tribal king"

Vignette (cont.)

Václav Havel, originally a censored intellectual, then a leading dissident, was the author of the idea of the "life in truth". In his writings, he used to express the truth without pathos and with humour. In his life, he stood for the truth, up to being persecuted and jailed. He won back for people the self-respect they lost under totalitarianism. After the "velvet revolution" in 1989 he served as the Czechoslovak and later as the Czech president.

Václav Havel passed away on December 18, 2011.

As the news of his death spread masses of people spontaneously flooded the streets of Prague; soon burning candles covered Wenceslas Square ... "Wenceslas" is an ancient form of the name Václav, Havel's name was Václav and the "Good king Wenceslas" of Christmas carols was the medieval Bohemian king ... So, the possibility for symbolisation was at hand. But what sort of ritual to use? The Czechs by a two-thirds majority refuse any Church ...

However, the need to merge with others in some collective ritual was evident ... Tens of thousands spontaneously came together to mourn; crowds slowly moved through the Prague streets and over the river up to the castle ... No music was heard, no songs, no words, only silence lasting for hours and the footsteps of so many. But such a shared silence is a part of music too, it is its complementary and meaningful part ...

After the funeral a group of Havel's friends collected all the flowers and wreaths, loaded them on a boat and floated them down the water ... as a self-made ritual.

Václav Havel's death was like the loss of the "tribal king", a very traumatising event. Yet this trauma did not invite any social pathology, did not weaken the group. The group members felt the freedom to invent their own rituals to mourn—and thus to heal the group. The experience of communitas supported the true collective self ...

When did the group members experience it, this time of communitas?

In May 1945, when the war ended.
During the Prague Spring, in 1968.
During the Velvet Revolution, in 1989.
Then—when Václav Havel passed away, in 2011 ...

Always within the span of one generation. Just as though the collective self was expressing its need for time rhythmisation, for rebirth as a truthful collective being.

The longing for the life in truth is a spiritual and healing phenomenon

Truth cannot be owned as an object, as "a thing"; it should not serve any other goals. Truth cannot be reached definitively, it is always to be sought anew. To accept this final inaccessibility of the truth means protection of the collective self against totalitarian temptation.

The inaccessibility of the definite truth and the longing for identification with the truth—these two phenomena belong to what is felt as sacred. The human longing to identify with the truth, to find one's own meaning, is a very powerful one. It is of the same urgency as:

> "As the hart panteth after the water brooks, so panteth my soul after thee, O God. My soul thirsteth for God, for the living God: when shall I come and appear before God?" (Psalms, 42: 1–2)

People may be longing and struggling for life in truth with the same urgency, once they are able to formulate the truth as the meaning of their collective self.

Note

1. "Samizdat" was one of the words transplanted into the Central European languages from Russian, as a part of the totalitarian influence; samizdat books were written or translated by underground authors, then typewritten many times, bound and distributed secretly, free of charge, and under threat of severe punishment; these home-made books often were lacking any bibliographical data—such data as well as the "editors" names, and the times and places of manufacturing had to stay hidden.

These manuscripts and handmade books were later collected by one of the underground editors Jiří Gruntorád and established as a library named Libri Prohibiti; in June 2013 this collection was accepted into the UNESCO register Memory of the World.

References

Cassirer, E. (1946). *The Myth of the State*. New Haven, CT: Yale University Press.

Hopper, E. (2003). *Traumatic Experience in the Unconscious Life of Groups* London: Jessica Kingsley.

Hopper, E., & Weinberg, H. (Eds.) (2011). *The Social Unconscious in Persons, Groups, and Societies: Volume 1: Mainly Theory*. London: Karnac.

Hus, J. (1412). *Výklad viery*. Cs.wikiquote.org/wiki/Pravda, accessed March 30, 2017.

Klímová, H. (2011). False we—the false collective self as a dynamic part of the social unconscious in a totalitarian system. In: E. Hopper & H. Weinberg (Eds.), *The Social Unconscious in Persons, Groups, and Societies: Volume 1: Mainly Theory* (pp. 187–208). London: Karnac.

Lorenz, K. (1992). *Takzvané zlo*. Prague: Academia, 1992.

Pines, M. (1996). The self as a group: the group as a self. *Group Analysis, 29*(2): 183–190.

Roubal, P. (2009). Jak se dělá lid? Prague: Dějiny a současnost.

Scholz, R. (2012a). The social unconscious and the foundation matrix—some thoughts. *Group-Analytic Contexts, 56*: 27–28.

Scholz, R. (2012b). As time goes by—collective trauma and memory. Prix Irene Conference 2012, Prague.

Stone, W. (2009). *Contributions of Self Psychology to Group Psychotherapy: Selected Papers*. London: Karnac.

The Holy Bible (1611). *Psalm 42: 1–2*. London: The British and Foreign Bible Society.

Turner, V. W. (1969). *The Ritual Process: Structure and Anti-Structure*. London: Penguin.

Winnicott, D. W. (1960). *Ego Distortion in Terms of True and False Self*. London: Hogarth.

CHAPTER SIX

The musical foundation matrix: communicative musicality as a mechanism for the transmission and elaboration of co-created unconscious social processes

Linde Wotton

In this chapter I would like to bring insights from the field of communicative musicality to contribute to our understanding of the co-created unconscious social processes of the foundation matrix. I provide a brief outline of the theory of communicative musicality developed by Malloch and Trevarthen (2009), which holds that our innate musicality is the foundation of all human communication, and I refer to the work of Gratier and Apter-Danon (2009), which demonstrates the crucial importance of improvisation to the process of belonging. They describe the co-creation of the early protohabitus within infant-carer interactions in terms of expressive timing and implicit knowing, and the way in which these are shaped by the wider community. The notion of protohabitus is clearly related to the concept of habitus used by Nobert Elias (1939), whose ideas about interconnectedness were, of course, an important influence on the development of Foulkes's thinking about the social unconscious and the foundation matrix. As I have discussed elsewhere (Wotton, 2012), I view the matrix as a musical process—a complex reflexive process that rests on our innate communicative musicality. The matrix is the "music" of the group, emerging from the creative space of interactions between members.[1]

In writing of the matrix as a network of communication, Foulkes said:

> We must accept that the language of these [communications] is not confined to words, but extends to inflexions of voice, manner of speaking, looking, to expressions, gestures, actions ...; emotional reactions of all sorts ... These primary levels correspond to the foundation matrix, based on the biological properties of the species, but also on the culturally firmly embedded values and reactions ... developed and transmitted in ... the social network. (1975, p. 131)

I am attempting to theorise further the non-verbal aspects of this "language", with particular reference to music—and paradoxically thereby offering a vocabulary that has so far been lacking—in order to contribute to the ongoing discussion of the foundation matrix and the unconscious social processes that emerge from and shape our communication and, hence, our "selves".

Unlike the discursive symbolism of verbal language, which breaks experience up into identifiable elements, music has the capacity to communicate presentational knowledge, that is, information about wholes, relationships, and events in context. It is perhaps this capacity that makes the non-verbal aspects of the language of the foundation matrix particularly powerful in transmitting unconscious social processes—information about social relations and figurations—and therefore warrants our attention. The theory of communicative musicality offers a way of conceptualising how we come to embody our past and that of our community (those "culturally firmly embedded values and reactions") as well as the potential for future change, through the construction of musical narratives based on our innate musicality (a "biological property of the species"). Musicality is understood here in terms of a sensitivity to embodied rhythms and patterns of tension and release, based on a shared, biologically derived sense of timing. This musicality is fundamental in allowing human bodies to be radically open and responsive systems—open to the transpersonal processes that form us, while at the same time those processes are formed by our interactions.

Our implicit knowledge about belonging and the power figurations that govern social interactions—the rules of the game of communication, as it were—derives from and is embedded in the musical narratives improvised within the earliest exchanges between infants and their close kin. A secure attachment style, for instance, is linked to the expressive timing of such exchanges, as I shall go on to describe. However, the patterning of interactions and the co-construction of their meaning continue throughout life and, in turn, influence the nature of future interactions. The theory of communicative musicality suggests an understanding of communication—not as some sort of a message being passed from a sender to a receiver—but rather as a co-creation, providing information about the state of the relationship to all participants simultaneously. This is a basic relational characteristic.

The foundation matrix can be seen as the shared implicit experiential knowledge of the restraints and constraints within which it is possible to improvise new meaningful communications and relationships. However, improvisation also pushes the boundaries of what is possible, and might, therefore, gradually and recursively change the nature of the communication matrix from which it derives.

Presumably, some restraints are fundamental to all music, created by all people at all times and in all places (a system of relationships built around intervals of rhythm and pitch)—in the way that the biological properties of the species are fundamental to the foundation matrix—but within this, other constraints very much reflect the particular socio-historical context and perhaps—by analogy—if we are to speak of "the" foundation matrix we should imagine it as a process involving the various "musics" that have emerged in different communities—the eight note scale of Western music, the microtones of Indian music, the powerful rhythms of South American music, the pentatonic (five note) scale of Chinese music, and so on—and which form the basis for further improvisation (of dynamic matrices) within and between communities.

Communication

Communication, and in particular, attending to the *total* communicational field as a co-created process and its fundamental and recursive role in shaping the so-called individual and her social context, became the cornerstone of Foulkes's work. He used musical metaphors to convey what he could not otherwise express—and perhaps could not be expressed in the theory and concepts of his time.

It was the work of Theodore Adorno that led Foulkes to adopt the term "conductor" in relation to group analysis. Adorno, the critical theorist and member of the Frankfurt school, was himself a pianist and follower of avant-garde music and he saw the structure of different musical ensembles as representing different types of social organisation. Adorno viewed the orchestra as "a microcosm … where the tensions of society are repeated and may be studied concretely" (1962, p. 115). His interest in authoritarianism led him to investigate the relationship between conductor and orchestra, where the location of authority fluctuated between the two and it was this model of leadership that appealed to Foulkes (Behr & Hearst, 2005). Adorno attempted to revoke the fatal separation between feeling and understanding and the privileging of content over form and was therefore, like Foulkes, interested in wholes and total situations.

Hopper and Weinberg (2011) have pointed to the fundamental importance of verbal language in conveying unconscious social processes:

> Language is the primary tool by which and through which social reality is perceived and constructed. Language defines, names, and describes objects. It moulds and shapes the perception of all external phenomena. It structures the formation of concepts and, therefore, of thinking itself. These are reciprocal and recursive processes (Derrida, 1974; Lacan, 1977). (p. xxxiii)

They refer to the ideas of Ernst Cassirer, who criticised Aristotle's substantialist view of concepts as being grounded in the "natural order" and offered instead a functional and relational view (cf. 1910). Thus, scientific concepts represent ideal relations—they form a conceptual network, which itself *constitutes* the order of things, and he applied this to linguistics in his philosophy of symbolic forms.

However, as Hopper and Weinberg also acknowledge:

> The internalisation of social, cultural and communicational arrangements is based on many neurobiological processes, ranging from social instincts to patterns of infant mother communication, including the use of all of the senses and the apparatus. For example mirroring based on mirror neurones is of special importance but so, too are many other barely understood aspects of the social brain. (ibid.)

It is some of these barely understood aspects that I wish to explore more closely—and doing so challenges the notion of internalisation in this context.

Susanne Langer, the American philosopher of mind and of art, was greatly influenced by Cassirer. She argued that symbol formation is a natural property of the mind, transforming sensation into meaning—and, crucially, that that meaning is derived from the community within which it is developed. Interestingly, when she translated Cassirer's 1925 work into English in 1946 she employed the term "matrix"—", "every one of them [symbolic forms] must first be emancipated from the common matrix of myth" (p. 44). And this was just about the time at which communication was becoming central to Foulkes's theories, although he did not use the term matrix until his 1957 book with James Anthony (Nitzgen, 2010).

Langer (1953) distinguished between the discursive symbolism of verbal language (that can be comprehended by progressively building up an understanding of its parts, which have a fixed meaning in isolation; naming, defining, and describing objects)—and the presentational symbolism of non-verbal aspects of human communication (including music) that is experience-like, dealing with wholes, relationships, and contexts, and cannot be understood on the basis of its parts, at least not independently from one another. For example, the notes of a piece of music have no meaning except in the context of their entire presentation. In the context of presentational symbolism, meaning is unsaturated and has to be constructed anew, perhaps continuously.

By virtue of its internal structure—the way the notes relate to each other, the significance of the intervals, the way both of these change according to context, the hierarchy of keys and so on—music develops patterns of tension and release and Langer described these patterns as "feeling forms" (1951). It is important to be clear that in this chapter, I am using the term "musical" to describe that kind of patterning of tension and release over time and not merely its representation in sound, which we would normally call music. Langer also developed a theory of isomorphism, which holds that every affect has a particular form or shape and that the auditory contours of music can evoke emotion directly (something we have surely all experienced)—because the pattern of sound directly represents the shape of an emotion with which we are familiar. This is presentational symbolism. The act of listening to a group singing has recently been shown to have as much immediate impact on mood as being part of the singing group itself (Unwin, Kenny, & Davis, 2002).

The distinction between the two types of symbolism—discursive and presentational—seems to correspond with what we have come to understand about the different types of attention paid, respectively, by the left and right hemispheres of the brain (McGilchrist, 2010). The left hemisphere attention is specific and directed to what is already known to be important, to the concrete, what is graspable, to distinctions, classification, and analysis, whereas that of the right is broader, applied to things in their context, implicit meaning, patterns, and relationships, and the unexpected. We could say, for instance, that the individual can only be abstracted artificially from her context, from the interactions that form her, by the left hemisphere's capabilities in verbal language, which chop experience up into discrete elements and provide symbols that can be manipulated. And manipulated so successfully that this kind of thinking has come to dominate over experiential knowledge. McGilchrist suggests that historically, periods during which there is a balance of right and left hemisphere thinking are gradually overtaken by a tendency to favour the left (the rise and fall of Graeco-Roman civilisations; the Renaissance to the present day).

Clearly, we need both types of attention and symbolisation in order to survive and function as human beings, but each deals with different types of information. Presentational symbolism, dealing with meaning in context and operating largely outside our awareness, has great potential for the unconscious sharing of social processes and arrangements that are taken to be of "the natural order". This area has been much less well explored than the link between verbal language and "the social unconscious"—perhaps as a result of the dominance of left hemisphere thinking or simply because it is much more difficult to describe in words; the right hemisphere, which is sensitive to wholes, is silent as it lacks verbal language. Before discussing several important insights from the field of communicative musicality I will turn to the concept of habitus and the related notion of protohabitus.

Habitus

Nobert Elias, the sociologist, who had a great influence on Foulkes, and with whom he remained in conversation throughout his life, used the term habitus (1939) to describe the habits of mind, social preconceptions, values, modes of relating, and their inherent power figurations, that derive from the time and place in which we live, and that we come to "inhabit", but of which we are not even aware and so do not question, yet which make us feel at home in our community. This is discussed in more detail elsewhere in this volume. Elias traces the way in which practices developed within one particular social group spread gradually over time to the wider society and move from their original status as very deliberate choices to become unconscious prejudices about "normal" behaviour. The term habitus has become widely used in sociology and human geography, particularly through the writings of Pierre Bourdieu, to refer to the automatic, unacknowledged attitudes and practices of any given socio-historical context that come about through the interaction of social processes around notions such as gender, race, and class. These collective cultural "sediments" become embodied and structure the minds of individuals living in that context who reproduce them through their preferences and actions and in turn influence future interactions and relations. Embodiment is fundamental to the process—even sensory perception itself is shaped by the social context in which it is developed. Gad Yair (2015) describes the particular sensitivity of the vision and hearing of young Israelis now living in present day Berlin, to shapes and sounds reminiscent of the Holocaust. Habitus is clearly a term that refers to transpersonal processes and is closely related to Foulkes's notions of the foundation matrix and social unconscious (E. Foulkes, 1990).[2]

"Mothering practices" are part of any habitus, and in the field of communicative musicality the term protohabitus is used to describe the shared temporal structure that develops between mother and infant, within which interactions take place and find their meaning—the earliest version of habitus. Although heavily culturally determined, it is uniquely improvised by each pair, as I will go on to illustrate. The process can be seen both in terms of Merleau-Ponty's (1959) concept of "*intercorporéité*" (where bodily interaction, including speaking and listening, means partaking in a joint intercorporeality) and of Stacey's (2000) view of the matrix as a complex responsive process emerging from the interaction of bodies.

Communicative musicality

The theory of communicative musicality—which holds that we have an innate musicality that is the basis of all human communication, allowing us to be in time and in tune with others and so to construct joint meaning out of experience—was developed by Stephen Malloch and Colwyn Trevarthen (2009). It links the biological with the social because our biologically based communicative musicality plays a significant role in the simultaneous formation of the self and society, in how we embody co-created unconscious social preconceptions and practices in the circular process of belonging and creating meaning. As such, it has particular relevance for group analysis.

Researchers from a range of theoretical backgrounds—paediatrics, child psychology, ethnography, anthropology, and social linguistics have observed mother–infant interactions in an attempt to understand how it is that human emotion and intention are immediately shareable through gestures of the body and the voice. They were struck by the dynamic nature of the non-verbal communication that they observed, the shared rhythmic quality of turn taking, and the contribution of the infants, from their earliest days, to pulling their mothers into the flow of the exchange. It seemed that the vitality of the communicative gestures was sufficient to forge memorable stories within a co-created relationship, made up of delicate expressions and sensitive responses forming musical or dance-like patterns. These patterns convey information about the state of the relationship to all the participants simultaneously, with no particular message being transmitted. This statement is reminiscent of Foulkes's description of resonance as "communication taking place without any particular message being sent or received, being in fact purely instinctive" (E. Foulkes, 1990, pp. 299–300).

Wherever mother–infant interactions were observed—in Germany, Nigeria, Scotland, Japan, or Sweden, mothers spoke to infants with similar rhythms and intonation, and the infants moved in sympathy. In 1996 Stephen Malloch was a postdoctoral researcher in Edinburgh and he began to listen to recordings that Colwyn Trevarthen had made some years previously, of mothers and babies (from as early as eight weeks old) "chatting" and this is what he noticed:

> As I listened, intrigued by the fluid give and take of the communication, and the lilting speech of the mother as she chatted with her baby, I began to tap my foot. I am, by training, a musician, so I was very used to automatically feeling the beat as I listened to musical sounds. There was no doubt in my mind that the melodious speech of the mother had a certain musical quality to it. It suddenly dawned on me that I was tapping my foot to human speech—not something

> I had ever done before, or even thought possible. I replayed the tape, and again, I could sense a distinct rhythmicity and melodious give and take to the gentle promptings of the mother and the pitched vocal replies from the baby .... A few weeks later as I walked down the stairs to [the] lab, the words "communicative musicality" came into my mind as a way of describing what I had heard. (Malloch & Trevarthen, 2009, p. 4)

Malloch subjected recordings of mother–infant interactions from around the world to acoustic analysis and this bore out his original experience—there is a constant pulse underlying these interactions and it is always in the range of one to three per second. Trevarthen (1999) postulated that humans have an intrinsic motive pulse (IMP), a time keeping, energy regulating control and he suggested that this was based on the biologically determined rhythms of processes in the brain, which are common to the species.

The presence of an intrinsic motive pulse means that we can develop a shared sense of time passing—what we might call "intersubjective time". This allows us to synchronise our experience and coordinate our, initially non-verbal, communication to build up a shared meaningful narrative, in which the meaning of the gesture becomes apparent in the response (as Mead (1934) has it). This is what Daniel Stern (2004) calls "affect attunement"—the aligning and sharing of bodily states within the intersubjective domain.

He suggests (2010) that our experience is made up of "vitality affects" (more recently termed "dynamic forms of vitality")—*forms* or *shapes* of tension and release, which are repeated and varied over time so that they combine to make up our sense of self. The pulse underlies the vitality affect, allowing us to sense the temporal contour of experience as it arises. The patterns of tension, often involving heightened excitement, followed by a final resolution, build up to form a narrative of gesture and response. These multi-modal vitality affects are the equivalent of the predictable and yet variable "feeling forms" that Susan Langer postulated in the 1950s. She suggested that these feeling forms are *presented* to us in music—symbolised in the shape of their auditory contours. Crucially these forms are developed *between* people and the narrative that is constructed will be unique to each relationship. Affect attunement is not just simply aligning emotional states but also jointly making sense of them in the light of previous experience and current intentions.

A neuro-biological basis for the parallels between vitality affects and music is now apparent in the overlap between those areas of the brain activated in response to emotion and to music (Panksepp & Trevarthen, 2009). The non-verbal, bodily (including vocal), rhythmical exchanges between mother and infant form proto-conversations that permit the development of a shared awareness of emotional states and organise our earliest experience along musical lines. In their rhythmical interaction, mother and infant are forming the social—the patterning of their conversation of gestures—while at the same time they are being formed by it (for the mother's sense of self is surely changed in the process, as well as the infant's). The *form* of the experience and its capacity to bring order give it the status of a transformative aesthetic experience (Bollas, 1987), one where sensation, emotion, and intellect all come together, where emotion becomes affect that can be shared. As adults, verbal language takes precedence in much of our communication but the musical aspects crucial to achieving mutual understanding persist in non-verbal features such as tone of voice, inflection, rhythm of exchange, facial expression, and posture (Wotton 2012).

The evidence from the field of communicative musicality demonstrates that we humans have the capacity to pick up and respond to variations of pitch and rhythm in speech and multi-modal bodily gestures, as patterns of tension and release over time. These patterns are in turn built up into narratives about the nature of experience and relating. The rhythmicity of these exchanges is universal, with a pulse or beat that falls within a narrow range—so, clearly, it is based on the biological properties of our species. At the same time, when the rhythms are compared across communities, there are subtle variations that reflect the speech patterns of that community—so they are also culturally derived and elaborated. This is precisely the pattern of similarities and differences that we would expect to characterise a fundamental co-created unconscious social process of the foundation matrix—having normative, cultural, and communicational dimensions—and very close to any definition that we might provide of "the social unconscious". It is within such rhythmical exchanges that we make meaning together, building our sense of self and our implicit knowledge of relating, through the cultural practices and modes of expression that we come to embody and which provide us with a sense of belonging.

Gratier and Apter-Danon (2009) compared first, vocal interactions in French, Indian, and American mother–baby dyads living in their own cultures. They demonstrated that while there were cross-cultural similarities, in terms of pulse, quality, and narrative—in line with Malloch and Trevarthen's original findings—there were also culturally specific variations, which could be seen as consistent with tacit rules of verbal conversation in each culture, such as turn taking and the length of pauses between exchanges.

The researchers then studied dyads where the mother had immigrated, taking as their example Indian mothers who had immigrated to America. In the case of immigrant mothers who felt confident and well supported, whether they adopted Indian or American mothering practices or a combination of both, the alignment of mother–infant vocal interactions was as close as that found in dyads living in their own cultures, and the cultural specifics such as turn taking fell *between* the Indian and American patterns. However, in cases where mothers showed signs of cultural conflict and a lack of confidence in their own style of mothering, the vocal interactions showed much less coherence; fewer narrative episodes were developed and the interactions lacked a sense of improvisation. They tended to have a rigid rhythmical pattern—mothers' expressions were more predictable and infants' were less creative and adventurous.

The researchers concluded that:

> When a mother loses her confidence in her own community's cultural practices, a shared protohabitus with her infant, uniquely improvised within well established cultural traditions, is harder to define, and so too is an intersubjective sense of belonging ... Mothers and infants share a set of culturally derived expressive forms that are both predictable and afford playful variation .... An interaction that lacks the creation of a shared structure (protohabitus) does not foster a sense of belonging, and for similar reasons, neither can an interaction that lacks a temporal improvisational quality ... Belonging requires a balance between the known and the new, repetition and creativity, structure and variation. (ibid., p. 305)

So, expression unfolds within shared temporal frames that depend on biological processes and on the relational and cultural context, to sustain both a sense of belonging and a sense of adventure, and we come to embody our past and that of our community as well as the potential for future change. It is thus that we can say with Foulkes, that the individual is social to the core—emerging from a habitus/foundation matrix that is maintained and developed through the musical interactions of the members of the community, a process that is paradoxically forming and formed by itself at the same time.

Gratier and Apter-Danon state that:

> Belonging is based on interactive motifs and styles shared by the community into which the infant is born, and that the infant begins to embody spontaneously through regular and intimate communication with close kin. But belonging goes beyond what is culturally given as a right of birth. It allows the infant to explore new inventive ways of expressing and sharing experiences. (ibid., p. 304)

Improvisation

It is the improvisatory quality of communicative musicality that is particularly linked to belonging. We are not just talking about a pre-existing system into which the individual must fit slavishly or else founder, but about truly co-created relationships and social groups. Improvisation implies a familiarity with the conventions that govern the relationships between the notes, the hierarchy of the keys, the musical form—or in the case of the family or group, the sociocultural conventions that govern interpersonal relationships—so that one can create the unexpected, to depart from the form while still having regard to it, to offer a gesture that will call forth a subtly different response and take the form in a new direction, without destroying the sense of connection. We hear it in a good jazz group where themes and motifs are exchanged and "played" with, within the shared temporal structure that alone allows participants to introduce meaningful changes.

The link between interactive timing and the sense of belonging is even more subtle than I have so far indicated. It depends on the co-creation of flexible yet predicable patterns that are clearly structured yet variable, which provide both regularity and exciting nuance and foster intersubjective engagement and learning. The term "expressive timing" is used to describe the way a performer brings a piece to life by playing a note just before or just after the beat and a similar micro-variation is also found to be most engaging and creative in mother–infant interactions. It implies a knowledge of the beat and of the limits beyond which you will lose contact. Both rigid regularity and extreme movement away from the beat result in disengagement. It has been found that of the mother–infant interactions studied when the infant was four months old, only those where the expressive timing fell in the mid range—neither rigidly regular nor wildly divergent—were correlated with a secure attachment pattern at twelve months. It seems that we need a degree of "temporal elasticity" to leave room for creative expression and collaborative exploration, where purposes can be negotiated.

Daniel Stern writes: "There is something about the deviation from the beat, the irregularity or variation from the expected regularity that is expressive of feelings and thoughts" (1982, p. 104). Not surprisingly he relates this to music making in jazz groups. Interestingly, jazz groups tend not to have a conductor—with the exception of big bands—instead everyone contributes to the sound (literally) and "authority" moves around among the players, although there may be one who, as it were, "grounds" the group, starting and ending the pieces. This is closer to my own notion of the group analyst as the tonic or home note within the scale, rather than as conductor (Wotton, 2012).

Dynamic patterns of repetition and variation have *flexibility*. They allow us to push the boundaries of what is allowed within the conventions of the interaction. "Mistakes" are often made in jazz ensembles but their final status depends on the cooperative flexibility of the group to contain them within the form—to blur the boundary between expectation and creativity. The ability to "repair" these mistakes can be related to the notion of rupture and repair in mother–infant interactions and in psychotherapy.

Musicality can be seen as providing a form of Winnicottian "holding" (1971). Mothers hold their infants' attention, regulate their emotions, and create predictable styles and routines through the handling of the baby and thereby provide the psychological holding that lays down the foundations of health. However, Gratier and Apter-Danon suggest that it is the *expressive timing* of the interaction that constitutes the primary source of the experience of holding. If they are right—and the link between secure attachment and expressive timing, referred to earlier, supports this—then holding is not just something that the mother does for the infant but rather, it is co-created.[3]

Implicit knowing

The non-discursive, presentational, procedural knowledge that is grounded in the intersubjective sense of time is summed up in the term "implicit knowing". This is woven into belonging in the first six months of life. The infant's expressive movements are guided by a set of culturally derived and musically shaped habits and practices. The knowledge that is transmitted and elaborated (through improvisation) in this way would have to do with social arrangements, attitudes, and power figurations. A community's history and traditions are embodied in the movements and rhythms of exchange of its members but these are hard or even impossible to separate out and subject to scrutiny—we can only become aware of them through contact with another community ("not us"). The theory of communicative musicality presents us with a picture of a wonderfully subtle and creative process for developing a sense of belonging and a sense of self within the foundation matrix, a process that is at the same time intensely delicate and fragile, fraught with possibilities for near misses, for failure and exclusion. We can see how trans-generational trauma, for instance, might be passed on through such transpersonal processes, as a way of being rather than a form of words, embedded in familial rhythms of interaction and thus, incidentally, offering a very different view of the phenomenon from the idea of something unbearable being forcibly projected into the infant. The lack of a secure sense of the family's place within the community (as in certain cases in the migration study described earlier) that might result from trauma, or the need for traumatised individuals to protect themselves from overwhelming feelings, is likely to restrain the flexibility and creativity of interactions between caregivers and infants and lead to the perpetuation of certain rigid forms of communication down the generations. Conversely, when music is used as ritual, it is the rigid repetition of familiar themes, specific to the history of the community and expressed in sound, that can bind people in a sense of "communitas" (Turner, 2012). It provides a feeling of sameness, safety, and predictability that is more necessary than creativity in threatening times. (See the work of Helena Klimova in this series.)

A further example comes from a small study of mothers with borderline personality disorder, which showed that they tend to stick to rigid repetition and do not adapt to variations in the rhythm of interaction introduced by their infants, who then seem to disengage (Gratier & Apter-Danon, 2009). The study demonstrated a highly specific style of vocal interaction, characterised by a high degree of repetitiveness—in content, phrasing, and timing. Repeatedly the infants seemed to sense a point where they might join in the exchange, which was then cut short by the rigidity and repetitiveness of the interactive format established by the mother. The researchers suggest that what they saw represented a disruption of intersubjective time. They inferred that the mothers—whose own implicit knowledge of relating was characterised by abandonment, impingement, and emptiness—had a disrupted sense of intersubjective time that hindered their ability to put their own experience into a narrative form and to establish a clear sense of belonging. This would naturally contribute to a general lack of meaningfulness that would continue into the next generation.

As the infant develops, meaning becomes increasingly public and conscious, and based in verbal language. The presentational field, however, continues to constitute the foundation for all meaning-making activity and co-exists with linguistic referential meaning throughout life. The implicit knowledge of relating within the family is extended and adapted, its meaning constructed anew according to context—in the nature of presentational symbolism—through the joint improvisation of the dynamic matrix of each new group of which the individual forms a part.

The musical foundation matrix

The foundation matrix consists of communication processes that derive from a shared biological and cultural inheritance. The evidence from the field of communicative musicality would suggest that our innate musicality has a fundamental part to play in the transmission and elaboration of this inheritance, through our interactions and the way in which those interactions form both our social context and our sense of self at the same time. Within the broad shared patterns of the foundation matrix, subtle differences are developed and transmitted in each community, and within these, each protohabitus is uniquely improvised between infant and carer along musical—bodily yet social—lines. And hence too, collectively the members of the "group" (or social system) constitute the norm from which individually they deviate (Foulkes, 1948). The shared musical process of interaction forms both "the social" and the "individual" simultaneously so that any distinction between inside and outside is untenable. "Internalisation" is an inadequate (and indeed misleading) term to convey the formative dynamic process of *improvisation* around cultural motifs and patterns within a shared, co-created temporal structure, providing both a sense of self and a sense of belonging, which the theory of communicative musicality attempts to describe. And of course, those cultural motifs, patterns, and social arrangements are themselves developed within the same process. It is this emphasis on the lively, dynamic, recursive, and responsive co-constructed nature of the communicative process that I find such a useful addition to ways of thinking about the matrix.

It is important to remember, as Stacey (2000) points out, that the matrix is a process that *organises* our experience of being together. That is to say it is not neutral, it is made up of concord and contest at the same time—which music conveys so well. What emerges is hierarchical, full of similarity and difference with the potential for inclusion and exclusion. And around these, power figurations arise that determine the possibility of further communication. The process emerges from interactions between particular bodies, but results in a transpersonal process evolving over time. (This does not imply, of course, that the process has any separate existence outside such interactions.) And it is precisely this order of complexity—with all its contradictions—that music "presents" and that our innate musicality allows us to appreciate and perform through the improvisation of belonging. The implicit knowledge of relating, and the experience of expressive timing acquired through interacting with others from infancy onwards, provide us with an awareness of the shared patterns and motifs in the foundation matrix around which we can improvise new interactions as well as the shared temporal framework within which to do this, and the limits beyond which we will lose connection.

The patterning of "feeling forms" that makes up music can be seen as a mnemonic, directly describing our social arrangements (Sloboda, 1985). So too, and more fundamentally, the narrative patterning of dynamic forms of vitality, which makes up our sense of self, also conveys the implicit knowledge of the "rules of engagement"—the intertwining power relationships and values—of a community and its broader context. The resonance of the wider community will always be represented within the interactions of any of its members. At the same time the precise meaning of any communication is improvised anew in each new group that arises within that community. The "musical" patterns of tension and release, the feeling forms, the interactive motifs, which are present in the matrix and to which we are sensitive due to our innate musicality, also form the basis for resonance. Foulkes understood resonance to be biologically based and the term is, of course, derived from physics, describing the way a system oscillates with greater amplitude in response to certain frequencies of vibrations depending on the material of which it is constituted. In the case of sound, the system will amplify a sound whose frequency matches one of its own natural frequencies of vibration, and colour it with overtones, or harmonics. The experience of resonance within a group is so rich because the response evoked in each individual is subtly different (as each habitus has been uniquely improvised). This kind of presentational symbolism is appreciated directly, without any particular message being sent or received, and the meaning has to be co-constructed according to context. Jointly constructing the meaning of an event at a particular time in a particular group contributes to our sense of belonging to that group. The rhythm of interpersonal exchange and its expressive timing present information about the state of the relationship as a whole (including the power figurations) directly and to all participants simultaneously.

The variety within unity of possible human motifs and styles that is present in the musical foundation matrix means that belonging to one community shows just how much you do not belong to the one next door (in a very direct and bodily way, the timing *feels* wrong)—and indeed we hold on to such distinctions in order to maintain our sense of identity, particularly when under threat. This dialectic within the matrix of me/not-me, I am and I am not, as well as us and them, we are and we are not, and so forth (Hopper, 2003) could be conceptualised in terms of musical counterpoint. Moving beyond the family group means clashing with other styles—being out of step—and having to work to create new inclusive ones with their own power figurations and facing questions of whose style will prevail. You have to know—in the experiential sense—the underlying form in order to be able to improvise on it and create a sense of belonging—and implicit (or resonant) within each community's matrix are the shared underlying temporal patterns of the foundation matrix from which it has been improvised. The theory of communicative musicality offers exciting potential for understanding and describing these non-verbal processes that operate outside conscious awareness.

Conclusion

It is curious to find that I have written so much about change in relation to the foundation matrix—the "givens" of human communication—but it is perhaps a useful reminder that the foundation matrix is not a thing but a process—a complex responsive process—and not fixed but paradoxically forming and being formed by itself as it emerges from our interactions over time. It is constrained by the biological properties of the species—our musicality in this case, which allows the culturally embedded values and reactions to be transmitted and elaborated along musical lines. The particular patterning of embodied communication within each community presents the social arrangements of that community and is expressed—and at the same time subtly changed—through the improvisation of belonging. Thus, too, is the foundation matrix reflexively and recursively altered over time.

Notes

1. Other writers who have specifically explored the links between group analysis and music include: Sabina Strich (1983), who suggested that music constructs a virtual group; Andrew Powell (1983, 1990), who compared the development of a therapy group to the historical development of Western music and pointed to the necessary attunement of the group analyst to the harmonics of the matrix; and Rocco Pisani (2014), who discussed the similarities between conducting an orchestra and conducting a group.
2. How are we to understand the proliferation of terms—habitus, foundation matrix, social unconscious? Do they describe the same or different things? Or does the proliferation have more to do with the power figurations within and between psychoanalysis, sociology, and group analysis? Social unconscious clearly positions itself in relation to psychoanalytic concepts, establishing both a distinction and a connection. The foundation matrix perhaps speaks more to the notion of the network and transpersonal processes, while the term habitus emphasises the effect on the individual—though Elias's view of interdependence renders any such dichotomy unnecessary.
3. The observations from the field of communicative musicality would indicate that the capacity to play in the transitional space and a sense of me/not me is present much earlier than Winnicott's theory suggests and it would be interesting to explore this further.

References

Adorno, T. W. (1962). Einleitung in die Musiksoziolgie. Frankfurt: Suhrkamp. (Quoted in Rothe, S. (1989), The Frankfurt school: an influence on group analysis? *Group Analysis, 22*: 405–415.

Behr, H., & Hearst, L. (2005). *Group Analytic Psychotherapy: a Meeting of Minds*. London: Whurr.

Bollas, C. (1987). *The Shadow of the Object*. London: Free Association.

Cassirer, E. (1910). *Substance and Function and Einstein's Theory of Relativity* W. C. Swabey & M. C. Swabey (Trans.). New York: Dover, 1953.

Cassirer, E. (1925). *Language and Myth*. S. K. Langer (Trans.). New York: Harper & Bros., 1946.

Elias, N. (1939). *The Civilising Process*. Oxford: Blackwell, 1994. Foulkes, S. H. (1948). *Introduction to Group Analytic Psychotherapy*. London: Karnac.

Foulkes, S. H. (1975). *Group Analytic Psychotherapy: Method and Principles*. London: Karnac.

Foulkes, E. (Ed.) (1990). *S. H. Foulkes. Selected Papers: Psychoanalysis and Group Analysis*. London: Karnac.

Gratier, M., & Apter Danon, G. (2009). The improvised musicality of belonging: repetition and variation in mother–infant vocal interaction. In: S. Malloch & C. Trevarthen (Eds.), *Communicative Musicality: Exploring the Basis of Human Companionship*. Oxford: Oxford University Press.

Hopper, E. (2003). *Traumatic Experience in the Unconscious Life of Groups*. London: Jessica Kingsley.

Hopper, E., & Weinberg, H. (Eds.) (2011). *The Social Unconscious in Persons, Groups and Societies: Volume 1: Mainly Theory*. London: Karnac.

Langer, S. K. (1951). *Philosophy in a New Key; A Study in the Symbolism of Reason, Rite and Art*. Cambridge, MA: Harvard University Press.

Langer, S. K. (1953). *Feeling and Form*. London: Routledge & Kegan Paul.

Malloch, S., & Trevarthen, C. (2009). Communicative musicality: communicating the vitality and interests of life. In S. Malloch & C. Trevarthen (Eds.), *Communicative Musicality: Exploring the Basis of Human Companionship*. Oxford: Oxford University Press.

McGilchrist, I. (2010). *The Master and His Emissary: The Divided Brain and the Making of the Western World*. New Haven, CT: Yale University Press.

Mead, G. H. (1934). *Mind, Self and Society*. Chicago, IL: University of Chicago Press.

Nitzgen, D. (2010). Hidden legacies. S. H. Foulkes, Kurt Goldstein and Ernst Cassirer. *Group Analysis, 43*(3): 354–371.

Merleau-Ponty, M. (1959). *Phenomenology of Perception*. D. Landes (Trans.). London: Routledge, 2013.

Panksepp, J., & Trevarthen, C. (2009). The neuroscience of emotion in music. In: S. Malloch & C. Trevarthen (Eds.), *Communicative Musicality: Exploring the Basis of Human Companionship*. Oxford: Oxford University Press.

Pisani, R. (2014). The art of conduction an orchestra. *Group Analysis, 47*(2 suppl.): 33–45.

Powell, A. (1983). The music of the group: a musical enquiry into group-analytic psychotherapy. *Group Analysis, 16*: 3–19.

Powell, A. (1990). Words and music: an unsung therapeutic alliance. *Group Analysis, 23*: 225–235.

Sloboda, J. A. (1985). *The Musical Mind*. Oxford: Oxford University Press.

Stacey, R. (2000). Reflexivity, self organisation and emergence in the group matrix. *Group Analysis, 33*: 501–514.

Stern, D. (1982). Some interactive functions of rhythm changes between mother and Infant. In: M. Davis (Ed.), *Interaction Rhythms: Periodicity in Communicative Behaviour*. New York: Human Sciences Press.

Stern, D. (2004). *The Present Moment: In Psychotherapy and Everyday Life*. New York: W. W. Norton.

Stern, D. (2010). *Forms of Vitality: Exploring Dynamic Experience in Psychology, the Arts, Psychotherapy and Development*. Oxford: Oxford University Press.

Strich, S. (1983). Music and the patterns of human interactions. *Group Analysis, 16*: 20–26.

Trevarthen, C. (1999). Musicality and intrinsic motive pulse: Evidence from human psychobiology and infant communication. *Musicae Scientiae*, special issue 1999–2000: 155–215.

Turner, E. (2012). *Communitas: The Anthropology of Collective Joy*. New York: Palgrave Macmillan.

Unwin, M., Kenny, D., & Davis, J. (2002). The effect of group singing on mood. *Psychology of Music, 30*(2): 175–185.

Winnicott, D. W. (1971). *Playing and Reality*. London: Routledge.

Wotton, L. (2012). Between the notes: a musical understanding of change in group analysis. *Group Analysis, 46*(3): 48–60.

Yair, G. (2015). The Germans: Cultural trauma and the Israeli habitus. *American Journal of Cultural Sociology, 3*: 254–279.

PART III

EMPIRICAL STUDIES OF THE SOCIAL UNCONSCIOUS AND THE DYNAMIC AND FOUNDATION MATRICES OF MIDDLE EASTERN PEOPLES AND SOCIETIES

CHAPTER SEVEN

The social unconscious of Israeli Jews: described and analysed by an Israeli living in North America*

Haim Weinberg

Moving from Israel to California in 2006, I was surprised to experience the respect with which people in the USA relate to authority. Patients in my private practice, participants in my groups, and students in my classes call me Dr Weinberg, while in Israel they call me Haim, which is my first name. In the USA they seemed to accept my authority, respect my knowledge and opinions, and comply immediately with my instructions, while in Israel I am used to immediate arguments, complaints, and resistances. I am not sure how aware of this I was while living in Israel. Although I had written about the social unconscious before moving to the USA (e.g., Weinberg, 2006, 2007) and actually focused on this topic in my PhD dissertation during 2000–2006, becoming an immigrant in a new society and going through acculturation processes led to my becoming keenly aware of the fine nuances and tacit assumptions that distinguish North American from Israeli cultures. To be more precise, I am concerned here with Californian culture, which might certainly be compared with, for example, New York culture, and

*This is an elaborated version of a chapter in my PhD dissertation (Weinberg, 2006). Some of the hypotheses and ideas in this chapter have been developed in the Introduction to Hopper & Weinberg (2011) and in Nuttman-Shwartz & Weinberg (2012).

the subcultures of these two states or regions of the United States may be as different from each other as they are from Israeli culture.

In this chapter I summarise my understanding of the social unconscious (SU) of Israeli Jews, through the lens of an Israeli Jew who lived in Israel for fifty-three years, who has become an American resident. Some of the insights about the SU of Israeli people came from my private practice which includes Israelis who live in the USA. In this unique setting of Israelis treated in Hebrew by an Israeli therapist, both living out of their homeland, hidden attitudes and values common to Israelis and belonging to their SU emerge. Such a situation reminds us of what Puget and Wender (1982) called "overlapping worlds", or the idea of "shared reality" (Nuttman-Shwartz, 2016; Tosone, 2012) where therapist and patient share a common social space, or are exposed to the same traumatic situation (Tubert-Oklander, 2014), but can only be partly aware of this.

Some of the phenomena, attitudes, and behaviours described in this chapter are not only unconscious, but also non-conscious and preconscious and even conscious. However, even if people are conscious of a particular pattern of behaviour they may be unconscious of its full motivations, and may not even acknowledge the existence of it or the impact of it (Hopper, 2001; Hopper & Weinberg, 2011). For example, Israelis might not be aware that they react to threats in an extreme way, and when they become aware of this, they may even try to justify it in terms of it being syntonic with their reality, while at the same time deny its traumatic origins in the experience of social trauma.

My analysis and discussion are limited to Israeli Jews in Israel. Although Israel is a multicultural society composed of many subcultures and ethnic groups, the evidence suggests that those groupings hold in common many unconscious and preconscious assumptions. Some readers might wonder about the evidence base of the hypotheses and assumptions about the deep unconscious codes of Jewish Israelis in this chapter. In his qualitative research, Yair (2011, 2015; see also in this volume), pointed out how the Holocaust constitutes a national Israeli habitus—an embodied amalgam of worldviews and sensations that mould contemporary perceptions and actions. He also detailed "the ten commandments" unconsciously affecting the behaviours of Israeli Jews. Most of his findings validate the ideas expressed in this chapter and the themes I identified as embedded in the social unconscious of Israeli Jewish people. We also have data from case studies of organisations in Israel (Nuttman-Shwartz & Weinberg, 2012). Another source of information about the foundation matrix of Israel and the social unconscious of Israeli Jews are group analytic and psychodynamic large groups (Weinberg & Schneider, 2003) and social dreaming matrices held in Israel (Biran, 2015). Also important are myths from the Bible and various themes in Israeli art.

I will now explore some of the constraints and restraints of social, cultural, and communicational arrangements in Israeli society of which its people are unaware. Being a member of the Israeli society creates shared anxieties, fantasies, defences, myths, and memories, and these elements of the SU are common to many Jewish people in Israeli society (Hopper & Weinberg, 2011).

General aspects of the social unconscious of Israeli people

In the Introduction to *The Social Unconscious in Persons, Groups and Societies* (2011, 2016) it was emphasised that in the study of the social unconscious, social trauma is of particular importance. If we want to describe the SU of the Israelis in one simple sentence, it is: Israel is a traumatised and traumatising society (Nuttman-Shwartz & Weinberg, 2012). Memories of centuries of persecution, the long shadow of the Holocaust, and the recent past of ever-present wars and threats exist in the Israelis' consciousness and unconsciousness. From the inception of Israel it has been preoccupied with wars or threats of war with Arab countries. In the last decades the Israeli-Palestinian conflict deeply affects Israeli society: its horrors of terror are part of everyday life. Many Israelis feel surrounded by enemy countries, and hated by the world. Many of the behaviours of Israelis can be understood against the background of unelaborated historical traumas and as a kind of a PTSD reaction (Yair, 2011). Deep anxieties (on the verge of paranoia) about annihilation, expulsion, and persecution; overreaction to any threat as if it would lead to destruction; a need to always be strong and show no weakness: all these are reactions to a history of expulsion from Zion, hundreds of years of persecution, and, of course, the trauma of the Shoah-Holocaust.

Israel is a multicultural but polarised society, conflicted internally and externally, struggling with difficult questions of social and national identity. Issues of territory, identity, security, rigid outside boundaries, and blurred inner boundaries contribute to its current situation. It is a melting pot for Jews coming from the diaspora to "the Promised Land". Even this short sentence conveys shared fantasies and yearnings transmitted for hundreds of years through generations of Jews. "Next year in built Jerusalem," Jews would say annually when reading the Hagada in the traditional Passover Seder, transferring this yearning from father to son. The result is that immigrating to Israel for the Jews is saturated with emotions, longing, expectations, idealisation, and shared fantasies. Indeed, there is a special word for this act—making "Aliya", which means "going up", as opposed to the act of emigrating from Israel which is called "Yerida", meaning "descending", with all associated negative connotations. The social unconscious of Israeli Jews is strongly connected with the Jewish fate and history. In fact, we cannot understand the current social and political situation in Israel without relating to historical events of the Jewish people and to the fact that Israel is a melting pot for many ethnic and cultural groups. Questions of diversity and multiculturalism are ubiquitous.

The idealisation of Israel and Israeli society was part of the myth of Jews coming back to their former homeland. A famous Israeli poet (Bialik) once said, "We will be a normal state only after we have the first Hebrew thief and a Hebrew whore," This idealisation contributed to the denial of many unjustified acts occurring in Israel in its first decades. The world participated in creating the myth of the "halutzim" (pioneers, settlers) who came to the desert to make their land flourish. This myth ignored the existence of another people in Israel who had been settled for years in Palestine.

In addition, in order to establish a new identity unifying different ethnic and social groups, and in contrast to the image of the weak Jew in the diaspora, certain social-cultural myths and narratives were developed. The most important of them was the image of the "Sabra", the newborn in Israel. It required the creation of a new entity based on a common past (dismissing communities who did not suffer the Holocaust, which therefore privileged the experience of European/ Ashkenazi Jewry), and a united illusionary identity with no differences of religion or tradition (including denying the Arab minority living in the country) and with a clearly identified external enemy (Moore & Bar-On, 1996). This creation prevented the working through of traumas from the Holocaust and immigration. The focus on activity and doing, such as the combination of building a new country and going to war, impeded the working through of emotional issues such as mourning the loss of families in the Holocaust and elaborating guilt feelings. The Sabra image involved classical heroic (and culturally masculine) features, including the focus on physical strength and denying of weaknesses. Historical events in Jewish history representing chosen glory were illuminated and praised, while chosen traumas were denied and repressed. Emotional expression was considered a weakness. Life in the shadow of war also contributed to the difficulty in dealing with these traumas. This need for a new identity in the midst of an existential threat encouraged seclusion and strengthened outer boundaries while blurring inner ones.

As an anecdote, a clear difference in people's attitude I encountered when moving to the States relates to the behaviour of Israelis when they become sick. My impression is that in the USA people stay home and avoid coming to the workplace or class when they feel under the weather, out of concern not to infect other colleagues with their germs. In Israel you are expected to come to work even when you are feverish. This behaviour of Israelis might be seen as inconsiderate to North American, while it is actually a manifestation of the need to appear strong and not yield to physical weakness.

The kibbutz and its ideology of equality, where everybody works according to her or his ability and receives from the community according to her or his needs, is an example of these processes (irrespective of its actual practices). There was a felt need to create an illusion of a new society with modern humanistic social norms praising the image of the enlightened Israeli "Sabra" warrior (Gretz, 1995). This was in stark contrast to the image of the Jew as Holocaust victim, or physically frail intellectual.

Another aspect of the social unconscious of Israeli Jews is expressed in the profound and repeated phrase of "I am not going to be a sucker". Israelis argue about everything, they are keen on getting a deal, and will not let anyone play tricks with them. They always know better than the other does especially when the other is an authority. If the authority comes from abroad they are in conflict. On one hand they invite the famous guest and want to hear what he has to say. On the other hand they compulsively need to undermine his expertise and authority. Half jokingly, when discussing cultural differences with my students in the USA, I comment: "Israelis come to lectures (especially if the presenter is someone from abroad) to show the presenter that she or he knows nothing and that they know better." Once an Israeli philosopher

(Yeshayahu Leibowitz) explained this as "We are fed up of being ruled by the goyim [gentiles]." It seems that this sentence reverberates in the Israeli social unconscious. The revolt against the shared memory of the Jew who is controlled and governed by others creeps into daily acts, manoeuvring Israelis into a paranoid position of wanting to show "who is in charge here". Maybe this is one of the reasons why Israelis tend to break any rule, test the limits, and reject authority. This attitude has its impact even in issues of foreign affairs, starting with Ben Gurion (the first Israeli prime minister) who said that "What the goyim have to say is not important."

This tendency of Israelis "not to be a sucker" and their sensitivity around being perceived as such, could also explain Israelis' strong reactions to public threats (in addition to the annihilation anxiety mentioned above). A non-Israeli and non-Jew might not understand those reactions, perceive them as overreactive, and easily label Israelis as aggressive. Actually, it stems out of a deep fear of being humiliated like the Jew in the diaspora. It can be attributed to a narcissistic vulnerability of many Israelis based on collective memories of centuries of humiliation.

The Israeli collective memory

The role of the collective memory (sometimes called "social memory") in consolidating the SU is enormous (see Halbwachs, 1980; Hopper & Weinberg's Introduction, 2011). It is strongly affected by stories and myths from the Bible, which every Israeli studies again and again from kindergarten to high school. It is also influenced by historical events and traumas routinely over-told both in formal education, frequently mentioned by political leaders and through the media. According to the Bible, God promised the land of Israel to Abraham (the first Jew) and his descendants: "Le'Zaracha eten at haraetz hazot" ("I will give this land to your descendants" (Genesis 12:7)), and this sentence is memorised and engraved in the SU of Israelis. Unfortunately, Israelis lost their homeland more than 2000 years ago, were exiled for centuries, and could only yearn to return to Zion (the land of Israel) until the establishment of the Jewish state in 1948. The over-emphasis of ownership over the land is not only a way to politically justify the settlements, or the ruling of Palestinians, but also a defensive reaction to a profound trauma of loss (Atlas-Koch & Kuchuck, 2012).

Israelis have a very strong and unique connection to their motherland, calling it Haaretz (The Land), being strongly attached to "her" (Haaretz is feminine in Hebrew). This bonding reflects memories of living in the diaspora for centuries, longing to return to Zion "when the Messiah comes". My clinical observations of Israeli patients in the USA confirm those of Atlas-Koch and Kuchuck: "They deal with powerful emotions over leaving The Land, missing her, loving and hating her" (2012, p. 96). The sense of "ownership" is prevalent far beyond the issue of the land (including the Palestinian lands). It prevails in the Israeli's car driving (as if the road belongs to the driver, especially for men), in public service, and even while being abroad.

The collective memory of a nation is represented in part by the memorials it chooses to erect (Lene Auestad, unpublished paper). The preoccupation with memorial ceremonies and with perpetuating the memory of the deceased is well known in Israel, and memorial monuments can be seen almost everywhere, whether it is for Jewish communities exterminated during the Holocaust or for fallen soldiers in Israel's wars (Malkinson & Witztum, 2000). Summarising the main elements that are repeatedly engraved in the collective memory of Israelis, either by educational institutions, political leaders, or the mass media, it seems that they are related to historical roots (we were here 2000 years ago), centuries of sufferings and persecutions (from pogroms to the Shoah), and perpetuating the fallen (from past and present). Paradoxically, living in the shadow of death and the deceased only strengthens defences of denial and dissociation, helping Israelis to deal with daily threats of terror. However, these repressed/dissociated/disavowed parts inhabit the Jewish Israeli social unconscious.

Discussing the social memory, we should also take into account collective defences concerning what is not remembered, forgotten, and otherwise denied (see Doron's chapter about "black holes" in the Israeli SU in this book). The Nakba, the Palestinian disaster of being expelled from their land (see also Tali's chapter in this book), during the Israeli War of Independence (historians still debate whether it was an organised and deliberate exile) is not mentioned in Israeli history textbooks. Weegmann (in this book), states that one of the characteristics of the Palestinian social unconscious pertains to forgotten memories, partly due to Israeli efforts (conscious or unconscious) to deny the existence of a Palestinian people.

Myths in the SU of Israelis

The myths in Mediterranean countries such as Greece or Italy are often taken from Greek mythology and the myths in Israel are often taken from the Bible. They are part of the Jewish culture and legacy. One of the most influential biblical stories is that of Isaac's sacrifice. The story is presented as a proof of Abraham's and Isaac's deep faith in God, but beyond it we read about the readiness to sacrifice a son due to some superior value or belief (for the deep influence of this myth on Jewish people in general, see Stephen Frosh's chapter in Volume 2 of this series, 2016). The possibility of sacrificing their children by sending them to the army, knowing they might be killed in wars, haunts Israeli parents day and night. The "Promised Land" should have been accompanied with a promise for quiet peaceful life. Instead of leaving a better place for their children, the next generations have to deal with the same issues of life and death. In the name of national-secular ideologies the death of sons becomes sacred.

We can learn a lot about the social unconscious from art works. Many Israeli writers and poets expressed the theme of the sacrifice. From the poets, I chose Yehudah Amichai, a famous Israeli poet, who takes up Isaac's binding a second time in the poem, "Three sons had Abraham, not just two" (in his book, *Open Closed Open*, 2000, pp. 21–22). (Hebrew-English translations that might help understanding of this poem: Yishma = will hear. El = God. Yitzhak (the Hebrew name of Isaac) = will laugh. Yivkeh = will cry. To those not knowledgeable about the Bible—Abraham had two sons: Isaac (Ytzhak) and Yishmael (or Ishmael, who is considered the father of the Moslems).)

> Three sons had Abraham: Yishma-El, Yitzhak, and Yivkeh.
> First came Yishma-El, "God will hear,"
> next came Yitzhak, "he will laugh,"
> and the last was Yivkeh, for he was the youngest,
> the son that Father loved best,
> the son who was offered up on Mount Moriah.
> Yishma-El was saved by his mother, Hagar,
> Yitzhak was saved by the angel,
> but Yivkeh no one saved.
> When he was just a little boy, his father
> would call him tenderly, Yivkeh,
> Yivkeleh, my sweet little Yivkie

but he sacrificed him all the same.
The Torah says the ram, but it was Yivkeh.
Yishma-El never heard from God again,
Yitzhak never laughed again,
Sarah laughed only once, then laughed no more.
Three sons had Abraham,
Yishma, "will hear," Yitzhak, "will laugh," Yivkeh, "will cry."
Yismah-El, Yitzhak-El, Yivkeh-El.
God will hear, God will laugh, God will cry.

Another Israeli artist who is haunted by the theme of Isaac's sacrifice is the famous painter and sculptor Menashe Kadishman. He painted hundreds of innocent sheep during his artistic career. But when his son was drafted into the army he started painting and sculpting works protesting against sending the boys to death. Picture 1 shows one of his sculptures. In this artwork Abraham does not appear at all, probably because he is the leader sending the sons to war. The decapitated head is of Isaac, not the ram, while the ram itself is threatening from above.

Picture 1. Kadishman: Isaac's sacrifice.

Friedman (2015) described the binding of Isaac as a scapegoating process, and referred to its connections with sacrifice. Lavie (2017) connected it to the Oedipus complex (focusing on the aggression of the father towards his son) and explained how the hierarchical-aggressive aspect of Judaism is reflected in the social unconscious of Israeli Jews, as fathers send their sons to be killed in battles. Hanni Mann-Shalvi (2016) explored the feelings of Israeli parents-to-be towards their unborn child, and found high levels of anxiety related to the danger that their sons would be drafted eighteen years later. She concluded that this anxiety resides in the social unconscious of Jewish-Israeli parents and influences their parenthood as being overly involved, overprotective, and too interventionist.

The SU of Israeli people systematically analysed

Brown (2001) suggested four ways in which the social unconscious is manifested, which can be explored in the Israeli context:

1. Assumptions: what is taken for granted or as "given" (Hopper, 2001)
   a. The Chosen People—The Jewish nation is often referred to as "the Chosen People". They were chosen by God to influence the rest of mankind, a "light unto the nations" (Isaiah 42:6). However, the sense of being a *chosen people* occurs in both religious and non-religious contexts. Views of being a chosen people convey a meaning of superiority and are sometimes connected with ethnocentrism and racism. At the same time the "chosen status" also claims to carry greater responsibility and sacrifices than others. For some Israelis this taken-for-granted assumption in their social memory means that Israelis should portray higher moral codes and values, hence their tendency to be overly self-critical (the world surely joins this attitude of judging Israel in different criteria than other nations). For others it means superiority and justification for acts which ignore other people's rights.
   b. The Promised Land—As mentioned before, according to the Bible (Genesis 17:8), the land of Israel was "promised" to the descendants of Hebrew patriarchs by God, making it the *Promised Land*. This is another assumption in the Israeli social conscious and unconscious. Religious and right-wing Jews consciously use it

to expel Palestinians from their land, but being unconscious too, it can also explain the amazingly lenient attitude of left-wing government and public opinion towards the settlers in the West Bank (Zertal & Eldar, 2004).

c. The Jewish state—The state of Israel was established after the Holocaust as a safe home for the persecuted Jewish people. A special law was passed at the inception of Israel about the right of every Jew to immigrate to Israel. The taken-for-granted assumption that Israel is the Jewish state, a natural place for Jews, can be understood in the light of the above, but it also deprives other ethnic groups living in Israel of some civil rights. Being the state of the Jews, Israel persistently discriminates against other minorities. This might be done consciously and deliberately, or sometimes it might be done without awareness.
d. All Israelis are friends—This idiom ("Kol Israel Haverim" in Hebrew) reveals an assumption that impacts on interpersonal and inter-group relationships among Israelis. On one hand it establishes a clear boundary between those who belong (all the Jews) and those who are "not friends" (Arabs and other minorities). At the same time it establishes a sense of togetherness and unity, sometimes artificial and sometimes very real. When a Jew meets another Jew somewhere in the world they have a strong sense of connection due to long-standing traditions and beliefs, partly based on this idiom. The norm of mutual help, which is very strong in Jewish communities, also has its roots in the belief that "all Israelis are friends". Israelis continue this tradition in many ways, from gathering in groups whenever they meet abroad, to creating mutual help and interdependency between community members, for example in the kibbutzim. This assumption might be the reason why even when Jews split, or enter a conflict, there is always a sense of togetherness that prevents the conflict from deteriorating into a war between "brothers".

The idea that "we are all friends and together", resonates with Hopper's fourth basic assumption (1997) of incohesion, especially with its massification pole. One aspect of the "one-ness" (Turquet, 1975) of massification is how much Israelis disrespect the privacy or boundaries of the other, and this attitude is evident in daily actions, from intervening in people's conversation to telling strangers what to do. Such aggression is typical of massification (Hopper, 2003). However, these processes have defensive qualities against aggregation and the fear of annihilation, which is important in the social unconscious of the Israeli people. Doron (2014) pointed out that Israelis shift between two poles, expressing two conflicting assumptions coexisting in the unconscious of Israeli Jews: the Israeli motivation towards fitting in, as opposed to the Jewish historical motivation for standing aloof. By being unconscious, the Jewish-Israeli social unconscious is capable of containing such conflicts simultaneously.

Questions about boundaries and disrespect for privacy in the Israeli culture remind me of another way in which California differs from Israel. In my American therapy groups it takes time for members to enquire of others about personal issues, while in my Israeli groups, members ask penetrative, intruding questions without hesitation. While in California the respect for privacy is high, sometimes leading to isolation and alienation, in Israel lack of boundaries governs the scene. In terms of the SU, I assume that in California it reflects the deep theme of individualism rooted in "the American way", in contrast to the too deep, almost enmeshed, involvement of Israeli Jews with one another.

2. Disavowals: disowning knowledge or responsibility and other denials (Hopper, 2001)

   Because Jews considered themselves morally superior to their neighbours from early history, Israelis could not see themselves as creating injustice. Thousands of years of helplessness and victimhood made it difficult for the Israelis to accept that they too can be aggressive, and not only as a response to annihilation threats. In addition, due to centuries of persecutions and anti-Semitism, every criticism from other nations was rejected and labelled anti-Semitic. The possibility of a deep mechanism of identification with the aggressor, which might explain how the persecuted people became persecutors, is hard to perceive for Israelis, narcissistically hurting their self-image as merciful people. Even today many Israelis still disown and have difficulty accepting the fact that they have done harm to Palestinians too. An attempt to discuss this possibility encounters an immediate reaction that "… the Palestinians are all terrorists and that either we did nothing wrong, or we only protected ourselves from their aggression, or that all we have done is nothing compared to their cruelty."

A strong disavowal of responsibility exists in Israel for its part in the Palestinian-Israeli conflict.

Traumatised societies, such as Israel, tend to create rigid ideologies (Staub, 2000). Zertal (2002) shows how the central voice in the Israeli social unconscious has always been characterised by an endless accounting of the Jewish historical role as victims, and with the tendency to split. Whoever experienced such traumatic persecutions must protect himself from the recurrence of the past. The victim is never an aggressor; he is a survivor.

In an academic course in Israel about group processes, the teacher asked the students to write a memory about their "first group". One of the students shared with the group her memory from kindergarten where the sadistic nursery teacher made them sing "Jerusalem of Gold" for hours and deprived them of food until they sang it well. The group was quite shocked. Associations followed about the Holocaust and Nazis abusing Jews. Another association was about Israeli soldiers in the army basic training boot camp where the officers abuse their power to make them stand for hours in the hot sun and sing. No one had an association to the concurrent stories written in the newspapers about Israeli soldiers at the roadblocks, forcing Palestinians to sing national Israeli songs. When the teacher (actually group leader) asked about it, the students (all Israeli Jews) admitted that they couldn't think about Israeli soldiers as abusers.

There is another side of the split in which Israelis are flooded by guilt feelings and view their aggression as aimed towards helpless and innocent Palestinians. This is no less ignoring a complicated reality. Benjamin (1988) refers to the tendency to split action into two extremes: either you do or are done to. Israelis strongly believe that injustice is only done to them. The possibility that each side can become both an aggressor and a victim cannot enter the discourse.

3. Social defences

Various primitive defences based on splitting and projective identification are highly active in the Israeli social unconscious (Nuttman-Shwartz & Weinberg, 2012). Based on Jewish tradition, Israeli society is expert in using splitting and exclusion (Doron, in this book). They say that wherever there are two Jews—there are three synagogues. Israel is supposed to be a melting pot for the different ethnic groups from the diaspora, but it is still divided into social subgroups with substantial cultural and class differences. The main division is between Ashkenazim (whose origins are mostly from European and American countries) and Sephardim (who generally came from Africa and Asia). This general division does not fully describe the diversity of subgroups and their features.

This disintegration is expressed also between religious and secular Jews. Ultra-orthodox Jews are exempted from military service, creating a sense of exploitation for secular Jews and contributing to deep splitting. This issue becomes even more complicated because many of the religious Jews (not extreme in the religious area) are identified with a politically extreme right-wing ideology and populate the settlements behind the green line (the border before the 1967 war). Thus religious variation becomes political differentiation as well.

But of course, the issue that involves mostly splitting and projections is the relationship with the Arabs. For years, the Arab countries were Israel's main enemy, enhancing annihilation anxieties and paranoid feelings about Israel facing another holocaust. In more recent times, the Palestinians changed from terrorists to legitimate partners for negotiation. This process engendered upheaval for many Jewish Israelis, for whom negotiation with the Palestinian Liberation Organization had been taboo. During the last forty years, peace agreements and settlements were signed with two Arab countries and with the Palestinian Authority, but the complete longed-for peace is still far away. The building of the fence between Palestinian and Israeli territories (although helping to increase security and stop terrorist intrusion), especially because of its political abuse, is a concrete symbol for the splitting mechanism practised in Israel.

Splitting involves exclusion as well: one social subgroup excludes the other and unconsciously marginalises it. Thus, Israelis in the centre of the country excluded the southern citizens near the borders of the Gaza strip who were for years bombarded by Hamas missiles, and ignored their suffering. Together with that, Israeli society uses projection and projective identification quite often. Arab countries were perceived for years as evil and wanting to destroy the Israeli state and "throw all the Jews into the sea". This was not totally untrue but also helped the Israelis develop a distorted perception that they are a peace-loving country while the Arabs are bloodthirsty. The peace treaty with Egypt (and later with Jordan) and the escalation of violence between Israelis and Palestinians shifted this perception from Arab countries to the Palestinians, using the same defence mechanisms. Now the Palestinians became the warmongers, and Arafat was understood to have proved that "we have no partner for peace talks".

4. Structural oppression: control of power and information

   Manifestations of this dimension of structural oppression are very difficult to observe directly in any democratic country, but they can be deduced from the distribution of resources, such as governmental budgets. The amount of money allocated for education, construction, welfare, etc. for Arab villages in Israel is definitely less (actually one third) compared to the amount invested in the Jewish population. This might be due to a directed and intentional governmental plan to discriminate between Arabs and Jews, but it can also be due to an unconscious racial attitude towards minorities. Smooha (1978) in his book *Israel: Pluralism & Conflict* claims that Zionism does not go together with an equal status and equal rights for the Arabs. This claim is connected to the assumption that Israel is the state of the Jews.

The different attitude towards Israeli Arabs and the discrimination against them can be seen in the approach of the Israeli police, which became clear in the events of October 2000, after the beginning of the second Palestinian intifada. Israeli Arabs joined their Palestinian brothers starting riots in Israel, blocking main roads and threatening free transportation. The police opened fire on the Arab crowd, killing thirteen citizens. Never before had policemen in Israel opened fire on a crowd, and it is generally agreed that they would not have taken such extreme measures had it been a Jewish crowd.

Control of power reveals itself also between genders in Israel through comparing salaries of men and women in Israeli society. On average men earn more than women who do the same jobs. Gender stereotypes are hidden in the image of the Sabra which is based on a masculine stereotype of physical strength and the repression if not suppression of emotions. The importance of the family and its stability has slowly changed in some sections of the population but not in religious families. According to the stereotype, Jewish mothers are perceived as castrating, not letting children grow up and get away from their control (Raufman & Weinberg, 2016). Modern Israeli mothers are still expected to fulfil their nurturing role in the family while also developing a career outside the family, thus exerting quite a pressure on them to become a superwoman.

The hidden double gender role standards are revealed in therapy when even modern, financially independent, and career Israeli women still feel that they have not actualised themselves if they are not married. Even if disguised, the quest for the male partner is always there, with a hidden assumption that a woman is not really worthy without a man she has obtained. In contrast, Israeli men do not feel that their worth depends on whether they have an ongoing relationship and are more prone to draw their sense of worthiness from their professional status.

Although mass media communication in Israel seems to be free of any censorship, as is common in other democratic countries, articles relating to military actions and national security issues still need to be approved by the military censor. The Israeli newspapers also have their own inner self-censorship, deciding which news should not be revealed to the public in order to avoid damaging actions against terrorists. Although this attitude can be understood when talking about a country that is under a real threat of terror, it reveals a semi-conscious trend to use security as an excuse for undemocratic acts and possible abuse of power.

Israeli chosen traumas and chosen glories

"Chosen trauma" is an echoing trauma, becoming a paradigm that reassures against existential threat, and exists in the national memory (Volkan, 1997). Surely the most echoing trauma in the life of the Jewish people is the Holocaust. The murder of six million Jews by the Nazis reduced the Jewish population of the world by a third. Moreover, the way it was so orderly carried out, and the seeming helplessness of the victims, left its marks on many survivors and their families. The state of Israeli was mainly conceived because after the Holocaust it became self-evident the Jews needed a safe place. Many Holocaust survivors had immigrated to Israel even before it was formally established in 1948. A lot of survivors tried to overcome the horror they had been through by repressing the memories, avoiding any discussion about them, and ignoring the death camp prisoner number tattooed on their wrist. Those who were born in Israel joined this "conspiracy of silence", avoiding confrontation about the painful past with "those who were there". In the early days of the Israeli state (the 1950s and 1960s) no public discussion about the Holocaust existed. Denial governed the scene. The memories were still too painful, and an element of shame for being helpless and not resisting the massacre prevented an open discussion. Israeli youngsters were brought up either with the myth that all the Jews went like sheep to slaughter or that they all fought like brave warriors in the revolt of the Warsaw ghetto. At any rate the absence of a public discourse about what really happened there left the survivors feeling isolated and misunderstood. They were not able to mourn the losses, and focused on surviving without touching the painful memories. Sometimes it resulted in nightmares, sometimes in hidden guilt feelings, and mostly was transferred to the second generation of the Holocaust survivor children. According to Volkan (ibid.) this is the natural platform for the emergence of a chosen trauma that cannot be elaborated and worked through in the nation's memory. The image of the strong Sabra appearing within the Israeli social unconscious can be explained as a counter-reaction to the weakness of the Jews who—in the dominant social unconscious—went as sheep to slaughter.

From the 1970s on it seemed as if the opposite phenomenon occurred: overuse of the Holocaust in the public discourse. The Holocaust memory was associated with almost everything, sometimes cynically used by politicians for their purpose, but no doubt creeping into the Israeli social unconscious. In the first Gulf War (1991) Israel was attacked by missiles that were suspected of carrying chemical warheads, and all Israelis had to enter "sealed rooms" to be protected from this threat. Many anxious responses and exaggerated acts were not only because of the real threat but because of the shared memory of the Holocaust, combining a threat of annihilation with a gas attack and entering a sealed room. The association to the gas chambers of the Nazi camps was strong not only for Holocaust survivors but for second generation children of survivors.

Holocaust memories penetrate through the Israeli public discourse no matter what the subject is about. Sometimes it is stated clearly, but it can also be covert and only deduced from what is said. Deep inside themselves, Jews are well acquainted with persecution and being a suffering minority. The other side of this equation is the need to deny this experience because it is too painful, and so we can see opacity and insensitivity as a response to Palestinian suffering as well. Biran (2015) illustrates that in one way or another the Holocaust is always the social trauma in Israeli social dreaming experiments.

The Holocaust is not the only chosen trauma in Jewish history. As horrible as it was, it might be used as a "collective screen memory" (Hopper, personal communication). Centuries of persecution preceded this unperceivable event and probably echo intensively in the national memory as well. Jews were persecuted for their strange clothes, traditions, behaviours, etc. for hundreds of years. They became the perfect "other", an object of projection and hate. Fears of annihilation accompanied Jews and Jewish communities from their first exile from Israel. Other traumas of persecution and of an anti-Semitic nature are well remembered in Jewish history and taught in Israeli schools again and again. Small wonder that every act of terror in Israel reconstructs a primary threat to Jewish survival, from the destruction of the second temple, exile from Spain in 1492, the Holocaust, etc. (Gretz, 1995).

Additional comparisons

Israeli society is an immigrant and multicultural society, but in contrast to the North American immigrant and multicultural society, and although both societies hold the myth of making the desert flourish and civilising the wilderness (and in both places while ignoring the presence of indigenous people: Palestinians in Israel, Native Americans in the USA), the main narrative in establishing the USA is not about forced immigration of refugees like in Israel, but of a voluntary one. Immigrants to the United States always looked to the future, hoping and believing that the country of unlimited possibilities will help them achieve and actualise themselves, while the face of the refugees and Holocaust survivors was turned to the past, the place they left and the memory of those exterminated, with limited public discourse around it. The unspoken and unelaborated fugitive and survival experience has a direct impact on the creation of a similar refugee experience for another nation, the Palestinians.

Another difference between these two cultures, related to multiculturalism vs. multiple cultures, is how strongly people from those cultures are connected among themselves. Despite the differences between Jews of different ethnic and cultural origins, they are all connected through the collective memory of a common origin and the assumption of "all Israelis are friends", meaning that they are guarantors for one another. The glorious past historical memories of the Israelis, never forgotten and never denied, deeply bonds Israeli Jews from different descents. The situation in the US is different and there is no deep connection between people immigrating from different countries. Actually, this diversity created the need for something new to deeply connect people and create a foundation matrix strong enough for a united identity. On the surface these are the principles of freedom and equality common to the States, together with dreams and fantasies of a boundless future. However, on a deeper level it is the idol of money and financial success as an "objective" criterion for social comparison, and as a common value that unites diverse cultures of immigrants.

The need of Israelis to be (and show themselves as) strong is a reaction (formation?) to their past in the diaspora, and their fear of becoming victims again has created complicated relations with aggression. While US citizens are very diverse in their attitude towards conflict and aggression (New Yorkers tend to be more assertive and conflict oriented, while Californians shy away from direct conflicts), Israelis seem as if they are looking for conflicts (but are oblivious to why they are perceived so). I believe that deep unconscious mechanisms of identification with the aggressor and splitting off and denying "weak" parts are involved in this behaviour. At any rate, the aggressive attitude of Israelis in incidents that can be resolved peacefully is already a world famous stereotype, unfortunately having a grain of truth. The real situation is more complicated because at the same time Israelis feel and show immediate compassion towards victims around the world (as part of their deep identification with victims as well) and are the first to send aid in many natural disastrous events.

Summary and conclusion

Two parallel narratives predominate in the establishment of the state of Israel in the twentieth century: the pioneers and the Holocaust. The myth of the pioneers is "the chosen glory" of the revival of the Jews in their homeland (so that the settlers in the West Bank are half-consciously considered the new pioneers and the attitude towards them is dictated by this factor), while the Holocaust and centuries of persecution is "the chosen trauma" of the Jewish state (so that any threat is considered an annihilation one, and Israelis vow not to go again as "sheep to the slaughter").

Israelis integrate a rare mixture of individualism ("no one will tell me what to do", "I am not a sucker") and grouping ("all Israelis are friends"). As stated above, they move between the poles of fitting in and being unconsciously overly influenced by public opinion, to standing aloof and sometimes rebelling against consensus. By being unconscious, the Jewish-Israeli social unconscious is capable of containing such conflicts simultaneously.

References

Amichai, Y. (2000). Open Closed Open: Poems. Orlando, FL: Harcourt. Translated from Hebrew by Chana Bloch and Chana Kronefeld.

Atlas-Koch, G., & Kuchuck, S. (2012). To have and to hold: psychoanalytic dialogues on the desire to own. *Psychoanalytic Dialogues, 22*: 93–105.

Benjamin, J. (1988). *The Bonds of Love: Psychoanalysis, Feminism, and the Problem of Domination*. New York: Pantheon.

Biran, H. (2015). *The Courage of Simplicity: Essential Ideas in the Work of W. R. Bion*. London: Karnac.

Brown, D. (2001). A contribution to the understanding of the social unconscious. *Group Analysis, 34*(1): 29–38.

Doron, Y. (2014). The Israeli social unconscious as revealed to me during the GASI International Summer School in Serbia. *Group Analysis, 47*(2): 128–141.

Friedman, R. (2015). The best and worst feelings in the matrix. Republished as: The group analysis of the Akeda: the worst and the best feelings in the matrix. In: R. Friedman & Y. Doron, *Group Analysis in the Land of Milk and Honey* (pp. 61–73). London, Karnac, 2017.

Frosh, S. (2016). Born with a knife in their hearts: transmission, trauma, identity and the social unconscious. In: E. Hopper & H. Weinberg (Eds.), *The Social Unconscious in Persons, Groups and Societies: Volume 2: Mainly Foundation Matrices* (pp. 3–20). London: Karnac.

Gretz, N. (1995). *Captive of a Dream: National Myths in Israeli Culture*. Tel Aviv, Israel: Am Oved. (In Hebrew.)

Halbwachs, M. (1980). *The Collective Memory*. New York: Harper & Row.

Henderson, J. L. (1984). *Cultural Attitudes in Psychological Perspective*. Toronto, Canada: Inner City.

Hopper, E. (1997). Traumatic experience in the unconscious life of groups: a fourth basic assumption. *Group Analysis, 30*: 439–470.

Hopper, E. (2001). The social unconscious: theoretical considerations. *Group Analysis, 34*: 9–27.

Hopper, E. (2003). Aspects of aggression in large groups characterised by (ba) I:A/M. In: S. Schneider & H. Weinberg (Eds.), *The Large Group Revisited*. London: Jessica Kingsley.

Hopper, E., & Weinberg, H. (Eds.) (2011). *The Social Unconscious in Persons, Groups and Societies: Volume 1: Mainly Theory*. London: Karnac.

Hopper, E., & Weinberg, H. (Eds.) (2016). *The Social Unconscious in Persons, Groups and Societies. Volime 2: Mainly Foundation Matrices*. London: Karnac.

Lavie, J. (2017). Beyond Oedipus in group analysis: sacrificing the sons in the Israeli social unconscious. Republished as: Beyond Oedipus in group analysis: sacrificing of boys in the social unconscious of the Israeli people. In: R. Friedman & Y. Doron, *Group Analysis in the Land of Milk and Honey* (pp. 47–60). London: Karnac, 2017.

Malkinson, R., & Witztum, E. (2000). Collective bereavement and commemoration: cultural aspects of collective myth and the creation of national identity in Israel. In: R. Malkinson, S. S. Runin, & E. Witztum (Eds.), *Traumatic and Nontraumatic Loss and Bereavement: Clinical Theory and Practice* (pp. 295–320). Madison, CT: Psychological Press.

Mann-Shalvi, H. (2016). From ultrasound to the draft: Unconscious track of Israeli Masculinity. Tel Aviv: Resling Publishing House (in Hebrew). Published in English as *From Ultrasound to Army: The Unconscious Trajectories of Masculinity in Israel*. London: Karnac, 2016.

Moore, Y., & Bar-On, D. (1996). Narrative biography analysis: Life story of a second generation to Holocaust survivors. *Sihot-Dialogue: Israel Journal of Psychotherapy, XI*(1): 36–48. (In Hebrew.)

Nuttman-Shwartz, O. (2016). Research in a shared traumatic reality: Researchers in a disaster context. *Journal of Loss and Trauma: International Perspectives on Stress & Coping, 21*(3): 179–191.

Nuttman-Shwartz, O., & Weinberg, H. (2012). Organizations in traumatized societies: The Israeli case. In: E. Hopper (Ed.), *Trauma and Organizations* (pp. 215–231). London: Karnac.

Puget, J., & Wender, L. (1982). Analista y paciente en mundo superestos [Analyst and patient in overlapping worlds]. *Psicoanálisis, 4*(3): 503–536.

Raufman, R., & Weinberg, H. (2016). Early mother–son relationships, primary levels of mental organization and the foundation matrix as expressed in fairy tales: The case of the "Jewish mother". *Group Analysis, 49*(2): 149–163.

Smooha, S. (1978). *Israel: Pluralism and Conflict*. London: Routledge & Kegan Paul.

Staub, E. (2000). Genocide and mass killings: Origin, prevention, healing, and reconciliation. *Political Psychology, 21*: 367–382.

Tosone, C. (2012). Shared reality. In: C. R. Figley (Ed.), *Encyclopedia of Ttrauma: An Interdisciplinary Guide* (pp. 624–627). Thousand Oaks, CA: Sage.

Tubert-Oklander, J. (2014). *The One and the Many: Relational Psychoanalysis and Group Analysis*. London: Karnac.

Turquet, P. (1975). Threats to identity in the large group. In: L. Kreeger (Ed.), *The Large Group: Dynamics and Therapy* (pp. 87–144). London: Constable.

Volkan, V. D. (1997). *Bloodlines from Ethnic Pride to Ethnic Terrorism*. New York: Farrar, Straus & Giroux.

Weinberg, H. (2006). Group analysis, large groups, and the internet unconscious. PhD dissertation. Manchester Metropolitan University, UK.

Weinberg, H. (2007). So what is this social unconscious anyway? *Group Analysis, 40*(3): 307–322.

Weinberg, H., & Schneider, S. (2003). Introduction: Background, structure and dynamics of the large group. In: S. Schneider & H. Weinberg (Eds.), *The Large Group Revisited: The Herd, Primal Horde, Crowds and Masses* (pp. 13–26). London: Jessica Kingsley.

Yair, G. (2011). *The Code of Israeliness: The Ten Commandments for the 21st Century*. Jerusalem: Keter. (In Hebrew.)

Yair, G. (2015). The Israeli existential anxiety: Cultural trauma and the constitution of national character. *Social Identities, 20*(4–5): 346–362.

Zertal, I. (2002). *Death and the Nation*. Or Yehuda, Israel: Dvir. (In Hebrew.)

Zertal, I., & Eldar, A. (2004). *Lords of the Land: The Settlers and the State of Israel 1967–2004*. Tel Aviv, Israel: Kinneret, Zmora-Bitan, Dvir. (In Hebrew.)

CHAPTER EIGHT

"Black holes" as a collective defence against shared fears of annihilation in a small therapy group and in its contextual society

Yael Doron

In this chapter I will discuss the "black hole" as a collective or social defence against extremely painful shared anxieties. "Black holes" can exist in the small therapeutic group as well as in the wider society. I will illustrate the dynamics of the collective black hole with clinical data and with sociological reports.

For various reasons, social trauma is of particular importance in the formation of the social unconscious of societies and other social systems such as organisations (Hopper, 2012). It is, therefore, especially important to consider collective defences against shared anxieties that have been caused by social trauma, such as secrecy and normative taciturnity (Hopper, 2003). Black holes are another collective defence.

"Black holes" as a collective defence

In astronomy, a black hole is a region of space-time which exhibits such a strong gravitational pull that no particle or electromagnetic radiation can escape from it, not even light. Since they do not emit light, black holes cannot be observed, and their existence can only be deduced from phenomena that are caused *by* them. This resembles Freud's view of the unconscious as "… an unconscious conception … of which we are not aware, but the existence of which we are nevertheless ready to admit on account of other proofs or signs" (Freud, 1915e, p. 89). As the product of a denial, the "material" of a psychological black hole is neither available for narrative nor readily visible. This material can be apprehended only through indirect indications of it, such as slips of the tongue and other parapraxes, the repetition of mal-patterns of relationship, etc. which can be regarded as symptoms of anxiety associated with matters that have been repressed and/or denied. Nevertheless, just like other phenomena that have been made unconscious, psychic black holes control our actions as well as our feelings and thoughts related to what has been made unconscious.

Psychoanalysis has utilised the image of the "black hole" several times in the past. Ullman (1975) argued that the processes which occur in a dream that transforms implicit material into explicit material begin in the "black hole" of the psyche and end with words and meaning. Drawing on the theory of negative hallucinations, Bion (1970) used the term "black hole" to describe the "infantile catastrophe" of the psychotic patient. Glasser (1979) conceptualised the black hole as the characteristic defence of the "core complex" of perversions as a defence against psychosis. Grotstein (1990, p. 378) understood the black hole as "the ultimate traumatic state of disorganization, terror and chaos". Hopper conceptualised (1991) a process of "encapsulation" as a form of protective disassociation with respect to the fear of annihilation, separation, and death, following the traumatic experience of catastrophic loss in the earliest stages of development. He argued that an encapsulation was associated with a psychic black hole, and that it was unclear whether the black hole existed within the self or within the other, or within both. Hopper (1995) used clinical data to show that the black hole was typical of the defensive structures of drug addicts of various kinds. Eshel (1997, p. 195) described the gaps between sessions in psychoanalytic treatment, especially the therapist's vacations, as "black holes of discontinuity in the containment and in the holding environment of the treatment". In summary the concept of the black hole has been used to refer to the consequences of denial and/or disavowal as a disassociative defence against the fear of annihilation as a consequence of the experience of strain or cumulative and catastrophic trauma. The "black hole" has also been used to refer to the defence itself.

I would hypothesise that black holes exist not only in the mind of an individual person, but also in the dynamic and foundation matrices of his groupings, ranging from small groups who meet for the purposes of psychotherapy to organisations and their contextual societies. These collective black holes are associated with material that the members of a particular social system deny and/or disavow, because the recognition of such material would give rise to guilt and shame, various distorted patterns of relationship, and even the fear of annihilation, separation, and death. Actually, the recognition of these feelings and the open discussion of the phenomena that cause them can also precipitate attempts to change the situation, which is likely to set up a further set of anxieties (Hopper, 2000).

How does this kind of collective defence develop? In her discussion of the relationship between a therapist and the patient, Eshel (1997, p. 199) asks: "How can the therapist experience the patient's emotions … when the experience is one of a 'black hole'—of being gripped, sucked into, distorted and annihilated by enormous forces of death and destruction?" Bollas (1987) while writing about the "un-thought known" in the context of the analytic situation, suggests that the suffering of one person becomes the illness of two persons.

Similarly, in a therapeutic group, the mental pain of a person and especially the mental pain of two persons in a relationship can become the pain of the group as a whole, or at least of a subgroup of it (Friedman, 2007). If we wish to build a bridge between psychoanalysis and group analysis we need to remember that "… groups become the personal and collective transitional, mediating and self-objects of their members" (Hopper, 2009, p. 412). Hence, processes that exist in persons are enacted and recapitulated within the "here and now" of the group through projective and introjective identification, and group specific processes, such as resonance, mirroring, condensed phenomena, and so on. Thus, we can see the collective black hole as a collective defence against shared anxieties of the people in the group. This is especially relevant to clinical group work with traumatised patients, especially within the context of organisations and societies that might themselves be traumatised, such as Israel (Nuttman-Shwartz & Weinberg, 2008).

Clearly, groups can and do co-create collective representations within their dynamic matrices of situations from the "there and now" and "there and then" that are characterised by feelings of helplessness and loss involving chosen traumas and chosen glories (Volkan, 2001) as elements of the foundation matrix. Hopper (2007) has discussed these processes in terms of equivalence, group microcosm, and traumatophilia.

Black holes also exist in larger, more complex social systems, such as organisations and societies. Together with their collective terror, they also re-enact their shared defence mechanisms, such as their collective black holes. Collective black holes are highly likely to endanger the group as a whole as well as every individual member of it, because they are unconsciously relived and re-enacted in the "here and now", long before the material emerges consciously. Whether in an individual person or in a social system, the black hole develops in order to protect against feelings of shame, guilt, and annihilation anxiety.

A black hole in a small therapeutic group: "friendly fire attack"

I will now illustrate the phenomenon of a collective black hole in the dynamic matrix of a small therapy group, in the context of the foundation matrix of the wider contextual society in which the group was embedded.

My group was seven years old. It was composed of three men and two women, between twenty-five and fifty years of age. All of them were members of this group for at least one year. Three of them were in combined therapy with me, one was in individual therapy with me before entering the group, and the last one was in individual therapy with another therapist before joining this group. About two years ago, I introduced a new participant to my group, Barak.

Barak was severely wounded six years previously, during his military service, in a "friendly fire" incident. (The expression "friendly fire" describes a situation in which a military or police force opens fire on its own soldiers due to misidentifying the target as hostile.)

The context of Barak's injury was the war in Gaza in 2009 in which approximately 1300 Palestinians were killed. The Israeli forces had ten casualties. Four Israeli soldiers were killed in two "friendly fire" incidents. In addition to them, dozens of other soldiers were physically and psychologically injured during these incidents. Barak was one of those severely injured soldiers. After a difficult and intensive day in battle, he and his comrades went to sleep in an empty building in a Gaza city neighbourhood. A communication failure led to their misidentification as a hostile force and the incident ended with an Israeli tank shelling them. Two soldiers died on the spot, whereas Barak was severely injured. He was unconscious for many weeks, and after he had regained consciousness, most of his body remained paralysed for a long time, during which he had numerous operations. His right arm was amputated below the elbow, and with time, replaced with a prosthetic arm. His capacity to move his left hand remained limited. He also suffered from a head injury, due to shrapnel pieces sprayed into his brain. In addition to all these injuries, there was also the psychological trauma.

Six years had passed since the injury, during which Barak underwent physical and psychological rehabilitation. I met him when he participated in a group of Israel Defense Forces disabled veterans, which I facilitated in the Ministry of Defense. A short while afterwards, he approached me for individual therapy, and after a year, I invited him to join my "normal" group therapy.

Barak's joining of, and adaptation to the group was not simple, to put it mildly. I (Doron, 2017) have described elsewhere the traumatic way in which the group accepted him; this was despite the fact that we had a very long and irregular preparation period before he entered the group (more than a month). The first session of Barak's arrival was a complete disaster. The group members ignored him completely in the waiting room, and when the session began they went on with their stories as if nothing new had happened. They gave him a kind of a "performance", showing off their achievements, without really looking at him, and eventually, when they did try to introduce themselves to him, it sounded even worse. I left the session feeling that it was the wrong decision to introduce Barak into the group and that we were all going to pay for this mistake. I knew that I had already been shaken several times before by the introduction of new members to the group (Doron, 2014), but this time, it seemed more extreme. I was angry with myself; I thought that I had not prepared the group and Barak well enough and that I had damaged all the people concerned.

The next sessions were no better: Barak, who I knew from the past as a talkative and friendly person, hardly said a word for entire meetings. The rest of the group members almost never looked at him. In the few times they did try to approach him they only asked about his plans for recovery, what he was going to do in the future, what did he want to learn, and so on. It took them three months(!) to ask him for the first time what happened to him and how he was injured.

Nevertheless, in those first three months, although the group did not know anything about the terrible circumstances that led to Barak's injury, at least consciously, the group was re-enacting time and again in the "here and now" the intolerable experience of a "friendly fire attack": group members started to attack Barak, and then attacked each other, a process that continued for many long months. The group as a whole, including me as its conductor, was trapped in an everlasting cycles of attacks, victims, and perpetrators. No one stayed clean. Everyone was under fire. Within a short time this group, which had been warm and friendly, became dangerous for all of us. Almost every week someone got hurt, and went home feeling humiliated, insulted, or depressed.

In the next months the group space was filled with feelings of guilt, anxiety, and aggression, and with mutual vulnerability of all the group members. The term "friendly fire" hovered in the air, "attacking" us. Using Foulkes's ideas we could say that the symptom (the friendly fire attack) was "mumbling to itself secretly, hoping to be overheard" (Foulkes & Anthony, 1957, p. 259). Using intersubjective perspective we would say the group re-enacted it over and over in the room, hoping to create a better solution through the relationships (Grossmark, 2015). Thus, for example, the group members repeatedly tried to get closer and help each other, but it only resulted in more reciprocal attacks. Over time the friendly fire was present in the room, expressed in thoughts—but no less in the emotions: in the aggression, anxiety, and mostly in the guilt that controlled us. We all attacked and suffered attacks, injured each other and were injured.

And then, two years after he entered the group, one day Barak opened the group session and announced that he had decided to leave the group. "You don't help me at all. I didn't get anything from sitting here with you for the last two years," he told the others. He meant to leave at the end of that session—an "illegal" step in our group, where people stay for at least a month upon announcing their intentions and before leaving the group. Barak's speech felt to us all like a sudden attack, without a warning. The group members tried to convince him to stay and process his wish to depart, but he didn't agree. They tried to use the rest of the session to talk with him about his achievements in the group—he no longer wanted to kill himself every morning, he had found a girlfriend and was deeply in love, he had started to work and had managed to keep his job, although he hated it. They felt, as I also did, that many of his accomplishments were achieved thanks to the group's support and therapeutic work with him. But Barak didn't want to listen; he was very cynical and remote, and even mocked the others and insulted them until they stopped talking to him. Although they asked him to continue to come—he never showed up again. At the end of that session I felt that in his way out of the group Barak had re-enacted the same event that brought him into it. His "unresolved" trauma and troubled psychological state were relived in the "here and now" of the group (Doron, 2015).

One of the roles of the group conductor is to "translate" the symptoms to the group in a way which offers them insight and understanding, which is considered by Foulkes and Anthony (1957) as the beginning of the healing process. In contrast, the term "friendly fire" implies the blindness of the leader of the forces, that is, the group's therapist, and indeed, part of the processes that took place in the group resulted from my blindness as a group conductor—beginning with how I prepared the group for Barak's joining, followed by my panic and guilt when I felt that the group "was not okay" and did not welcome Barak sensitively and appropriately. During his first months in the group I had a hard time being patient and letting the process of Barak's entry to the group evolve. As a result, not infrequently, it was also I who attacked the group and participated in the friendly fire process, which resulted in a state of deep insecurity for all participants.

Looking now at this period of my group's life, with Barak, it seems that the group and I were caught in the basic assumption of incohesion (Hopper, 2003), oscillating between aggregation and massification. In an extraordinarily painful way Barak became a scapegoat and through this he enabled the massification to continue (Friedman, 2017).

"Friendly fire" as an example of a black hole in the social unconscious

With time, I began to think about the term "friendly fire" as a fundamental element of the foundation matrix of Israel which controlled and affected us in the group. All the group members (including me) are Israelis, who served in the army, and we all have siblings or children serving in the IDF. We are all living in a "soldier's matrix" (Friedman, 2015), and as such, were all raised on slogans connecting us directly to states of war, survival, and glory, such as "It is good to die for our country," "You do not leave wounded on the battlefield," and the officer's command in the battle: "Follow me." We all occasionally hear of disasters occurring in the military service and are overwhelmed with anxiety. But as opposed to the heroic stories, we have almost no myth, song, or national memory that deals with the friendly fire issue.

I believe that the very term "friendly fire" resides in the dark part of the foundation matrix, within its deep, hidden areas of collective black holes. Thus, the exposure of a collective black hole elicits anxiety, aggression, guilt, and shame, and exposes the feelings that have been blocked from perception. These feelings attack all the more forcefully those people who survived such events and stayed alive. The feeling of losing the "safe place" remains with them for the rest of their lives (Friedman, 2013). This was Barak's personal experience, but it resonated with experiences shared by all of us—Israelis who send their children to war time after time, reliving the heroic and tragic story of Isaac's binding—the Akeda—a Jewish and Israeli myth that lies in the foundation matrix of the nation (Friedman, 2017; Lavie, 2017; Weinberg, 2009).

The therapeutic group can turn out to be the place in which the severe injury is re-enacted over and over in the "here and now", but it can also become the safe place that enables reparation and growth (Friedman, 2007), a positive social psychic retreat (Mojovic, 2011). In the months that followed the events just described we have tried to understand how to stop being caught in the hurtful dynamics of black holes that originate in the foundation matrix but which are recapitulated within the dynamic matrix of the group. We tried to make the group a safer place, and indeed for some time it really felt safer. But Barak's sudden departure implies that the process did not end successfully. At least not for him.

Yehoshua (2007), a famous Israeli writer, wrote a novel named *Friendly Fire*, in which he tells the (fictional) story of Yrmi, a man who lost his son in the army, in a friendly fire incident. Yrmi (shorter name for Yirmeyahu—the name of the important biblical prophet Jeremiah, who foretold of Jerusalem's destruction) asks to cut himself off from all his former connections, from his family, and from Israel as a whole. The only way he feels he can deal with the pain of his son's unnecessary death is through total erasure of anything that connects him to Israel. When I read this book I was thinking about Barak and his departure from our group. Is he doomed to relive time and again his trauma in new connections, without any other (happy or at least normal) ending?

Writing this chapter I was thinking about the term "friendly fire" and its parallel in Hebrew—"Esh Kochotenu"—which means, literally, "the fire of our forces". When I checked the most popular Hebrew dictionaries, I was amazed that I could not find this term—not under the word "fire" and not under "force", although the phenomenon of friendly fire is so common, and occurs, unfortunately, in every war and many military routines. So, why do the Hebrew dictionaries omit it? Is it an accident? I think not. In my opinion, ignoring friendly fire is not a matter of conscious, deliberate policy. Instead, it represents a black hole as a social or collective denial and/or disavowal—within the social unconscious of the Israeli people and the foundation matrix of Israel as a nation.

Black holes within the social arena

Black holes, as a collective defence mechanism against extremely painful shared anxieties, also exist in the community, and in society at a national level. This can be illustrated by the way the state of Israel deals with the "Nakba". The displacement, dispossession, and dispersal of the Palestinian people is known to them as the Nakba, meaning "catastrophe" or "disaster". In 1948, after the Israeli Declaration of Independence, during the war between the Jews and Palestinians, an estimated 700,000 Palestinians fled or were expelled, and hundreds of Palestinian towns and villages were depopulated and destroyed. These refugees were divided between Jordan, Lebanon, Syria, the West Bank and the Gaza Strip.

The complex attitude of Israeli society towards the Nakba is manifested through the void—the Nakba is not taught at Israel's schools, and Israeli Jews know almost nothing about it. It doesn't have almost any traces in art—in poems, stories, TV shows, etc. The silence around the subject is screaming. It is as if (or exactly because) Israelis don't want to remember it or think about it at all. Tali (in his chapter in this book) argues that "The 'Nakba', in all its many aspects, is for the Palestinians a defining event in their history." He concludes that the story of the Palestinian people exists more in their social unconscious than in their conscious. Weegmann (in his chapter in this book) strongly agrees that the Nakba is denied and not recognised. But not only by the Palestinians. Ben Zur (2015) claims that the Nakba is also a part of the history and identity of those who committed it. She thinks that the Nakba is a traumatic event for Jewish Israelis as well, with shameful and difficult memories which haunt those who were soldiers back in that time, their families, friends, and in fact all of Israeli society. There are formal governmental forgetting practices which deliberately minimise the existence of traces of that trauma—old Arab names of neighbourhoods and cities in Israel are renamed in Hebrew new names, forests are planted over the ruins of the Arab villages, and the official state maps omit the old Arab names, although many of the older citizens still use them. In this way, the Israeli wider society, much like the members of my small analytic group, using massive defence mechanisms, such as collective black holes, against their unbearable feelings.

A unique example of the denial, guilt, and shame the Israelis feel regarding the Nakba can be traced in the social storm that developed when in 1977 the Israeli Broadcasting Authority (public government body that governs Israeli radio and television broadcasts) wished to screen the film *Khirbet Khizeh*. The film followed a book with the same name, written in 1949, by S. Yizhar, an important Israeli writer, dealing with the expulsion of the fictional village Khirbet Khizeh—representing the many villages which were evacuated during the Nakba. The book tells about the immorality of the soldiers who executed the expulsion. Although it was a part of the Israeli high school curriculum, when it was made a TV drama it sparked a public debate, whether it should be broadcast or not. The Knesset (the unicameral national legislature of Israel) asked to postpone the broadcasting and the minister of education declared it was postponed. The broadcasting authority saw these events as steps which limited its freedom of expression, its workers darkened the TV screens for the time the film was originally scheduled to be broadcast, and the high court was asked to intervene. The Knesset had five more special meetings before it reached the conclusion that the film could be broadcast.

More personally, I would add that as a child and adolescent growing up in Israel, I did not hear anything about the Nakba, not in films, books, debates, and so on. Moreover, I think I heard the word "Nakba" for the first time only during my service in the army. This is so bizarre and unbelievable that I must consider the Nakba to be a collective black hole in the Israeli social unconscious.

What can we do with collective black holes?

This chapter deals with a very strong, severe, and extreme phenomenon that "attacks" individuals and groups from inside, while they wish to defend themselves from real or fantasised catastrophe. What can we do, as group analysts and as individuals, to diminish this phenomenon or reduce its impact on us? How can we teach ourselves to trace the unconscious parts which are missing? How can we "see" what is not out there? The void? The empty? The "black holes" in our mental lives? We need others to be with us, talk with us, and reflect to us our inner mental lives (Foulkes, 1964). Together, in small analytic groups as well as in larger groups (Schneider & Weinberg, 2003), we can start to notice the missing, silent, and perhaps silenced parts in our societies and minds. We can learn about them from what is said, and not said, from what is done to us, or done by us, as part of the relationships between the members of the small and large group. When we see those parts, acknowledge them, give them names, tell their stories, to others as well as to ourselves, there is a better chance that they will stop governing us from the depth of our social unconscious.

References

Ben Zur, E. (2015). The Israeli unconscious and the Palestinian Nakba. A lecture given in the international conference of the Israeli Institute of Group Analysis, "The Road Not Taken", Tel Aviv.

Bion, W. R. (1970). *Attention and Interpretation*. London: Tavistock.

Bollas, C. (1987). *The Shadow of the Object*. London: Free Association.

Doron, Y. (2014). Primary maternal preoccupation in the group analytic group. *Group Analysis, 47*: 17–29.

Doron, Y. (2015). Sudden departure in group. *Group, 39*: 295–302.

Doron, Y. (2017). The black hole in the social unconscious: a collective defence against shared fears of annihilation. In: R. Friedman & Y. Doron (Eds.), *Group Analysis in the Land of Milk and Honey*. London: Karnac.

Eshel, O. (1997). On "black holes", death and analytic existence. *Dialogues ("Sihot"), 11*: 195–205. (In Hebrew.)

Foulkes, S. H. (1964). *Therapeutic Group Analysis*. London: Karnac.

Foulkes, S. H., & Anthony, E. J. (1957). *Group Psychotherapy: The Psychoanalytic Approach*. London: Karnac.

Freud, S. (1915e). The unconscious. In: *S. Freud: Beyond the Pleasure Principle and Other Writings* (pp. 89–94). Tel Aviv, Israel: Dvir, 1988. (In Hebrew.)

Friedman, R. (2007). Where to look? Supervising group analysis—a relations disorder perspective. *Group Analysis, 40*: 251–268.

Friedman, R. (2013). Overcoming shame through dreamtelling. *International Journal of Counseling and Psychotherapy, 10–11*: 39–44.

Friedman, R. (2015). Soldiers matrix. *Group Analysis, 48*: 239–257.

Friedman, R. (2017). The worst and the best feelings in the matrix. In: R. Friedman & Y. Doron (Eds.), *Group Analysis in the Land of Milk and Honey*. London: Karnac.

Glasser, M. (1979). Some aspects of the role of aggression in the perversions. In: I. Rosen (Ed.), *Sexual Deviation*. Oxford: Oxford University Press.

Grossmark, R. (2015). The edge of chaos: Enactment, disruption and emergence in group psychotherapy. In: R. Grossmark & F. Wright (Eds.), *The One and the Many. Relational Approaches to Group Psychotherapy* (pp. 57–74). New York: Routledge.

Grotstein, J. S. (1990). Nothingness, meaninglessness, chaos and the "black hole" II. *Contemporary Psychoanalysis, 26*: 377–407.

Hopper, E. (1991). Encapsulation as a defence against the fear of annihilation. Appendix II. In: *Traumatic Experience in the Unconscious Life of Groups: The Fourth Basic Assumption: Incohesion: Aggregation/Massification or (ba) I:A/M*. London: Jessica Kingsley, 2005.

Hopper, E. (1995). A psychoanalytical theory of drug addiction: Unconscious fantasies of homosexuality, compulsions and masturbation within the context of traumatogenic processes. *International Journal of Psychoanalysis, 76*(6): 1121–1143.

Hopper, E. (2000). From objects and subjects to citizens: group analysis and the study of maturity. *Group Analysis, 33*: 29–34.

Hopper, E. (2003). *The Social Unconscious*. London: Jessica Kingsley.

Hopper, E. (2007). Theoretical and conceptual notes concerning transference and countertransference processes in groups and by groups, and the social unconscious: Part II. *Group Analysis, 40*: 29–42.

Hopper, E. (2009). Building bridges between psychoanalysis and group analysis in theory and clinical practice. *Group Analysis, 42*: 406–425.

Hopper, E. (Ed.) (2012). *Trauma and Organisations*. London: Karnac.

Lavie, J. (2017). Beyond Oedipus in group analysis: the sacrifice of boys in the social unconscious of the Israeli people. In: R. Friedman & Y. Doron (Eds.), *Group Analysis in the Land of Milk and Honey*. London: Karnac.

Mojovic, M. (2011). Manifestations of psychic retreats in social systems. In: E. Hopper & H. Weinberg (Eds.), *The Social Unconscious in Persons, Groups, and Societies: Volume 1: Mainly Theory* (pp. 209–232). London: Karnac.

Nuttman-Shwartz, O., & Weinberg, H. (2008). Organizations in traumatized societies: The Israeli case. *Organizational and Social Dynamics, 8*: 138–153.

Schneider, S., & Weinberg, H. (2003). *The Large Group Revisited*. London: Jessica Kingsley.

Ullman, M. (1975). The transformation process in dreams. *Journal of the American Academy of Psychoanalysis and Dynamic Psychiatry, 19*(2): 8–10.

Volkan, V. D. (2001). Transgenerational transmissions and chosen traumas: an aspect of large-group identity. *Group Analysis, 34*: 79–97.

Weinberg, H. (2009). The Israeli social unconscious. *Collection ("Mikbatz"), 14*: 11–28. (In Hebrew.)

Yehoshua, A. B. (2007). *Friendly Fire*. Bney-Brak, Israel: The New Library. (In Hebrew.)

CHAPTER NINE

The social unconscious of the Palestinian people

Sa'ed Tali

In this chapter I will try to trace the social unconscious of the Palestinian people in order to clarify and define it. What is in the "black box" of the collective Palestinian psyche? How has a history filled with turmoil, rulers, and regimes that have characterised our region, including the present Israeli reign, affected its formation? Attempting to answer such questions is a very challenging endeavour for me as a Palestinian. To the best of my knowledge, there has been little written about the Palestinian social unconscious.

From the moment I sat down to write I felt a great difficulty and heavy responsibility. At the beginning I did not understand what was happening to me, and I thought perhaps these were my familiar, personal difficulties in forming and writing my thoughts. However, as time went by I began to understand that something else was involved. I realised I was afraid of the public responses to the results of my investigation. I also understood I was afraid to write something that might jeopardise the Palestinian struggle for world recognition and the establishment of our state. I was afraid of the reaction of Palestinian readers in particular. Would they accept and identify with what I write? Or would they feel that I was contributing to their sense of humiliation? They might disagree with what I wrote, and I would have to face their anger.

The thought that I might have to do so reflects a central issue—personal honour—in the society from which I come.

My writing will be based on intersubjective assumptions and focus on that area which exists between the object I want to investigate and the subjective self who is responsible for the investigation. I cannot help but be involved. I will try, however, to maintain the objectivity necessary for looking at and analysing phenomena from outside the subject of my investigation. I will be carrying out a pioneer investigation of a closed society, one that does not like to expose itself, and in some ways is not coping well with an ongoing traumatogenic process. There is a shift between subjective and objective demands that I both feel and experience and at the same time freely interpret and analyse.

Many weeks went by from the moment I agreed to write about the social unconscious of the Palestinian people until I actually started writing. I quickly came to understand that the doubts that plagued me early on and which prevented me from starting to write were beyond my "personal psychology". I realised that they were a reflection of the Palestinian unconscious, which demands solidarity, togetherness, and loyalty to Palestinian issues. This is often at the expense of individual thinking. This tendency is particularly noticeable in meetings between Israeli Jews and Palestinians, in which the Palestinians have a need to present a united front, in addition to the fact that our society prefers the welfare of the collective over the needs of the individual, and we are in an ongoing war situation which pressures the individual to compromise and to sacrifice for the benefit of the society in which s/he lives.

The following excerpt is from a book by Sayed Kashua that illustrates the importance of the need for unity.

> I used to love Tira[1] during one of our major holidays, in which my uncles would slaughter a sheep, sometimes also a calf, in the courtyard of my grandfather's house. I also liked the holiday because I could play with my cousins, who had the same last name as mine. In Jaljulia[2] there was no one with our last name. Usually there were at least four children in the class with the same family name, and I was the only one in my class—in the whole school and later I understood, in all of Jaljulia—with a different last name. I was a foreigner in class and a foreigner in the village, with a strange family name, just as different as other foreigners in Jaljulia. (*Second Person*, Kashua, 2010, pp. 96–97)

This excerpt illustrates the importance of familial and group belonging among adults and children in Arab society. I myself remember that once when I was a child and walking with some friends through the fields of the village in which I grew up, we met some other children, older than us. I recall that I was afraid, even more than the others. I didn't know why. Usually I was the bravest child in our group. When we drew closer to the big kids, they asked each of us for his family of origin and who was his father. All the children answered and identified themselves. One by one the big kids let them go on their way. When they questioned me, they did not recognise my family or my father. I had to "work" hard so that they could identify me and the family to which I belonged. Only then did they let me go home. I understand now that the fear that overcame me was connected to the fact that unconsciously I knew that I belonged to a small family, and this left me with a feeling of not being protected. I didn't feel as safe as those who belonged to the larger families.

Palestinian society, aside from coping with the difficult implications of the creation of the state of Israel, also has to deal with isolation from the larger family of the Arab nation. It is noticeable that when Palestinians get together in Arab group meetings they try first to preserve their sense of belonging to the common family of Palestinians.

Who is a Palestinian?

This is a difficult issue, from which nonetheless I cannot run away. It involves a search for roots. I and others like me often wonder who should be considered a Palestinian and who should not. What sets us apart from other nations in the region? What are our roots? What is the Palestinian nation? Where did it all begin? Is this a history of the locality or of the nation and its people or both together? And what is the difference between Palestinians and other Arabs? Jews raise doubts about the existence of a Palestinian nation, which always evokes the anger of Palestinians. We should bear in mind that the Palestinians who are in fact citizens of the state of Israel are exposed to much data about Jewish history and the Jewish Israeli narrative. However, the Palestinian narrative is not only unrecognised in Israel, but often denied. This is one of the reasons for writing a short description of our history and trying to learn more about our social unconscious. The Palestinian unconscious is based on a history of the "place" and also of the people. According to the world's major religions, and particularly the religion of Islam, Palestine is the most sacred place on earth.

The Palestinians, like the rest of the Arabs, are a people who belong to the family of Semitic tribes. Around the fourth millennium BC, they wandered from the region which today is Saudi Arabia all the way to the Mediterranean basin. Beginning in the fourth century BC, the Semites began to abandon their nomadic life and started settling in areas they claimed for themselves. They spread out over different areas in the Middle East and became the foundations for various peoples. The Canaanites settled the region that later was called Palestine and together with tribes that migrated from the Greek islands, the Palestinian nation was woven together (according to the *Palestinian Encyclopaedia*, 1984). The Greek historian Herodotus gave the name Palestine to the region in which the Palestinians lived, which included the Greek islands all the way to the southern coast of what is today the state of Israel. The name Palestine was formally adopted by the Roman Empire, and it is with us until today.

Today there are eleven million Palestinians around the world. Many of them are refugees and about half of them do not have citizenship in the countries in which they reside. Five and a half million Palestinians live today in Israel, the West Bank, and Gaza. The Palestinians grew out of nomadic life and now they are wandering once again. Today, however, they are trying to unify themselves and create themselves anew.

At the beginning of my research I wondered which Palestinian population I should choose: those who were expelled and could not return (either because of Israel's refusal to let them come back or for other reasons) or those who stayed within the boundaries of the state of Israel in 1948 and live within them as citizens even today. I wondered, should I choose those living in Israel and form a national ethnic minority; or those who have lived since 1967 in the West Bank and Gaza under the Israeli occupation?

This question was highly relevant because over time, differences were formed between the various entities that make up the Palestinian nation, particularly between those who live in the state of Israel and those who live in the Palestinian territories or in the Palestinian diaspora. These differences are similar to those that exist between Ashkenazi and Sephardic Jews. There is no doubt that life characterised by Western or Eastern culture penetrates and influences the Palestinian population. It creates a dynamic similar to that of any nation coping with majorities and minorities. Ironically, it is similar to that with which the Jewish people have had to deal.

It is possible that these questions relating to the various sectors of the Palestinian population are connected to the need of the Palestinians to present a united front. There is a push to cover the many splits that exist within Palestinian society regarding status, religion, subgroups such as those who fled in 1948 and became refugees, and those who remained behind, residents of the territories and residents of Israel, residents of the north and residents of the south of Israel, etc. All this affects the question, "Who is a Palestinian?"

Until the establishment of the state of Israel, the Palestinian population was completely within well-defined boundaries. Today they are dispersed over many and distant boundaries in the Arab world, in Europe, and in America. Despite their dispersal and its ramifications on our ways of life, I think that we have much in common, mainly due to collective memories (Halbwachs, 1992) and our social and cultural background. These memories draw the various groups close to each other. (Comparison between Palestinians who live here and those who live outside the 1967 Israeli borders—and particularly with regard to the social unconscious—is an important subject for future research).

Definitions

In conducting a review of various definitions of the social unconscious, I came to the conclusion that the story of the Palestinian people exists more in our social unconscious than in our "conscious". It is denied more than it is recognised. Hopper's (2003) definition of the social unconscious seems appropriate to describe the situation of the Palestinian: "The concept of the social unconscious refers to the existence and constraints of social, cultural and communicational arrangements of which people are unaware; unaware, in so far as these arrangements are not perceived (not known), and if perceived not acknowledged (denied), and if acknowledged, not taken as problematic ('given'), and if taken as problematic, not considered with an optimal degree of detachment and objectivity." This definition focuses on the repressed and denied unconscious arrangements that unite people who belong to the same collective. (I feel close to and identify with Palestinians wherever they are without being able to explain why, which is another reason for writing this chapter.)

Weinberg (2007) developed Hopper's definition, suggesting that the social unconscious must refer to specific contents, especially in order to make them operational and more accessible to empirical research. Moreover, he argues, collective memories of social traumas and social glories, whether or not they are "chosen" (Volkan, 2001), should be regarded as the "building blocks" of the social unconscious. They shape the identity of the system and the social identities of its members.

Halbwachs (1992) points out that collective memories can be defined as the reflections of the past that are adopted by all members of a system. These representations contribute to the formation of a coherent narrative of the history of the system. Although they may not provide an accurate historical account of what happened in reality, they come to answer particular needs, crystallise the consciousness of the system, create a sense of continuity, and build a sense of solidarity. These cultural legacies may be transformed into myths, which are more elaborated stories of important events, usually containing heroic and wishful elements. Myths are neither true nor false, but contain a mixture of fact and fantasy. Some myths have existed since time immemorial, but some are created quite quickly in an attempt to make sense of more recent, important collective events. Myths have many functions and can be explained in a myriad of ways. The elaboration of collective memories and the making of myths are like secondary revision in dream work (Hopper, 2015).

The Palestinians have a long and common history, including cuisine, poetry, language, and leadership. These commonalities set them apart from the rest of the Arabs in the Middle East. However, I would add the notions of a shared destiny and collective hope to the previous definitions of the social unconscious of any nation (Hopper, 2003). Anxieties, defences, fantasies, myths, and collective memories are of special importance to the acknowledgement of a shared destiny. Nonetheless, the main issue giving all Palestinians a sense of common destiny is the Israeli occupation. The Declaration of Independence and the founding of Israel have intensified and accelerated the separation and differentiation of the Palestinian people from other Arab nations. Palestinians live under a foreign regime, and there is a common desire for liberation. As in Europe today, the entry of immigrants awakens feelings of nationalism and hostility towards those who are "different". The Palestinians are looking for a cohesive and distinct identity to help them survive the majority rule of the Jewish Israelis and of course to maintain their long-standing tradition as a nation.

Imagined communities: imagined and implanted unconscious memories

Benedict Anderson (1983) discusses the growth of the nationalist idea and its development as a universal phenomenon. He uses the notion of "imagined community" to describe large groups of people who have come together around a unifying idea that causes them to act as a community even though in fact the connection and similarity among the individuals that make up the large group and smaller groups within it are minimal or do not even exist. Awareness of the community is so strong in these groups that they have the power, for example, to mobilise members to go and die on far away battlefields, as though their doing so was a matter of protecting their own homes and families.

According to Anderson, nationhood and states built on the nationalist idea are present-day examples of "imagined communities". Such imagined communities were often substituted during history by other imagined communities, such as large communities of Christian, Muslim, and Buddhist believers. The Palestinian community—and not only it—is an example of a community that just 100 years ago was subjugated to the Islamic-Arabic ruling regimes. Since the establishment of the state of Israel in 1948, the major community has become the Israeli one. According to Anderson, awareness of the "imagined community" includes not only the need for collective memory that is nourished by the national language, but also the need for "collective forgetfulness", that is, historic events that the national group is supposed to recognise as traumatic and that are better forgotten.

These ideas have led me to the uncomfortable feeling that my people and I might be searching for something unconscious that might in fact be totally false. I think that it behoves all of us—Palestinians, Jews, and members of other religious groupings—to doubt memories and facts forced upon our awareness. We should not accept them as real without testing them out. This is not an easy task for a person within the society being examined. It requires great courage and the ability to cope with pressure and criticism, but it is nonetheless a worthwhile and significant one.

Majorities that feel they are a minority and minorities that feel they are a majority!

"Nakba", expulsion, "refugeeism", "awada" ("return"), honour, minority, weakness, persecution and oppression, defeat, "intifada", "Shaheed" (martyrdom) and vision: it is hard for me to admit, but reading the above words brings heavy associations to my innards. This is perhaps a sign that I belong to a people that have experienced many difficult events. These have left a negative imprint on me and the rest of my people, even on the body/somatic level. We have internalised inferiority, catastrophe, and abandonment. We were left to ourselves, with no connection to near and far away brothers and no connection to powerful parents. We became split off from the big tribe.

In his book, *State of Siege*, written in 2002 in an encircled Ramallah, Mahmud Darwish expressed some of these feelings, and particularly to the issue of aloneness:

> Alone are we, alone to saturation
> If it weren't for the occasional rainbow.
> The siege is a gift on a ladder planted in the heart of a storm.
> We have brothers beyond this space.
> Good brothers, loving ones, who are watching us.
> And are crying in the secret corners of their hearts:
> "It's too bad that this siege couldn't be made public."
> And too bad they don't complete the sentence with:
> "… don't leave us alone."

The Palestinian people continue to act like a majority group because of their long connection with the Arab people, even though in fact we are a minority group in Israel. Palestinians see themselves as part of the Arab nation and they feel deep connection to it, however they have their unique characteristics that separate them from Iraqi Arabic or Egyptian. Palestinians feel pride and longing for the glory days of Islam, like other Arabs, while they felt frustrated and helpless in the face of the reality in which they live as a minority under foreign rule.

This dissonance—behaving as a majority when in fact we are a minority—is not simple. It greatly hinders the possibility of integrating and coping with the difficulties of the reality around us. I assume that the common Palestinian feels in his psyche that he is part of a majority, as the Jew feels in his psyche that he is part of a minority, even though in Israel he is part of a ruling majority. For the Jew, 2000 years of diaspora and life as a minority have not been erased and have a central place in the Jewish awareness. The encounter between two peoples who are motivated by unconscious aspects that actually contrast with the reality in which they are living only makes the possibility of finding solutions suitable for both sides more difficult and complicated.

The Palestinians became accustomed to being part of a larger bloc of peoples, ever since they became a part of other peoples of the area under Islam in the seventh century. Most recently, life in Israel has isolated them physically and culturally from other members of their group. The Palestinians, cut off from some members of their tribe and not yet organised as a distinctive group, find themselves for the first time responsible for their own future. Their situation is similar to that of a child who belongs to a big "hamula" (tribe) from which he is suddenly removed and sent to a private school for problematic children that is run under military conditions. Isolated, the Palestinians learned to repress shame and narcissistic injury resulting not just from their defeat by the Israelis but also as the weak link of the entire Arab world. In the last three decades, however, there has been a change. There are signs of a struggle for life, a sense of power and competence. These eventually become part of the "personal matrices" of Palestinians.

The individual, the uniqueness, and the mob

There is a widespread view that the Palestinians are in an ongoing process that began with a struggle for survival and continues in a struggle for recognition and rebirth. There is a movement away from dependency on the Arab world for help in achieving liberation and moving away from dependency on the state of Israel and its institutions: an attempt to use our own resources to achieve legitimate citizens' rights. There is a change in Palestinian self-image from a defeated people, without authority or leadership, to a people with a vision knowing who we are and what we want to achieve. We are a people that is maturing and developing, on the way to actualising selfhood, with a unique and separate identity.

Despite accelerated processes of change and transformation in the overall Arab world, that world is still one of a big collective in which, socially speaking, being noticed and unique is not desirable. Being so is difficult and sometimes dangerous. Hence, in Palestinian society, the individual tends to be swallowed up in the matrix. Therefore, it is often difficult to distinguish between the social and individual unconscious. The Palestinian unconscious is connected to the Arab one, and the Arab one connected to the Islamic one. The individual unconscious is connected to them all. And all these unconscious processes take place under the Israeli/Western/foreign occupation, that on the one hand represses it, and on the other, challenges it. The Palestinian collective wants to exercise its right to self-actualisation alongside Israel, while the Palestinian individual wants to fulfil himself alongside and under the Islamic and Arab identities.

The Palestinian struggle for independence and freedom accelerated the formation of nationality and the Palestinian narrative. This process was influenced by materials that are submerged in the Palestinian unconscious. But these developments, however one looks at them, have also been interrupted and repressed by the Israeli occupation, as has been the case with other nationalist movements.

The Israeli occupation has challenged Palestinians to define themselves more precisely, and in many ways to disconnect from the Arab and Islamic world. The Palestinian people are strengthening their uniqueness as a defence against assimilation and, thus, their disappearance as a minority in the Jewish state. There is anxiety about becoming an unnoticed minority in the Arab-Islamic world.

Khalil Jubran wrote in *The Broken Wings* (1912) that Redemption lies within the individual. He spoke about the Arab individual who grew up in a society in which the individual is always less than the collective and to a large extent its servant. In this regard the Palestinian people may be breaking a pattern common in the Arab states, for independence might only be achieved by separating from the larger Arab world with which until now they have always been a part.

Examples from conferences

Too few Palestinians who are citizens of Israel participate in professional conferences of the various non-profit organisations in the field of group therapy. For one thing the language of conferences in Israel is Hebrew and in some cases English but never Arabic. The approach and orientation is usually psychological, an orientation with which most Palestinians do not feel comfortable, rather than political/sociological.

This might account for a trend towards the abandonment of the Israeli arena in favour of involvement in the intra-Palestinian one.

First case

A recent conference of B'Sod Siach, an NPO whose goal is to advance dialogue between the various groups in Israeli society, took place in the heart of an ultra-orthodox neighbourhood in Jerusalem during a tense period between the ultra-orthodox and the state. A mother had been arrested because she was suspected of abusing her sick son by starvation. The large group was conducted by four conductors: two Jewish women, one who was secular and the other orthodox, and two men, one Jewish, who lived in a settlement and the second, myself, a Palestinian citizen of Israel. Fifty participants, who might be considered as representative of Israeli society, attended the conference: Jews and Arabs, leftists and rightists, ultra-orthodox and secular, Ashkenazim and Sephardim. There were only three Palestinian Israeli citizens: two older men and a younger woman. One Palestinian man left during the conference.

In the opening meeting of this "Dialogue" conference, during which all the organisers sat in one row facing the audience, a male Palestinian sitting in the first row of the participants looked at the director of the conference, a woman, and angrily complained that the welcoming speech had only been read in Hebrew. He requested it also be read in Arabic. He then told that on the way to Jerusalem he noticed that the name for Jerusalem in Arabic, Al Kuds, had been erased from the road signs. He said that here in a conference calling for dialogue, it was important to also have the Arabic language.

In my opinion the man was afraid that "Arabness" would be erased in the conference, as it had been on the road signs. He went on to express rage at the myriad of insults to male Arab honour in Israeli society. He was dismissed, belittled, and condescended to, and his verbal reactions were also dismissive and belittling. Some of the participants protested. The more they did so, the more he became aggressive, disrespectful, and violent towards the director of the conference. Most of the Jewish participants came out to support her, a woman who at the outset of the conference seemed to symbolise for them a big father-and God-like figure. The atmosphere was very tense and for some moments it seemed like a physical conflict between the Jews and the Palestinians would take place. The tension was broken after a few minutes when a Jewish female participant stood up, marched up to the Palestinian participant, put out her hand, introduced herself, and suggested that they get to know each other. They could speak among themselves as person to person, on a human basis. The Palestinian member, after some hesitation, accepted her offer. Then the female participant said that, in the name of the group, she wanted to move the discussion from the level of an encounter between "us" and "them" to one between "me" and "me" and from the level of nationalist groups to one of personal groups. The audience and organisers happily took hold of the lifesaver the female participant had thrown and supported a "hudna", that is, a temporary ceasefire between her and the Palestinian man.

Except for the lively moment at the outset of the conference, the Palestinians remained relatively passive, hardly speaking in the large group. Everyone spoke Hebrew, which had been proclaimed the official language of the conference, including the participant who had spoken at the beginning of his fear of being erased in the large group. Most of the informal subgroups seemed to disappear in the large group. The only group that "came out of the closet" and won recognition and sympathy were the homosexuals and lesbians. One gay man and one gay woman announced their sexual predilections and described their personal dilemmas. Perhaps the homosexuality in these transactions reflects the emergence of a "third" possibility. The "third" is neither a Jew nor a Palestinian, neither a man nor a woman, but rather a new, unrecognised entity that contains within it elements of all the various identities.

Conversation in the large group was in the language of "I" and not the language of "we". It was a neutral "I" that didn't belong to any group. In some paradoxical way, as feared by the angry Palestinian participant, the small groups unconsciously erased themselves within the large group and so, as with all the others, the Palestinian group was also erased.

One way to understand this is perhaps connected to annihilation anxiety. It is as though members of the small group acted out precisely what made them so anxious, that is, their annihilation. Perhaps members of the group were seeking to escape themselves and the conductors. Perhaps the gay man and the lesbian woman imagined a kind of relationship that would free them from the intense anxiety that each had to deal with. In this atmosphere of self-denial, the Palestinian group, like the others, was erased. So somewhat absurdly the nightmare of the original Palestinian member came true.

Conference participants, Jews and Palestinians, participated in the large group with an increased feeling of anxiety about the repetition of the old conflicts. There was also the experience of a positive encounter among themselves. The Palestinian participant who spontaneously protested against the erasure of the Arabic signs gave in to the strength and unconscious memories that brought him paradoxically to erasing his Palestinian identity, perhaps because he feared an attack both by the conference management and by the Jewish participants. Eventually, the Arab "we" and the Jewish "we" were erased from the matrix in favour of "me".

Second case

Another "Dialogue" conference and again the same seating arrangement. This time the chair of the conference was a Jewish male. He introduced the leaders and stated the goals of the conference and the method of working. The ceremonial part had finished and everyone was ready to begin work in the various small groups. Suddenly, just as in the prior conference, a male Palestinian participant stood up and began a long monologue with many accusations about injustice. He expressed hope that in this conference things would be different. As he went on, the other participants appeared more and more uncomfortable with his inappropriate sense of timing and place. As he sat in the front row with his face towards the leaders, in particular the director of the conference, everyone sitting behind him seemed to feel helpless.

At this conference there were actually two male Palestinian participants sitting in the first row who expressed rage and overt and covert aggression, directly and indirectly, towards the management. One might ask whether this was a coincidence or was there something unconscious influencing the male Palestinians. Perhaps sitting in the front row expressed the desire of the Palestinian men to reach the front row of Israeli society after feeling left behind for so long.

In the two cases, incidents involving Palestinian men took place at the opening of the conference. It was a kind of a starting-line, a declaration of purpose. But, as the conference went on, they found themselves in the back rows. This may have reflected a pattern in contemporary Palestinian society. The male Palestinians, accustomed to being the dominant gender in their society and in the Palestinian family, have been most hurt by the establishment of the state of Israel, as their status was damaged. In the conference there was an aggressive attempt by two men to reacquire a position of leadership and dominance. This dynamic might explain the rise of violence in recent years in Israeli-Palestinian society, violence that is turned inward, particularly towards women but also towards other men. The deteriorating status of Palestinian men and the inferiority they feel compared to Jewish men causes a feeling of great shame that sometimes creates rage but most of the time this must be covered and hidden. The alternative solution for this difficult position is for men to participate in a violent struggle which would compensate for these narcissistic wounds.

Palestinian society struggles, flees, and again struggles

Trotter (1916), who coined the notion "the herd instinct", claimed that in situations of war, survival instinct leads to increased group cohesion and subsequently to flight or fight (similar to Bion's basic assumption). From the point of view of evolution, this is the most efficient way to ensure continued existence. We cannot survive alone. Just as there is a nursing instinct and an instinct for sex and procreation, there is a flight or fight instinct in the herd.

The Palestinians turned from a proud nation as in the days of Salah al-Din, who defeated the Crusaders in the land of Palestine, to a shamed and defeated one, one that represses its sense of weakness and defeat. The way Palestinian men deal with their shame and denied weakness is to belittle others who are weak, such as women. A society that was accustomed to living in the shadow of a leader is now dealing with a new situation in which there is a lack of an authoritative father figure. Palestinian society is patriarchal, but the Arab father in it has lost control, fame, and significance.

In the two cases that I presented there were men expressing rage about the continuous injury to their personal honour. The importance of individual, familial, and tribal honour appears to replace national pride. It seems as though "moments of glory" on the national level (Volkan, 2001) are simply missing in the current Palestinian narrative.

Palestinian men are hurt and have difficulty coping maturely with the challenges of the Israeli reality. We could say that typically they have difficulty in resolving their Oedipus complex. This is expressed in their failure to cope with the powerful Jew, that is, the conqueror and oppressor (the father). It is also expressed in their inability to cut themselves off from their emotional dependency on the weak and unstable Arab side (the mother). The most prominent example of this is their admiration towards Arab leaders, such as the Egyptian Nasser and the Iraqi Saddam Hussein. Final autonomy will come only after they succeed in positively overcoming this conflict.

In patriarchal and collectivist Arab society and Palestinian society, the community is more important than the individual, and men are given a more important place than women. Many Palestinian men who were supposed to protect their society feel as if they have failed in regard to Israeli society and Jewish men. Palestinian men who are not used to expressing their feelings find themselves having to cope with an accumulation of repressed feelings. These repressed emotions are often expressed as "acting in" towards Palestinian society or "acting out" towards Israeli society.

Trauma and "chosen glory"

The establishment of Israel resulted in the destruction of normal life for Palestinians. Hundreds of villages were destroyed and hundreds of thousands fled, were expelled, and not allowed to return. Palestinians call these events "Nakba", an expression that means catastrophe. The Nakba is for the Palestinians a founding event in their history. It is a traumatic event that nearly erased them. But, instead of disappearing as a result of this national disaster, a process began leading to the establishment of the Palestinians as a nation.

Nonetheless, I feel we are still under the impact of having nearly been eradicated. Hope is still weak. Glory is still missing. There is no glory with which the Palestinian people can identify. There are only glories when linked together with the wider world of all Arabs and Muslims. Then, they can hark back—along with many Arabs—to the golden days of Islam in the Middle Ages, when Europe was still in the Dark Ages. Perhaps it is possible for Palestinians to relate their survival, in spite of the difficult war in 1948, to a life force and a continuous and determined process of nation building, with the coming Palestinian state envisioned as their "chosen glory" and the return of past Arab greatness. Palestinians have experienced life under a foreign regime, which to a large extent imposed itself on them. Instinctively they dream of freeing themselves and returning to a life they once had, life under Islamic rule. Jews are considered new Crusaders who have conquered the Holy Land.

What are the psychological influences of the absence of chosen glory on the Palestinian people? If we consider the process of development of the Palestinian people, we will discover that it fought for recognition, belonging, and their accompanying glories. One such case was Dahar el Omar who was the virtually autonomous Arab ruler of northern Palestine in the mid-eighteenth century and who established the first Palestinian state, and there was glory too in the days of Salah Al-Din at the beginning of the second millennium, who was successful in driving out the Crusaders from Palestinian land.

After the establishment of the state of Israel in 1948, most of the Palestinian cities were destroyed. What remained were peasants and villagers without social and political leadership. This situation was similar to that of a child orphaned from his father for many years. Palestinians are still yearning for the lost father and from time to time put faith in changing leadership. In retrospect, the new leadership may not have been the best "fathers". But the yearning and the search go on! Personally, I think that instead of looking for a father to crown and then be disappointed, we should give up this search and instead look for ways to begin taking care of ourselves and our own needs.

Shame

According to Sartre, "Hell is the other." For the Palestinians, "the other" is always the Israeli (and vice versa). The Palestinians and the Jews indeed have a "hellish" relationship. Each is an observing subject for the other; each arouses shame in the other.

The moment the Jew and the Palestinian are actually present for each other as two subjective beings—it is possible that destructive and uninhibited action towards each other can be reduced. Instead of living in isolation and disconnection side by side, living together should be encouraged where one party is present in the life of the other. In the story of the Garden of Eden, Eve and Adam eat from the Tree of Knowledge, and their eyes are opened. They become aware and at the same time ashamed. If the acquisition of knowledge sometimes brings one to upsetting realisations, it can also lead to shame. Because of this, some people forfeit the desire to know what is happening in the life of the other. They would rather not be exposed to the presence of the other so as not to be exposed to his difficulties and agonies or have him observe theirs.

I assume that there is shame both in the Palestinian and in the Jewish/Israeli social unconscious. In the Palestinian case the feeling of shame is contrary to the feeling of honour, which Palestinians hold in such importance. The feeling of shame is a particularly heavy burden, one that is nearly impossible to tolerate and manage. De Mendelssohn (2008, p. 393) wrote about the "heroic dilemma" and the "heroic solution". These refer to situations in which a person who feels humiliated takes on the defensive pattern of reaction formation, turning shame into pride and aggrandisement of the self. The latter part of this defensive manoeuvre is an "heroic solution" to the problem of shame. Daring to be proud of what was once considered shameful serves to restore those ego functions that have been damaged by shameful experience.

Edward Said, and the Palestinian unconscious

Out of my longing for a leader, I quote the words of Edward Said, a Palestinian father figure. In *Freud and the Non-European*, Said (2003), the father of post-colonial theory and the author of *Orientalism* (1978), and who together with Mahmud Darwish is a source of great pride among Palestinian intellectuals, discusses Freud's book *Moses and Monotheism*. The inherent paradox in the Freudian concept of identity stems from the inability to achieve a complete, integrative identity which develops after recognising that parts of the other are inside one's self. Identity belongs to those who are willing to include those cultural and emotional elements that actually undermine the sense of identity. In other words, identity is possible only if we recognise the presence of the stranger (or the "Other") inside ourselves.

In his book Said presents his thoughts about Freud's writings, including thoughts about establishing the identity of the One through that of the Other, whether the reference is to the nation or the individual. Said shows how Freud incorporates the Egyptian Other in the figure of Moses in order to establish the monotheistic identity of the Jewish people. He uses Freud's text in a comparison with the Israeli attitude towards the Palestinians. "When Freud dug into the archaeology of the Jewish identity," he writes (p. 43), "he insisted that its origin is not in itself but actually in other identities (Egyptian and Arabic). If so, of what is it composed and from where did it come? Is it in the Israeli/Jewish, the pan Arab, the Islam, the Canaanites or perhaps all of them?"

Said, the intellectual and Palestinian patriot who was born here but lived most of his life abroad, suggests a new perspective for understanding and coping with the complex situation in which the Palestinians are trying to build their modern identity, a perspective that opens a way towards a harmonious recognition of what we are today. It follows that national identity, whether we like it or not, is not something stable and inborn but something changing and evolving, something that is influenced by conscious and unconscious memories and by meaningful events and encounters with others throughout history. The Palestinian identity is carved from the conflict with the Israelis, in the same way that the Jewish identity began with other identities.

I ask myself if Said had participated in the conference in which the organisers were Jews, and sat in the front row like the two men described above, what would he have felt? How would he have reacted? What conscious and unconscious forces would be working on him? Would he sit and respond as a defeated and damaged Palestinian male or as a Palestinian male with pride, curiosity, and openness? What is common to Edward Said and other Palestinians who live in Western countries and to Palestinians who live here in Israel or in the territory of the Palestinian Authority? Do they all share a Palestinian social unconscious? I assume that there are many common elements but at the same time these Palestinians living apart geographically are also evolving differently. It is interesting to think how this will influence the future Palestinian identity.

It was difficult to begin writing this chapter but now, at its conclusion, I feel I have a better and clearer idea about the Palestinian social unconscious. If at the outset I experienced a blockage and disconnection (that I still do not fully understand), I now feel more connected. Within me a "fountain" of endless thoughts and ideas is bubbling. I will have to deal with them in future writings.

Notes

1. An Arab village in Israel.
2. Another Arab village in Israel.

References

Anderson, B. (1983). *Imagined Communities: Reflections on the Origin and Spread of Nationalism*. London: Verso.

Darwish, M. (2002). *State of Siege*. Beirut, Lebanon: Riad Al-rees.

De Mendelssohn, F. (2008). Transgenerational transmission of trauma: guilt, shame, and the "heroic dilemma". *International Journal of Group Psychotherapy, 58*(3): 389–401.

Halbwachs, M. (1992). *On Collective Memory*. Chicago, IL: University of Chicago Press.

Hopper, E. (2003). *The Social Unconscious: Selected Papers*. London: Jessica Kingsley.

Hopper, E. (2015). Personal communication.

Jubran, K. (1912). *The Broken Wings*. (In Arabic.)

Kashua, S. (2010). *Second Person*. Jerusalem, Israel: Keter.

Palestinian Encyclopaedia (1984). Damascus, Syria: Encyclopaedia Palestine Corporation. (In Arabic.)

Said, E. (1978). *Orientalism*. London: Penguin.

Said, E. (2003). *Freud and the Non-European*. London: Verso.

Trotter, W. (1916). *Instincts of the Herd in Peace and War*. London: T. F. Unwin.

Volkan, V. (2001). Transgenerational transmissions and chosen traumas: an aspect of large group identity. *Group Analysis, 34*(1): 79–97.

Weinberg, H. (2007). So what is this social unconscious anyway? *Group Analysis, 40*(3): 307–322.

CHAPTER TEN

"After the last sky":* Palestine, Palestinians, social memory

Martin Weegmann

Why write?

A negated history, a shrunken geography, and a barred, precarious existence. With no exaggeration, this is the condition of Palestine, not a state, a properly constituted society, but a small portion, a broken and separated fragment of a lost country, hemmed in and occupied. Israel's Other. A "placeless place", in the words of Darwish (2003).

This chapter was prompted by a degree of concern in relation to this book. Would there be, I worried, a place in this book, covering constituted countries, for those with no such security and boundaries, in this case Palestine and Palestinians, a place for a people marked by continuing exclusion and rightlessness? A place for a chapter that grants "permission to narrate" to such people? I take the phrase from an essay by Edward Said (1984), writing of systematic efforts to reduce Palestinian existence, a people moreover even invited to participate in the dismantling of their own history; history, as ever, is written by the victors, not the vanquished. This invites us to consider wider questions of who speaks

*"After the last sky", quoted in the chapter title, is from "The Earth Presses Against Us", by Darwish (2003).

and how, under what conditions, and with what implications? The vanquished do answer back, creating counter-narratives, however fragile and adverse their conditions of emergence. I knew that there would be a place for Israel in the book—there are many talented Israeli colleagues in our profession, eager to write—and was concerned that a confident Israeli narrative would either confine Palestinians to invisibility, conjured away, or reduce their appearance to cameo figures within a grander play, only ever and intractability associated with margins, with nuisance and violence. The equivalent figures of the "wretched of the Earth" (Fanon, 1983), those people on the receiving side of colonialism, state conquest, who, in all contexts, live the double disadvantage of primary subjection and secondary disparagement or discounting (Blackwell, 2003).

The psychoanalyst Christopher Bollas (2003) uses a graphic metaphor of "negative hallucinations" held by Israel about Palestinians, as a process of "not seeing what is there". It took decades to re-establish the word "Palestine" in diplomatic and wider public discourse, and to re-humanise Palestinians, at least relatively, rescued from the semiotic domination that ignored or referred to them obliquely, as mere Arabs, problem refugees, non-Jews, terrorists, and the like, their reduced land reconfigured as stripped-down "Territories" or biblically re-baptised. Israel feared the resurrection of the name: "Palestine" as a taboo word, its mention a contradiction in the face of what Shlaim (Shlaim & Sayigh, 1997, p. 177) calls the "doctrine of [Israel's] immaculate conception". "The Palestinian people does not exist" said and implied a succession of leaders of Israel, the same leaders often lauded in the West for their moral leadership and example. Even then, if Palestinians re-emerged as named people, with their flag no longer banned, Palestine as a place disappears progressively, with the world watching if not necessarily wanting to see (Cook, 2008; Frosh, 2015). Or indifferent. Most American leaders, for example, hardly concealed their lack of interest in a stateless people, without significant resources, including the view (wish) that the unhappy multitude who stood in the way of what might be called the "Israel legend" would eventually recede, as if in a Hollywood movie; Trump's ascendancy is a disturbing new low in how the rights of one people can be eliminated in favour of the power of another's. Although those who hold the power dictate the terms, the cracks cannot be concealed: "We wrested control of our name and etched it on the conscience of the world," writes Fawaz Turki (1998, p. 12) in his recollections of 1948 and its aftermath. Lack of space prevents any detailed account of this history and, in any case, the locus of my chapter is rather different—the passing of history into representation, into memory, and as refracted by the imagination.

I am aware of one Palestinian psychoanalyst, the late George Awad. I had the pleasure of some correspondence with him and was encouraged by his encouragement—"Write what you can, speak out," were his words. Against his own forgetting ("I tried to forget what it meant to be a Palestinian in order to get on with my life"), and surrounded by many who did not/would not see that aspect of who he was ("who wished to eliminate me as a person with a chosen identity, narrative and memories"), he attempted, late in life, to recover continuity with his past and achieve a more integrated cultural identity. "As I get older, I want to remember and record from a unique psychoanalytic perspective," he said. Born in Acre, he became a refugee in Lebanon at six, before moving to Canada where he died in 2007. (All quotes from personal communication; see also Awad, 2009.) I said I felt embarrassed, as a British person, to presume to write about a people far away, but about whom I have long been interested. Around the time, I was writing an article on Edward Said (Weegmann, 2005) and organising an IGA conference on his contribution, and was reaching out for help. Incisively, Awad added that everyone is far away if we place them so.

Britain, given its history as one of the "powers" (as the European empire states were called), bears heavy responsibility for some of the historical sequences that led to the eventual elimination of an entire country and for its role in the ruthless crushing of what could be called the earliest "uprising", the Arab Revolt: a further reason to write. British colonial rule broke the back of Palestinian society before its subsequent conquest (P. Anderson, 2001). Hughes (2009) sees in the response to the revolt patterns of collective punishment, shooting of rioters, crop destruction, and demolitions that are stunningly similar to contemporary military campaigns in the West Bank/Gaza. In the same way that we need to examine the history of British anti-Semitism, and related guilt, so too do we need to bring to light a long anti-Arab legacy and colonial condescension, one powerfully influenced by many "Orientalist" assumptions. I grew up fed on a familiar Israel romance story at school, with the "other side", if they were even acknowledged, tainted with implications of dark irrationality. The first shock to this image came at university, when I met actual Palestinians supported to be there by international funding bodies. And a few years ago, while trying to prepare for a professional visit, a psychology colleague from Ramallah pointed out, "We require witnesses."

This chapter is written in honour of such encouragement, albeit from far away, but nevertheless in close identification. Fearless speech is essential, and fearless writing too—one could call it "writing out".

Foundational rupture, social memory

From a brief description of the catastrophic nature of Palestinian experience, I consider one response to their multiple erasures over time, that of attempts to recover and maintain social memories. Unlike the social memory that is constructed within the bounds of nation states, equivalent Palestinian projects take place in many locations, including the occupied lands, widely dispersed refugee communities (many Palestinians have known nothing other than permanent stateless refugee status), and a wide diaspora. In other words, in many different present/absent, temporary/permanent, new/old locations, a task that requires an ability "to imagine and investigate in spite of barriers" (Said, 2001, p. 380). These projects take many forms, including memoirs, poetry, fieldwork, oral history, and construct a story of massive historical rupture and its complex refractions, transmissions, and transmutations down the years. It is a destruction that is difficult to represent because it is in some respects unique, is perhaps "unclassifiable" in Berger's (2011) phrase.

Groups and nations devise many ways of imagining their common existence, conceiving their unity, particularity, and peculiarity via images of a shared past (B. Anderson, 1983). The shared past is a horizon governed by a dialectic of living memory (or persons), cultural memory (within institutions, artefacts etc.) and history (which is a formal discipline) (Halbwachs, 1992; Winter, 2010). Memory is also history as seen through the domains of affect and identification—what moves us. The notion of "social memory" (social remembrance and its twin, forgetting or oblivion) is implicit in the concept of the social unconscious. After all, the concept of the social unconscious helps us to understand how groups and societies connect to a (now absent) past, how a "legitimate history" is authorised and its continuity is conceived. Such identities and social pasts do not emerge *sui generis*, present only to itself, but within fields that involve forever changing socio-discursive contexts and distributions of power. Social memories are by nature multiple and specific, articulated within time and space. If articulation is like a hinge, in which different elements of meaning are connected, boundary situations bond meanings in long-lasting, powerfully binding ways, constituting, if one wills, a mould, within which events that come after are seen and experienced (Hopper, 2001).

In the case of Palestine this is a shattered mould, a societal matrix premised on overwhelming erasure (Pappe, 2006; Piterberg, 2001). The term "foundational rupture" is proposed, though in this case it was not a singular event in time, but rather a structural and unfolding dispossession over the years. To this day, the threat and reality of annexations continues. In the absence of restorative justice and reparation, indeed, the reverse is the case: people remain caught in what seem inexorable and catastrophic historical moments. This includes appalling loss of life and a discriminated, marginal existence in refugee camps throughout the region, with Yarmouk camp (in Damascus) the latest example. In many areas (an isolated Gaza and parts of the dismembered West Bank), there is an alarming degree of what one American economist describing the region calls economic de-development and enclavisation (Roy, 1999). Such de-development and economic undermining and separation is normalised Israeli policy and a matter of cruel indifference and active neglect elsewhere (Medical Aid to Palestinians Report, 2013; Oxfam, 2014). An annexed (1967) East Jerusalem has been systematically cut off from its wider Palestinian connection since the early Nineties. The results affect all areas of life. Economic life truncated. Food insecurity. Medical insecurity. Natural resources reduced, controlled, or gone (Robinson, 2016). And with devastating cultural consequences.

When catastrophes happen

The contemporary history of the Palestinians rests on the date 1948, a year in which one country and its people disappeared from maps and names changed (Sanbar, 2001). Three quarters of one people's homeland was lost. *Nakba*, meaning "catastrophe", was not a singular event but the beginning of many subsequent acts of dispossession and displacement, and so experiences of *Ghurba* (estrangement, exile) are an inescapable and defining aspect of Palestinian life. We have noted other ways in which Palestinian realities were wiped away, emptied of content, and forgotten in the "political unconscious" (Eid, 2008). A history moreover that sits alongside another, that of Israel, which is a history of possession and creation. The Zionist project that inspired its creation as a nation has been successful and sustaining in all its variants, from religious to secular, left and right. The image of the redemptive, phoenix-like rise of a "small nation" (itself a signifier evoking vulnerability and promoting identification) is emotionally, consciously, and unconsciously resonant. A restoration in the face of unimaginable horrors.

The rise is associated with various founding and sustaining myths of Zionism: that Palestinians were not there, that "their" land was effectively empty, that "Arabs" had a primitive, insignificant existence and so forth. There are many euphemisms of conquest, each with its attendant narratives. Rose (2005) has done much to elucidate the sources of that deep appeal and the intractable allegiances to which it gives rise. Western guilt plays a role, although space does not allow me to elaborate (Kemp, 2015; Rose, 2013). At the end of the day, however, the making of one nation fired the imagination, while the unmaking of another did not, not at first anyway; one story that counted, another that did not. Not only this, but when the negated side was told, it was often a story about Palestinians as told by others, in Western countries, overlain by a colonial stance that saw in the Arab a "negative personality (Oriental, decadent, inferior etc.)" (Said, 1980, p. 37). The consequence of conquest and its discontents results in a precarious life for many Palestinians, who on top of dispossession are forever obliged to resist their elimination from knowledge and sight. Simply put, Palestinian conditions are an awkward aesthetic impediment to the self-image of a heroic, moral, and progressive Israel. And that is one reason why many, including in the West, look away, in discomfort, even though the contradictions are starker and harder than ever to conceal. Do group analysts do the same? None of this exonerates Palestinians from having to look into their shadows and divisions, albeit in a wider disaster that they did not choose, including leaderships all too often self-serving, violent, and corrupt; one way of viewing the emergence of more modern religious extremism is a result of the breakdown of a long, secular era of nationalist struggle that resulted in no actual gains. Such groups romanticise violence and endow it with "sacred" justifications; state violence, on the other hand, has no such requirements, given its self-justifying invocations of "security" needs. In some ways the history is one of two, intertwined "communities of suffering", each adding suffering to the other, as Said put it, although this formulation risks implying two equal partners locked in a "conflict", rather than as a conquest characterised by enormous disparities of power between the players.

In a remarkably short period of time then, Palestinian society, "fractured along multiple axes, was expelled and undone" (Jayyusi, 2007, p. 108). As a foundational rupture, with profound nullifying effects, Jayyusi argues that the past remains an unfinished project, a project premised on irresolution and unfolding dispossession. The novelist Khoury (2006, p. 384) puts it in the form of a persistent, repeating question, of why should Palestinians "have to invent our homeland anew, every day?". One issue arising from this is that a "haunted" past effectively replaces a "historical past", as the continuity that an unbroken historical past brings is severed (Lorenz, 2010).

Memory for forgetfulness: poem, book, memoir

Palestinians face that ultimate enemy of justice: forgetting. The late Mahmoud Darwish argued that in such circumstances it is essential to cultivate a "memory for forgetfulness". The poem and memoir are two mediums through which such forgetting is resisted, so let us turn our attention to the poetry of Darwish, and to the writer, Mourid Barghouti's memoir of a return visit to Ramallah. The aesthetic realm contains aspects of cultural capital—poems, novels, art, and so on—that play a key part in the make-up of social identities and their shaping role as instruments of narration (Bhabha, 1990; Bowman, 1994). In the case of massive social trauma there are always levels of knowing and not-knowing, with literary and metaphorical resources providing one of the ways in which such realities can be partially registered (Laub, 1993). As we shall see, such writings bear intimately on questions of social memory, as they offer articulations of experience, loss, and protest. In this way, one can suggest that they are efforts to limit the transmission of historic experiences into social unconscious life, and thereby to limit a process of oblivion.

Darwish (1941–2005) achieved remarkable presence in the Arab world and beyond. A cultural pioneer, Darwish wrote haunting, beautiful words from collective experiences of devastation. He did not like to be categorised as a "resistance poet", even though his work is full of resistance, and more. He prided himself upon artistic independence and did not wish to be "used" by anyone.

A few brief facts about his Orwellian life illustrate how an individual life and personal trauma become a collective one, how a story of one person can represent the story of the many. Darwish was born in the village of al Birwa, which was depopulated and bulldozed, like hundreds of others, its place taken by a substitute landscape. Indeed, on creeping back from Lebanon, where he and his family had fled, not only were homes gone but with them ways of life and words, including the Arabic names for places. His work is abundant in references to these and other catastrophes, as in one poem about the theme of departure, in which a woman laments, "My village is on my back" ("Athens Airport", 2003). Well documented by Palestinian scholars, the story of the villages and depopulated towns has been looked at anew by Kadman (2015), who examines the discursive means by which they were erased "from space and consciousness". Darwish lived by the ravages of chance as a "present absent alien" (an official designation of the era) within the new country of Israel, and was well acquainted with prisons and police stations. With his eventual departure and years of unsatisfactory exile, he was granted permission by the Israeli military powers, in 1996, to live in Ramallah. Just as his work has become part of the cultural weave and work of collective commemoration, so too, in death, a discourse of commemoration has built around his personage (Hassan, 2013).

In his exploration, Bowman (1994, p. 167) considers how Palestinians, from varied positions of exile, "discursively construct images of themselves", of which homeland is a central signifier. Images exist in many forms, including stories, songs, rhetorical themes, and reminiscences, but whereas these would normally be anchored and sustained by stable national structures, Palestinians do not have these. When Darwish wrote, "We travel like everyone else, but we return to nothing. Ours is a country of words" ("We Travel Like all People", 2003, p. 11), he underscores the remarkably thin and precarious nature of Palestinian existence. Addressing this fragility was his life mission, hence the obligation, stated in the same poem to speak out, to "Talk, Talk". And it is through poetic space, through that very insistence of "Talk, Talk", that a semblance of historical coherence is derived, a coherence bound to specific places and times, geography and aspirations. His poetry is richly referential, populated by the sensory and tactile, by landscapes, birds, and plants, the natural world imbricated by the cultural world, with all its proximity to issues of dwelling. He is saying—insisting—that certain worlds exist and existed, are and were actual, countering the many negations that surround Palestinian life, and producing counter-positions: "I belong there. I have many memories. I was born as everyone is born" ("I Belong There", 2003, p. 7).

Memory for Forgetfulness (Darwish, 1995) is a remarkable book of prose, mixed with verse and philosophy. Written as an account of a single day in the devastating siege and bombardment of West Beirut in 1982, which he dubs "Hiroshima Day", the book is an example of "writing under siege", as he pushes language to the limits, recording extraordinary times and the still ordinary accompaniments of those surviving on the ground, acts as simple as making morning coffee, chatting, and so forth. A protest against the possibilities of oblivion, the book encapsulates collective pain and expresses (im)possible yearning: "I don't see a shore. I don't see a dove" (p. 182)—the words that close the book. An outcry had become, he observes, a "poetic identity" (p. 174). In terms of social memory, this is an intriguing summation of how it could be that a suffering of old remains caught up within a current situation.

I Saw Ramallah (2004) is one of a genre of contemporary "visit" memoirs. In it, Barghouti, a poet and writer, details the places he has not seen since his protracted exiles, the plural deliberate given his exclusions from Egypt. Quietly observed, his questions gently accompany the journeys he conducts, from the crossing of Allenby Bridge into the West Bank, to those within and outside Ramallah. Then there are the blocked paths, the result of roadblocks, or a prevented entry to East Jerusalem. The bridge crossing is the first reminder of who it is who are in charge, of who and how many are allowed through: "And the world finds a name for us. They called us *naziheen*, the displaced ones" (p. 3). Borders and crossing points are painful reminders of their uncertainty, exposed as they are to "harassment, exclusion and sometimes worse, simply because of his or her identity" (Khalidi, 1997, p. 2). In commenting on the role of poetic expression, Barghouti says, "People like direct poetry only in times of injustice, times of communal silence. Times when they are unable to speak or to act" (p. 11). In such circumstances, poets are like deputies in an "imaginary and forbidden parliament" (ibid.). In seeing settlements dotted around the landscape, he knows that they represent, once more, "our absence" so that every aspect of Palestinian life is "temporary". He does not exempt the Palestinian authorities from criticism, from the "faults of our song", as he puts it, and does not wish to be bought by flattery. He asks, "Does a poet live in time or space? Our homeland is the shape of the time we spend in it" (ibid., p. 41). This distortion of time, part of the traumatic experience, is a point to which I will return.

"My measure is aesthetic," writes Barghouti (ibid., p. 43). Arguably there could be much more attention paid to the aesthetic aspects of social unconscious life, including the contribution of literary capital—poems, novels, myth, art—to the building of social memories and identities (Hopper & Weinberg, 2011; Kompridis, 2014). The spirit of such capital can be both "with" and "against" the grain of the times, and one important aspect of social memory in this case is that of the production of counter-memory, meaning the location and freeing of memories of the less powerful and marginal, "other" voices. For Barghouti, like Darwish, writing is in part an act of resistance, of defying domination from the outside as well as against the "chains of the tribe" within (Jaggi, 2008).

Barghouti's (2011) work continues with his powerful sequel, and revisit, *I was Born There, I was Born Here*. Its tone is angry, as he portrays a continuing displacement, ever more surreal. In the face of this, he is the first to admit just how difficult and exhausting it is to find the right aesthetic, as it were, and how to balance past/present, reminiscence/experience. Foundational rupture leaves the traces of the unrecoverable, and, quoting from a new collection of diaspora literature, Alyan (2016, p. 65), refers to "time-lapse photography in reverse". In another context, Volkan (1997) uses the evocative terminology of "time collapse".

The presence of lamentation and nostalgia in Palestinians' writing is common, as well as protest (Bernard, 2013). It could be called "nostalgic disorientation", in which people struggle to express unbridgeable gaps in reality, unsafety, and unpredictability (Papadopolous, 2002). Volkan (1999) uses the notion of nostalgia as a form of affective linking, a "linking phenomenon", which helps people to maintain contact with their pasts. One might see the role of legendary and allegorical references in Darwish as compensation for the absence of real, existing national space. Joudah (2007), a translator of Darwish, sees in his poetry a transformation of a lost land into an "unattained beloved", although in spite of, or because of this, Darwish also sought to express experiences that could transcend melancholy. But the efforts, and the lives they describe, are highly precarious. How then do writers deal with such an unresolved present, or an "undefeated despair" (Berger, 2007)?

Oral testimony: voices against time

Sanbar (2001) argues that history became an "emergency science" among Palestinians as a buffer to guard against disappearance. One could say the same for memory studies. Memory feeds into history, although it is not equivalent to it, and is a fragile resource, dependent as it is on the living and/or the recorded. Memory bears on issues of narrative legitimacy, and its absence, such as in situations where when one person's story can be told and another's cannot, where one group's experience is legitimised and another's ignored and de-legitimised (Lentin, 2008). An important trend in this respect are the growing number of oral history and witness projects aimed at gathering memories of ordinary Palestinians, under occupation and in wider exile.

Rosemary Sayigh is a noted social anthropologist who has spent a lifetime researching the impact of the Israel-Palestine conflict on Palestinian refugees (Doumani & Soukarieh, 2009). With great appreciation of context, Sayigh conducted interviews with refugees, camp dwellers, and those least likely to appear as individuals within history books or to figure within the heroic, "masculine" narratives of official leaders; it is popular history, "history from below". Many traditional Palestinian accounts of "the struggle" and of their identity have centred on the viewpoint of an urban, male, and elite leadership (Khalidi, 1997). Take the example of women. Sayigh (1997) points out that women in the refugee camps have a rich stock of historical experience, expressed as *qussas* (stories) and usually transmitted in women's gatherings and family settings. Such stories may not take a strict chronological form, or even one based on a familiar "life story" concept (which is itself perhaps a culturally relative notion), but may be fragmentary and particularistic, based on things witnessed, heard, and "handed down". Oral testimony in such circumstances has a vital role to play in substantiating the experiences of those who are marginal and acts as a way of honouring the different styles of speech and personal recounting. Accordingly, many of the stories were recorded in the presence of family, neighbours, and so forth, mirroring the conditions under which such *qussas* are told naturally; memory as told, as witnessed, as performed.

Sayigh (2007, p. 136) underlines the importance of appreciating differences and more marginal voices, "being written into the unwritten collective story". The gathering of domestic accounts, easily dismissed as "personal", and thus unimportant, is an essential part of a wider "permission to narrate" from within, especially important in view of women's less visible suffering, their role in social cohesion, even in the physical rebuilding of often completely destroyed camps; all semblance of domestic continuity goes under such conditions, here and elsewhere. In Lebanon they have grown up in conditions of civil war, invasions, loss of a "national leadership", and widespread impoverishment. In the absence of protective institutions, with lack of funds, and the dispersal of scholars, the preservation of records and the work of memory projects operate against the odds; an instance of this was the ransacking of official archive material in Beirut in the early 1980s, material subsequently removed to Israel (Sayigh, 2014). Sayigh also addresses the exclusion of Palestinian suffering and the Nakba from the field of trauma studies, thus reproducing the secondary "silenced suffering" that is a common experience.[1]

Diana Allan (2014), also a social anthropologist and co-director of The Nakba Archive, conducted field studies, with residents of the Shatila camp, looking at how refugees there come to terms with "radical exclusion, alienation, and the indignities of refugee existence, and the daily struggle with poverty, loss, and political disenchantment" (p. 27). She describes the camps presently as liminal spaces of neglect and political violence, places that are "stencilled out of post-war urban renewal" (p. 17). Their inhabitants remain a stateless people in a very profound sense of that term and, with the enormous waves of new refugees into Lebanon, are likely to be forgotten further.

Allan is focused on the everyday experience of the refugees, of how they see their lives and futures, which may vary considerably from the collectivised narratives constructed *about* them. Heroic and nationalist discourses do not cover and satisfy the exigencies of current struggles, daily demands, and domestic resourcefulness. While "social memory" can subsume "personal memory", the two are not equivalent.

Research illuminates but potentially changes a context, and Allan is mindful about the risks involved in witness projects and their impact on those interviewed; a "politics of solidarity" and a "politics of remembrance" are heavily intertwined (Allan, 2007). Forgetting is implicated, both that forgetting born of necessity (the simple requirement of getting on with one's life) and fear, fear that they are (already) forgotten by their leaders and regional powers.

On a philosophical note, Stolorow (2011) has addressed the complex area of trauma, affectivity, and its other subjective components. He refers to a sense of living in "worlds apart", with a narrowing of vision and concerns (e.g., to that of survival) and that one can no longer trust a usual sense of "time stretching along". Tellingly, Sayigh discovers, many older refugees describe life post-1948 as "death", "non-existence", "burial", and the like. So, in this sense camp memories serve their inhabitants as a grim relational bond—indeed, some have little more than memory to affirm their existence.

Zones of inhospitality: keep moving

Identities do not exist in mid-air but are wrapped around the exigencies of time and place. Space is (f)actual, and founded upon the corporeal—earth, land, dwelling, and so forth. So what happens when a group or nation or former country finds itself radically "out of place"? And when the spaces and sites which might normally anchor collective experiences and identity are removed and are (now) absent? Homes might be provisional, as Said (2001) noted, but some homes are more provisional than others. Foundational rupture manifests in many realms, including the subjective and the physical and it is to the confluence of these two that we turn. The word "uprooting" is one instance of this, insofar as uprooted people lose land, agriculture (e.g., the destruction of ancient olive groves in the West Bank), and a sense of security and mooring. Gone too is that sense of historical continuity, of "time stretching along". We have touched upon how literary and other resources attempt to preserve a level of dignity and meaningful connection to land, hearth, and home. As Masahla (2014) puts it, "Palestinian social and cultural shared memory has always been more than simply recollecting or recording of 'the past': 're-collecting' and 're-membering' serve to reunite, to bring the historical fragments together, recreate, sustain and nurture collective identity" (p. 34). As part of the "connective structure of societies" (Assmann, 2008), social memories can be a precious yet fragile resource, dependent on the circumstances.

Allan (2014) makes the point that—certainly in nationalist discourse—the signifier "Palestine" floats independently of any signified; the signifier has discursive presence but remains hypothetical. Palestine as placeless, as atopia. A central challenge for collective Palestinian life under occupation and separation is a continuing, indeed reinvigorated dispossession by settlement complexes and land appropriation. The matrix of high-tech control and "zoning" makes the occupation a remarkable instance of modern-day colonisation, a politics of urban/rural undermining and separation (Coward, 2009). Weizman's (2007) study examines the detail of such forensic control and how ideas which begin life on a drawing board are enacted on the ground with the help of an army bulldozer and barbed wire. This, many would see, is a powerful form of structural and procedural violence. Bowman's field research in West Bank villages refers to a "logic of encystation" that results in their progressive loss of viability and land. These policies are humiliations, diminishments, and a further reminder that "[E]very Palestinian has a border inscribed around him or her" (Bowman, 2004, p. 13).

Two aspects stand out here, that of the elimination of yet more space and that of the extendable, mobile border. On the former, Hanafi (2013) proposes the graphic term "spacio-cide". He argues that Palestinian living space, such as it now is, is treated in an arbitrary, disposable manner by those in charge, who act with immunity in a self-granted state of exception. Habitable space and the living security that goes with it become the target, the unstated message being something like "Don't assume security" and "Keep moving"; "sovereignty by stealth" is how Weizman (2007) puts it. This constitutes an industrialisation of Palestinian suffering and results in a state of "extreme precarity" for many (Butler & Athanasiou, 2013). A popular idea in the realm of social memory, that of "sites of memory" (*les lieux de mémoire*, Nora, 1989), falters under conditions when and if many of those physical memory sites are erased, which brings us back to the general theme of what is it that Palestinians can hold/hold onto in their lives (Lentin, 2008).

The closely related matter of fluid state borders has been addressed by many, including Kemp (1998, p. 92) who analyses the role of such borders as lines which can be breached with ease by the powerful. In this sense their crossing has enormous symbolic and actual power, having "the effect of both trivialising the border and instilling a sense of lordship over the territories across the lines". Although Kemp's focus is on the early stages of Israel's state building, its signification clearly applies now, to the building of settlements and displacements, barriers and checkpoints, and also land appropriations within Israel, as it affects Israeli Arabs and Bedouins (see Masalha 2005, on this Kafkaesque world); at the time of writing (summer 2015), new communities were demolished or threatened by the bulldozer. The usual "spatial envelope" (Hirst, 2005) of state power is, in this instance, a highly expandable one. Curiously for a term that was once used widely, "Greater Israel" is less heard now, one of the reasons being that it is being realised, normalised, and redrawn on the ground. One social-psychic consequence, linked to the exercise of such power, is that of the assertion and reinforcement of one people, in the solidity of their identity alongside the layer-upon-layer exclusion of (an)other(s). This is an invidious process with the passing of that which is "unpromising" to others, vulnerability decisively transferred to those who carry the burden of reduced being and lesser history.

Conclusion

The chapter has explored aspects of the unfolding tragedy of Palestine, the ruptures that were its unmaking and that continue to ruin its viability. Situated at the "edge of hope" and "edge of despair" (Barghouti, 2003), theirs is a story with no satisfactory end and with ever reducing options for the future. Power and powerlessness remain key, and as the Israeli dissident, Yitzhak Laor (2002, p. 119) starkly puts it, "The Israeli *imaginaire* is constituted, before anything else, on the belief in Israeli supremacy." Might, moreover, presented as right.

I have highlighted the role of social memories and the conditions under which these are produced and are qualified or disqualified, and looked both at the literary domain and that of oral history and witnessing projects. The case of the Palestinians, by contrast to the "allure" of an established Israel, is made more troubling by the degree of obliteration of their past, as it were, rather than just a connection to it; pasts too can be subsumed, dominated, and conquered (Van Dyke & Alcock, 2003). I have argued that social memories are important components of a social unconscious life, and, in this case, one in which the foundations of a society are irretrievably damaged and disrupted (Mojović, 2015). I have emphasised the importance of places and the erasure of the actual spaces around and within which lived experience and memory is bound, with a resultant "surreal" implication (Robinson, 2016). Literary and aesthetic resources are one means of trying to halt oblivion and restore a measure of recognition and dignity—the "trauma of diminished existence" (Achebe, 2000, p. 16).

It is not an easy area to review, not least because a degree of personal distress is involved, yet it is important for group analysis to continue to look at societal examples of profound rupture and displacement. Not only this but it is important for group analysts to have the courage to voice protest and to express solidarity in circumstances where it is urgently required. And to raise difficult questions. If it is an unsettling piece, I offer no apology, as it is one that needs to be written and told.

Acknowledgements

Thanks to:

George Awad, Dick Blackwell, Rachel Cohen, Glenn Bowman, Stephen Frosh, Martin Kemp, Edward Khantzian, Ronit Lentin, Rosemary Sayigh.

Note

1. When I asked Rosemary Sayigh how she kept a sense of hope alive she replied, "Researchers who work with people who are marginal, impoverished, handicapped, are known to suffer from burn-out. The sense of helplessness is particularly hard to cope with. I always feel that if they can live it, I ought to be able to write about it."

References

Achebe, C. (2000). *Home and Exile*. New York: Anchor.

Allan, D. (2007). The politics of witness; remembering and forgetting 1948 in Shatila camp. In: A. H. Sa'di & L. Abu-Lughod (Eds.), *Nakba: Palestine, 1948, and the Claims of Memory* (Chapter Ten). New York: Columbia University Press.

Allan, D. (2014). *Refugees of the Revolution: Experiences of Palestinian Exile*. Redwood City, CA: Stanford University Press.

Alyan, H. (2016). In dust. In: Y. Suleiman (Ed.), *Being Palestinian; Personal Reflections on Palestinian Identity in the Diaspora*. Edinburgh, UK: Edinburgh University Press.

Anderson, B. (1983). *Imagined Communities*. London: Verso.

Anderson, P. (2001). Scurrying towards Bethlehem. *New Left Review, 10*: 1–18.

Assmann, J. (2008). Communicative and cultural memory. In: A. Erll & A. Nünning (Eds.), *Cultural Memory Studies. An International and Interdisciplinary Handbook*. New York: Walter de Gruyter.

Awad, G. (2009). Psychoanalytic perspectives on the Palestinian/Israeli conflict: Festschrift in honor of George Awad. *International Journal of Applied Psychoanalytic Studies, 6*(3): 163–257.

Barghouti, M. (2003). The servants of war and their language. *Autodafe*, Journal of the International Parliament of Writers, *3*: 39–47.

Barghouti, M. (2004). *I Saw Ramallah*. A. Soueif (Trans.). London: Bloomsbury.

Barghouti, M. (2011). *I was Born There, I was Born Here*. H. Davies (Trans.). London: Bloomsbury.

Berger, J. (2007). *Hold Everything Dear*. London: Verso.

Berger, J. (2011). Come closer. Foreword to Barghouti, 2011.

Bernard, A. (2013). *Rhetorics of Belonging: Nation, Narrative and Israel/Palestine*. Liverpool, UK: Liverpool University Press.

Bhabha, H. (1990). *Nation and Narration*. London: Routledge.

Blackwell, D. (2003). Colonialism and globalisation: a group-analytic perspective. *Group Analysis, 36*(4): 445–463.

Bollas, C. (2003). Introducing Edward Said. In: Said, E. (2003), *Freud and the Non-European*. London: Verso.

Bowman, G. (1994). "A country of words"; conceiving the Palestinian nation from the position of exile. In E. Laclau (Ed.), *The Making of Political Identities*. London: Verso.

Bowman, G. (2004). About a wall. *Social Analysis, 48*(1): 14–20.

Butler, J., & Athanasiou, A. (2013). *Dispossession: The Performative in the Political*. Cambridge: Polity.

Cook, J. (2008). *Disappearing Palestine*. London: Zed.

Coward, M. (2009). *Urbicide: The Politics of Urban Destruction*. London: Routledge.

Darwish, M. (1995). *Memory for Forgetfulness*. I. Muhawi (Trans.). Berkeley, CA: University of California Press.

Darwish, M. (2003). *Unfortunately, It Was Paradise: Selected Poems*. M. Akash & C. Forche (Trans.). Berkeley, CA: University of California Press.

Darwish, M. (2007). *The Butterfly's Burden*. F. Joudah (Trans.). Hexham, UK: Bloodaxe.

Doumani, B., & Soukarieh, M. (2009). A tribute long overdue: Rosemary Sayigh and Palestinian Studies. *Journal of Palestine Studies, 38*(2): 6–11.

Eid, H. (2008). The Zionist Palestinian conflict—an alternative story. *Nebula, 5*(3): 122–139.

Fanon, F. (1983). *The Wretched of the Earth*. C. Farrington (Trans.). London: Penguin.

Frosh, S. (2015). Beyond recognition: the politics of encounter. *Psychoanalysis, Culture and Society, 20*(4): 379–394.

Halbwachs, M. (1992). *On Collective Memory*. L. Coser (Trans. & Ed.). Chicago, IL: University of Chicago Press.

Hanafi, S. (2013). Explaining spacio-cide in the Palestinian territory: colonization, separation, and state of exception. *Current Sociology, 61*(2): 190–205.

Hassan, S. (2013). Passing away: despair, eulogies, and millennial Palestine. *Biography, 1*(2): 27–50.

Hirst, P. (2005). *Space and Power: Politics, War and Architecture*. Cambridge: Polity.

Hopper, E. (2001). The social unconscious: theoretical considerations. *Group Analysis, 34*(1): 9–27.

Hopper, E., & Weinberg, H. (2011). Introduction. In: E. Hopper & H. Weinberg (Eds.), *The Social Unconscious in Persons, Groups and Societies: Volume 1: Mainly Theory*. London: Karnac.

Hughes, M. (2009). The banality of brutality: British Armed Forces and the repression of the Arab Revolt in Palestine, 1936–39. *English Historical Review, 124*(507): 314–354.

Jaggi, M. (2008). A life in writing: Mourid Bharghouti interview. *The Guardian*, 13 December.

Jayyusi, L. (2007). Iterability, cumulativity and presence. In: A. H. Sa'di & L. Abu-Lughod (Eds.), *Nakba: Palestine, 1948, and the Claims of Memory* (Chapter Four). New York: Columbia University Press.

Joudah, F. (2007). Translator's preface to Darwish, M., *The Butterfly's Burden*. Hexham, UK: Bloodaxe.

Kadman, N. (2015). *Erased from Space and Consciousness: Israel and the Depopulated Palestinian Villages of 1948*. Bloomington, IN: Indiana University Press.

Kemp, A. (1998). From politics of location to politics of signification: the construction of political territory in Israel's early years. *Journal of Area Studies, 12*: 74–101.

Kemp, M. (2015). Collusion as a defence against guilt; notes on the relationships between the West, Israel, and the Palestinians. *International Journal of Applied Psychoanalytic Studies, 12*(3): 192–222.

Khalidi, R. (1997). *Palestinian Identity: The Construction of Modern National Consciousness*. New York: Columbia University Press.

Khoury, E. (2006). *Gate of the Sun*. H. Davies (Trans.). London: Vintage.

Kompridis, N. (Ed.) (2014). *The Aesthetic Turn in Political Thought*. New York: Bloomsbury Academic.

Laor, Y. (2002). After Jenin. In: R. Carey & J. Shainn (Eds.), *The Other Israel: Voices of Refusal and Dissent* (Chapter Sixteen). New York: New Press.

Laub, A. (1993). Knowing and not knowing massive psychic trauma: forms of traumatic memory. *International Journal of Psychoanalysis, 74*(2): 287–302.

Lentin, R. (2008). *The Contested Memory of Dispossession; Commemorising the Palestinian Nakba in Israel*. London: Zed.

Lorenz, C. (2010). Unstuck in time. Or: the sudden presence of the past. In: K. Tilmans, F. van Vree, & J. Winter (Eds.), *The Performance of the Past: Memory, History & Identity in Modern Europe* (Chapter Four). Amsterdam, the Netherlands: University of Amsterdam Press.

Masalha, N. (Ed.) (2005). *Catastrophe Remembered. Palestine, Israel and the Internal Refugees*. London: Zed.

Masalha, N. (2014). Liberating methodologies and Nakba studies: Palestinian history and memory from below as sites of lifelong learning. *Holy Land Studies, 13*(1): 25–69.

Medical Aid to Palestinians Report (2013). *Twenty Years after Oslo: Palestinian Healthcare in the Interim* London: Medical Aid to Palestinians.

Mojović, M. (2015). The matrix disrupted: challenges and changes. *Group Analysis, 48*(4): 540–556.

Nora, P. (1989). Between memory and history: *les lieux de mémoire. Representations, 26*: 7–24.

Oxfam (2014). Cease failure. Gaza. Oxfam Briefing Paper 184. Oxford: Oxfam.

Papadopolous, R. (2002). Refugees, home and trauma. In: R. Papadopolous (Ed.), *Therapeutic Care for Refugees: No Place like Home*. London: Karnac.

Pappe, I. (2006). *The Ethnic Cleansing of Palestine*. Oxford: Oneworld.

Piterberg, G. (2001). Erasures. *New Left Review, 10*(2): 31–46.

Robinson, G. E. (2016). Whither Palestine? Weak state, failed state, or no state at all. In: M. Kanrava (Ed.), *Fragile Politics: Weak States in the Greater Middle East* (Chapter Ten). London: C. Hurst.

Rose, J. (2005). *The Question of Zion*. Princeton, NJ: Princeton University Press.

Rose, J. (2013). *The Last Resistance*. London: Verso.

Roy, S. (1999). De-development revisited: Palestinian economy and society since Oslo. *Journal of Palestine Studies, 28*(3): 64–82.

Sa'di, A. H., & Abu-Lughod, L. (Eds.) (2007). *Nakba: Palestine, 1948, and the Claims of Memory*. New York: Columbia University Press.

Said, E. (1980). *The Question of Palestine*. London: Routledge & Kegan Paul.

Said, E. (1984). Permission to narrate. *London Review of Books*, 16–29 February.

Said, E. (2001). Intellectual exile: expatriates and marginals. In: M. Bayoumi & A. Rubin (Eds.), *The Edward Said Reader* (Chapter Fourteen). London: Granta.

Sanbar, E. (2001). Out of place, out of time. *Mediterranean Historical Review, 16*(1): 87–94.

Sayigh, R. (1997). Palestinian camp women as tellers of history. *Journal of Palestine Studies, 27*: 42–58.

Sayigh, R. (2007). Women's Nakba stories; between being and knowing. In: A. H. Sa'di & L. Abu-Lughod (Eds.), *Nakba: Palestine, 1948, and the Claims of Memory* (Chapter Five). New York: Columbia University Press.

Sayigh, R. (2014). Oral history, colonialist dispossession and the state: the Palestinian case. *Settler Colonial Studies*. DOI: 10.1080/2201473X.2014.955945.

Shlaim, A., & Sayigh, Y. (1997). *The Cold War and the Middle East*. Oxford: Oxford University Press.

Stolorow, R. (2011). *World, Affectivity, Trauma*. London: Routledge.

Suleiman, Y. (Ed.) (2016). *Being Palestinian; Personal Reflections on Palestinian Identity in the Diaspora*. Edinburgh, UK:Edinburgh University Press.

Turki, F. (1998). Reflections on Al-Naqba. *Journal of Palestine Studies, 28*(1): 5–35.

Van Dyke, R., & Alcock, S. (2003). *Archaeologies of Memory: An Introduction*. Chichester, UK: Wiley.

Volkan, V. (1997). *Bloodlines: From Ethnic Pride to Ethnic Terrorism*. New York: Farrar, Straus and Giroux.

Volkan, V. (1999). Nostalgia as a linking phenomenon. *Journal of Applied Psychoanalytic Studies, 1*: 169–179.

Weegmann, M. (2005). Edward Said: his relevance to psychotherapy. *Psychodynamic Practice, 11*(4): 389–404.

Weizman, E. (2007). *Hollow Land: Israel's Architecture of Occupation*. London: Verso.

Winter, J. (2010). Introduction. In: K. Tilmans, F. van Vree, & J. Winter (Eds.), *The Performance of the Past: Memory, History & Identity in Modern Europe* (Chapter One). Amsterdam, the Netherlands: University of Amsterdam Press.

CHAPTER ELEVEN

The social unconscious of the Egyptian people: an application of some of the ideas of Bion and Klein

Mohamed Taha

This chapter explores the constituents, components, and manifestations of the social unconscious of the Egyptian people from two different perspectives. Noting that Bion's concept of basic assumptions is actually derived from Klein's concept of individual psychic positions (paranoid-schizoid and depressive, or PS–D), I assume that to some extent the same assumptions may apply to communities, societies, and cultures. Moreover, just as groups can move between basic assumptions and work dynamics, so can societies. In some of the discussion that follows, I will apply some psychoanalytic ideas that were developed with respect to individuals to consider aspects of social systems. This is very debatable and has its pros and cons, but I have to use what concepts are available to me.

Hopper (2003b) consistently argues that under certain circumstances a societal system is likely to regress into a very large group, and evince basic assumption processes, in particular the basic assumption of incohesion which is typical of the deep regressions that occur in large groups. Most of the time it is trauma that leads to regression, not only in persons but also in social systems (Weinberg, 2014). Thus, we can expect signs of regression in any traumatised society, and such a society will function as though it were a large group (Hopper, 2003a, 2003b).

Volkan (2002) describes societal regression occurring after a society has faced a massive trauma. It occurs when a majority of people belonging to that society share anxieties, behaviours, and thoughts typical of regression, and its purpose is to maintain or repair the shared social identity.

At the heart of Bion's ideas about groups (1961) is the observation that although groups are normally set up to pursue sensible and realistic goals—he calls this the "work group"—they from time to time fall into madness, which he calls "basic assumption" functioning, acting out primitive fantasies as a defence against fragmentation (Young, 2005).

Just as groups can move between basic assumptions and work dynamics, so can societies. At a certain point in time, a society can set itself up to pursue sensible and realistic goals and can be viewed as a work group. At another point in time the same society can act out primitive fantasies and defences and can be viewed as a basic assumption group.

An illustration of basic assumption group dynamics in the case of Egypt

In the past few decades, Egypt has experienced several massive traumatic events: the difficult years before the 25 January 2011 revolution, the revolution itself, the Brotherhood presidency, the 30 June 2013 revolution, and recurrent terrorist attacks. It seems to behave as a large group dominated by basic assumption dynamics. Curiously, this seems to be repeated throughout the history of Egypt.

Dependency basic assumption

The dependency basic assumption is operative when group members behave as if only someone else has the power, ability, and knowledge to satisfy their needs. Group members experience themselves as weak, ineffectual, and incapable of helping each other (Montgomery, 2002). In Egyptian society, this can be observed at many levels and contexts (Okasha, 2009). Children and adolescents depend on their parents until the third and sometimes fourth decade of their lives. Also, many married women are totally dependent on their husbands, who make all the decisions while they carry out only household duties. The family structure is traditionally patriarchal in that communication and authority flow vertically from top to bottom. In the workplace, clerks, officers, administrators, and other staff are mostly dependent on the boss, who gives and takes, punishes and promotes, and has to be pleased and honoured all the time. The workplace authority is usually treated as father of a family. Even at the psychotherapy level, a model of group therapy where the leader is more directive, prescriptive, and active was developed and proved to work better in Egypt than the group analytic model where the leader is less directive and more descriptive (Taha, Abd-El-Hameed, Kamal, Hasan, & Mahfouz, 2010; Taha, Mahfouz, & Arafa, 2008).

The unconscious role of history and religious understanding is obvious here. Fathers and ancestors have been held high above questioning and criticism since the time of the pharaohs. The Qur'an informs us that when the prophet Moses talked to Egypt's pharaoh about God who is in heaven and on earth, the pharaoh said, "I am Your Highest God!" Central authority and autocracy of pharaonic rulers over the ordinary population were the working rules in ancient Egyptian civilisation, and every new pharaoh was thought of as a new god. This assumption might be one of the explanations of what may be called "the chair syndrome" in Egypt, where a significant transformation in the attitude and behaviour of a person might occur once he becomes an authority figure, that is, chair of authority. He becomes grandiose and autocratic, and he deals with people as if he were a god. At the same time, parents have been given a much respected position by society and religion. So, in the social unconscious of the Egyptian people, fathers are represented as authorities, and authorities are mostly represented as god-like creatures. It is worth noting that the two words (god) and (father) in the Arabic language are nearly similar.

The late president Anwar Sadat used to call himself "the father of the Egyptian family". He used the traditional costume of an ordinary old Egyptian man in order to support that mental image for the Egyptian citizens (Abd-El-Hameed, 2012). The day he was assassinated, he had told his wife that he refused to wear his bulletproof vest because he was going to be among his children. And that is how Hosni Mubarak governed Egypt for thirty years, too. He was seen as a father who must be respected, idealised, and never devalued.

In many Egyptian contexts, people call one another pasha. Pasha is a Turkish word that means chief, head or master. It remains from when the Ottoman Empire ruled Egypt. It was formerly a title for high class people who had the power and money to buy the title pasha from the king.

This system was formally cancelled after Egypt's 1952 revolution; however, people seemed to have an unconscious agreement to keep calling their chiefs, work managers, or anyone in a position of authority, a pasha, as a sign of respect and honour.

Most ancient Arabian poets began their poems (even romantic ones) with an idealisation of the king, the ruler, or whatever authority they had. The same rule still applies in many Arab countries, where some poems, songs, and literary and artistic works are made only for the idealisation of authority. This could show how people may unconsciously participate in producing their dictators! In the shadow of their authority and fatherhood, they feel safe and secure (Rakhawy, 2014). "We deserve Mubarak. For 28 years, we accepted to be weak, vulnerable and negative. We gave up our dignity for the sake of a false sense of security. We deny our responsibility for our current situation and only blame others" (Eissa, 2008, p. 11).

A good example here is the doctored photograph that was published in *Al-Ahram*, the daily Egyptian newspaper, on September 14, 2010. It appeared to put ex-president Hosni Mubarak at the forefront of key figures in the Middle East peace talks in Washington, DC. The original photo showed US president Barack Obama walking in the lead on a red carpet, with Israel's prime minister Binyamin Netanyahu, Palestinian president Mahmoud Abbas, Hosni Mubarak, and Jordan's king Abdullah II slightly behind him. But the state-run *Al-Ahram* newspaper altered the image to show Mubarak in the lead, with Obama slightly behind him to his right, and then placed it over the article "The Road to Sharm El Sheikh", referring to the Egyptian Red Sea resort that hosted the second round of negotiations (Shenker, 2010).

The Egyptian revolution of 2011 and its successor of 2013 (initiated by the "Rebel" youth movement) were loud announcements that many Egyptians, especially the youth, have given up the patriarchal structure which involved idealisation of, and dependence on, the authorities. Note that one of the major characteristics of the revolution was that it had no leader! However, the dependency basic assumption in Egyptian society as described above may explain why, during the eighteen days of the Egyptian revolution of 2011, some, especially older Egyptians, were so sorry for Mubarak who was—in their view—devalued. They felt insecure imagining that he could leave, as if their own father was being forced out of his home and having to stand trial in front of his sons. It may also explain the situation in which most Egyptians have called General Sisi "to the flag" as a saviour of Egypt from its enemy, the

Muslim Brotherhood, and to lead the country not only as an Egyptian nationalist but as an Arab hero, on whom they depend.

Fight and flight basic assumption

Egyptian history is a history of fight and flight. Wikipedia (List of battles of Egypt, n.d.) lists as many as sixty-four big battles on Egyptian soil. They are classified as Pharaonic, Greco-Roman, Arabic/Islamic, medieval, modern, World War I, World War II, and post World War II. Ancient Egypt was one of the first civilisations to emerge as a consequence of the successful merger between two territories, the old Northern and Southern Egypt, under the leadership of King Mena the Unifier. Then came victories of King Ahmos over the occupying tribes, and the later defeat of the Romans by the joint forces of Arabs and Egyptians, followed by the victory over the Mongols and the glory of Saladin in winning back Jerusalem from the Crusaders. All these glories form cornerstones in the national Egyptian memory and foundation matrix. In the last century, there was the 1919 revolution, the 1952 revolution against King Farouk and the British occupation that led Egypt to take the leading role in the Arab and African liberation movements, and finally, the 6 October 1973 war against Israel, which is considered one of the most glorious victories in Egypt's history by Egyptians. It came after a painful defeat in the Six-Day War of 1967, which was humiliating and led to the full occupation of the Egyptian peninsula of Sinai (AbdEl-Hameed, 2012).

The geographic position of Egypt as a transcontinental country and a major power in Africa, the Mediterranean basin, the Middle East, and the Muslim world made it valuable and attractive to the whole world. In most periods of their history, Egyptians were either occupied by foreign countries or ruled by dictator regimes, fighting for their freedom. Moreover, the Egyptian people were mistreated by their rulers most of the time, and Egyptian fortunes in gold, petroleum, cotton, and so forth were abused. Egyptian land was not the property of its people for centuries.

On one hand, these national memories and inherited history have taught Egyptians to be cautious and paranoid, especially with foreigners. Conspiracy theory is a very common phenomenon. On the other hand, Egyptians have a characteristic sense of grandiosity and omnipotence rooted in their ability to withstand their invaders and abusers over time.

Fight and flight re-enactments in the 2011 revolution

Weinberg (2007) assumes that national crises (like revolutions) are chances for exploration of the contents of the social unconscious, where members of a social group may re-enact in the here-and-now relationships and pertinent emotions from their remote past. This seems to be the case here. Stemming from their traumatic history of being occupied and maltreated for centuries, many people—in the early days of the Egyptian revolution of 2011-thought it was a CIA or Mossad conspiracy to destroy the country. This may explain the aggression against some foreign reporters at that time. Dynamics of splitting (who is with us, who is against us) and persecution (they want to destroy us) were predominant at the early stage of the revolution. In later stages, supported by the national memory of great victories over their invaders and abusers, Egyptians unconsciously re-enacted the emotions associated with historical victories. In spite of government efforts to stop the revolution—from cutting off mobile phones and the internet to mass injury and killing—people withstood, resisted, and were assured of reaching their primary goal—the removal of Mubarak. The pharaonic myth of the Nile bride that encourages the Nile river to flow and to water the cultivated lands might have encouraged people to sacrifice their own physical well-being to the welfare of their people and children. The myth of Isis, the goddess of ancient Egypt who travelled across the country to gather the severed limbs and pieces of her husband's body so as to give life back to him after being murdered by his own brother, might have been at the back of protesters' minds in trying to bring Egypt back to life and dignity back to the Egyptian people. And the martyr's image and religious position in the social unconscious of believers (Muslim and Christian) might have made it a lot easier to face the government's police machine with empty hands and peaceful hearts. A demonstrator and a blogger said to a TV reporter in Tahrir Square: "I am going out there to get back my freedom or be killed with dignity" (Abd-El-Hameed, 2012).

The basic assumption of incohesion: aggregation/massification

Hopper (1997, 2003b) argues that a regressed traumatised society manifests behaviours stemming from the fourth basic assumption. This assumption is expressed in bipolar forms of incohesion. When activated, groups and group-like social systems oscillate between aggregation and massification. In the massification polarity, the group seems unified; members tend to merge in fantasy, present enmeshed characteristics, and deny differences; and an illusion of togetherness and sameness prevails. In the aggregative polarity, people feel alienated from one another; and indifference, hostility, and withdrawal from relationships are prevalent. In its extreme form, massive splitting mechanisms are active, and each subgroup is against the other subgroup.

It has been more than six years since the revolution, and after a long time of idealisation, I can see now that the fourth basic assumption could have been working in cycles in the Egyptian community since that time. The first round of the cycle was most active before the revolution of 2011 (incohesion), the second round was most active during the revolution (cohesion), and the third round was reactivated after the revolution (incohesion again).

First round: incohesion as aggregation

The years shortly before the revolution of 25 January 2011 manifested what was described as the greatest social and moral breakdown in the history of Egyptian society. Egyptians, usually described as kind, thoughtful, and helpful, were becoming an indifferent, unbound society, where each person cared most for his own happiness and welfare. People were turning selfish even in their relationships with their parents, families, and loved ones. Many felt alienated in their own country. Travelling abroad to work or emigrating was becoming the dream of many young people who felt isolated, helpless, and even angry with their fellow citizens.

Second round: incohesion as massification

During the eighteen days of the revolution (25 January–11 February 2011), people who were at Tahrir Square described a heavenly atmosphere. There were huge crowds of people, young and old, men and women, Muslims and Christians, from the full spectrum of Egyptian social and political life. They were not pushing or shouting at each other; they were respectful of their differences, and not a single complaint was reported about a quarrel, theft, or sexual harassment. They were also spontaneously but efficiently organised regarding security, supplying water and food, removing the sick and wounded, providing first aid, holding prayers, and regularly guarding each other (Christians guarding Muslims and vice versa). People seemed unified and merged in an "oceanic" fantasy. Differences were denied and a sense of togetherness prevailed. There was a failure to produce a leader; the sole leading figure was the idea, the purpose rather than the person, the hero, or the saviour. People from different parties and political groups found no difficulty living and standing together for long days. They all had a huge celebration *in situ* after it was officially announced that Mubarak was to step down on 11 February.

A key element of the form of aggression that underpins massification is scapegoating. Examples of scapegoating are mentioned later in a specific section as they took place after the revolution.

Third round: incohesion as aggregation

This, however, was not what had happened later on. No more than a month after Mubarak left, splitting was active and people started to withdraw from their square fraternity. Alienation and hostility took place over the vote on constitutional changes; Islamists took a corner against other revolutionary and political powers, who in turn opposed one another when some tried to make agreements and form alliances. Feelings of separation, hostility, and indifference supplanted the *apparent* togetherness, kindness, and reciprocal care that had prevailed in Tahrir Square (Abd-El-Hameed, 2012). This massive splitting is still active.

It seems that incohesion is probably the specific basic assumption that connects most with trauma and the fear of annihilation.

Pairing basic assumption

At the current time, the love of many Egyptians for their President Sisi seems to exemplify Bion's "pairing" basic assumption: create a messianic hope for the future of the group, promoting cohesiveness and mutual gratification of the members, and protection against the dangerous narcissistic and paranoid feelings underneath. On 25 July 2013, in one of the more prominent odes to Sisi, *Al Masry Al Youm* columnist, Ghada Sharif, wrote in a column titled, "Sisi, you just need to wink", that if he wanted to take four wives, she was available. In the same vein, Issa (2013) wrote a poem in praise of Sisi titled, "Wives are pregnant with your star". Mahmoud El Kardosy (2013) surprisingly titled his column in the *Al Watan* Egyptian newspaper, "Egypt to Sisi: 'I give you myself as your wife'".

Many Egyptians see President Sisi as the successor to Nasser, the Egyptian leader who fought the Muslim Brotherhood domestically and led Egypt to leadership of the Arab world and the non-aligned community. Sisi's revival of Nasser's memory was a good way to satisfy deeply buried longings for an era of Egyptian prominence in Arab and world politics. It also seems to satisfy a deeply buried longing in Egyptians for a powerful leader who will motivate them to work hard and face the failure of the economy and the debts accumulated after the collapse of the manufacturing and tourism industries. Current Egyptian reality includes the spread of terrorism, a threat of chaos that stalks all walks of life now. Many people feel that without a strong leader to impose his vision and his will, things will not get better, and confusion and chaos will continue for a long time (Al Sharnoby, 2013). This can also be viewed in the light of dependency basic assumption.

Current Egyptian social dynamics raise many questions. Is the Egyptian social unconscious repeating itself in the direction of fatherhood, in the direction of powerful leaders after a revolution that ended a thirty-year dictator regime? Has the dependency basic assumption been reactivated again so that Egyptians reconstruct, idealise, and depend on a new father after deconstructing an old one? Is this what we may term "social repetition compulsion"? Or do societies like Egypt perform better when ruled by powerful figures? There are many other questions, with no definite answers so far.

Social positions

According to Klein (1975), our individual minds are always in one or the other of two positions. One involves extreme splits, part object relations, brittle guilt, blaming, hating, scapegoating, paranoia, envy, and the tendency to aggression and fighting, whether verbal or physical. The other involves granting that life is not just extremes but consists of things all mixed up, some good, some bad. In this frame of mind guilt is not punitive but reparative. One is not in a manic state but in a rather subdued, depressive but not depressed one: live and let live (Young, 2005).

Hopper (2003b) argues that Bion's three basic assumptions are best understood in terms of the "interplay" between the paranoid-schizoid and depressive positions. Although Bion was not clear about this, he implied that, based on the death instinct, innate pathological envy is the source of irrational and destructive rage, and that primal processes of splitting, denial, and projection facilitate processes of idealisation and denigration in order to help the ego rid itself of painful rage and to protect its most important objects. Dependency develops from idealisation associated with the schizoid component of the paranoid-schizoid position, and fight/flight develops from denigration associated with the paranoid component. The basic assumption of dependency protects people from the experience of helplessness and fear that they will be unable to fulfil the requirements of those tasks the completion of which is essential to life, such as, in infancy, obtaining food. Feelings of unsafeness, uncertainty, being lost, of not knowing what to expect and what is expected, etc. are also involved. Pairing is based on sexualisation or eroticisation as a manic defence against anxieties associated with the depressive position, involving the conviction that goodness and perfection exist nowhere, not within and not without. In other words, pairing is not really a matter of genital sexuality. In any group, all the three basic assumptions and combinations of them emerge kaleidoscopically, as do the correlates of the paranoid-schizoid and depressive positions on which they are based.

Building on this, I would argue that societies and cultures can be viewed in terms of the psychic positions described by Melanie Klein. Moreover, cultures may oscillate and alternate between the two positions, which can be viewed as two poles of a dimension, during different periods of time and under different circumstances. And just like individuals, groups, societies, and cultures may stick for a while at one of these two positions, or at any point in between.

Supporting this assumption, Oklander (2014, personal communication) stated that the work of Klein includes another version of the positions, quite distinct from the developmental one, which poses them as alternative phases in an endless cycle of disintegration-integration in the working through of our experience, both conscious and unconscious, which follows, as Enrique Pichon-Rivière pointed out, an ascending spiral course (the dialectic spiral). This seems to be the way in which we interact with the world, of which we are a part and which is always part of us. New and problematic situations have a traumatic impact on mental processes, and this generates confusion; one way out of the confusion is splitting, which already represents one step forward, but must then be superseded by integration. However, integration never lasts, new situations emerge, and we have to start the cycle all over again.

Nevertheless the continuous exercise of this dialectic process develops in us an increasing capacity for dealing with life. But when the situations we have to deal with are highly noxious and beyond our capacity to deal with, or perhaps even unsolvable, we (as individuals, groups, communities, institutions, or societies) suffer major traumas, the normal cycle is disturbed, and we are stuck in one of its phases, which then acquires the dramatic psychopathological features that are the hallmark of Klein's descriptions. My example for clarifying these ideas is the society in which I used to live (Egypt) compared to other societies in which I have lived for some time (UK, USA, and some other Western countries). Here, I will have to analyse some negative aspects of my society, something that is disturbing and painful: trying at the same time—as a scientific researcher—to find a "neutral" position from which to observe my topic.

I think that on the PS (paranoid-schizoid)–D (depressive) spectrum, the current Egyptian society seems to be fixed at a point near the paranoid-schizoid pole, with most of its characteristic manifestations. Splitting, projection, idealisation/devaluation, scapegoating, part object mode of relating, grandiosity (inflated pride and craving for confirmation of dignity), and suspicion are predominantly used social defence mechanisms. This may be a regressive reaction to the many massive traumatic experiences that Egypt has faced and lived through in the last few years.

Splitting

One of the most obvious dynamics in current Egyptian society is splitting. Most Egyptians can be viewed/divided as *either* Sisi's (state president) supporters *or* Morsi's (Brotherhood) supporters. Every side idealises itself and devalues the other to the point of cold-blooded murder and terrorism.

Another example is the contradictory perception of the West. We Egyptians *either* idealise ourselves and our community while totally devaluing Western societies—viewing them as full of uncontrolled sexual behaviour, liberalism, non-religiosity, crazy fashions, and so forth—*or* devalue ourselves and our community and totally idealise Western societies—viewing them as perfect, and full of order, cleanliness, top technology, and so forth. The latter view is termed "the foreigner's complex".

There are many other examples in politics, sports, etc. Of course, such splits can exist in any society, but in Egyptian society these are more obvious, deeper, and frequently cross the boundaries of objective reality.

Such primitive splitting can partially explain the marked tendency for aggression in the current Egyptian community. It can also explain the extreme polarisation between good and bad in Egyptian media and drama that is often irrational, where there is usually a totally idealised figure and one who is totally devalued.

In many instances, splitting has led to disastrous outcomes. An example of the outcome of such splitting and tendency for aggression is the Port Said Stadium disaster of 1 February 1 2012, where seventy-nine people were killed after thousands stormed the field following a 3–1 victory by Al-Masry, an Egyptian football team. Rival fans attacked the other Egyptian football team players and their fans, using knives, swords, clubs, stones, bottles, and fireworks as weapons. More than 1,000 injuries were reported. Another example is the nationwide clashes between non-Brotherhood and Brotherhood members that took place in Cairo and several other cities many times in 2013, up until the termination of Mohamed Morsi's presidency by the 30 June 2013 revolution. The recurrent terrorist attacks on the Egyptian army by Brotherhood supporting organisations are other examples. They leave many injured and dead.

Scapegoating

The massive projection of "badness" onto "the other" has inevitably led to many instances of scapegoating. One recent instance is what happened in 2012 with Dr Ahmed Zewail, an Egyptian Nobel Prize winner in chemistry in 1999. For a few years after the prize, he was completely idealised and considered an Egyptian hero. TV hosts always treated Zewail like an idol, with much admiration. However, when Zewail suggested utilising the land and equipment of a private Egyptian university and converting it into a city for scientific research, he was suddenly devalued and scapegoated by some Egyptian media. He was described as lacking scientific integrity and stealing others' research (El Naschie, 2012).

Another example is what happened with Dr Sir Magdi Yakoub, an Egyptian cardiothoracic surgeon who established heart transplantation in the UK and became the world's leading transplant surgeon. When Dr Yakoub participated in some TV advertisements to support his non-profit health foundation in 2016, he was suddenly scapegoated by many extremists. They have devalued him and started a big debate on whether he deserves to enter heaven or hell based on his humanitarian work versus his Christian religion.

Part object relating

The part object mode of relating is another PS character, which is dynamically related to splitting. It is manifested in people's relation with themselves, their authorities, and, sometimes, their religion. Al Aswany (2008) thinks that many Egyptians relate only to some superficial aspects of their religion, such as how they should look, and deny deeper and more meaningful aspects that concern how they should behave. In his 2008 article "Why the manners of Egyptian have changed", he wrote:

> [T]he trouble got more complicated when many Egyptians adopted a very superficial understanding of their religion, an understanding that has spread like an infection from more primitive and retarded Bedouin societies. So, many Egyptians use manifest religious outlook to cover their latent behaviors ... societies can become sick just like individuals. (p. 19; my translation from Arabic)

Grandiosity, pride, and persecution

Analysing *Black Honey*, a 2010 Egyptian movie, Ibrahim Eissa, a political writer, elaborated on more PS manifestations in Egyptian society:

> [W]e are always self-inflated, and the movie tells us to stop being so self-inflated. We keep saying that "the Egyptian child is the smartest child in the world, that Egyptians are the best people in the world and that Egypt is the most beautiful country on earth" in an attempt to deny our current failures. Egyptian community is full of contradictions and extreme splits. Our society is full of bribery, deceitfulness, and corruption while we view ourselves as religious,

> kind and great. We have to go to a psychiatrist because we are in a paranoid state. We think that we are the best and that the entire world hates us, envies us and persecutes us. (2010; my translation from Arabic)

Eissa has mentioned some common examples of prevalent pride and grandiosity. Pride has a special position in Egyptian people's mentality and behaviour. An Egyptian likes to be respected, honoured, and valued. Egyptian people's sense of pride and dignity is—to them—untouchable. Numerous songs specifically express this sense of specialness are replayed at many societal events, such as when Egypt's football team wins a game. However, this mostly seems to be a defence against the unhappy Egyptian reality. Besides the dynamics of splitting and projection, this pride may account for the people's tendency to perceive criticisms or differences in opinions or ideas as insults, humiliations, and narcissistic injuries.

It may be interesting to present some preliminary results of a qualitative research study performed by Mohamed Ayman Abd-El-Hameed, and myself at Minia University. In Egypt, many people like putting bumper stickers containing proverbs, folklore sayings, cultural wisdom, jokes, or verses from the Qur'an or Bible on the back of their vehicles. We randomly collected more than one thousand bumper stickers written on cars, toktoks (large motorcycles), and mini-buses moving in the streets of the nine major cities of the Minia governorate. The collected sentences were translated from Arabic to English, then qualitatively analysed using interpretative phenomenological analysis (IPA) (Smith, 2003) in an effort to gain an insight into the Egyptian foundation matrix. The emerging themes of the analysed sentences seem to support the assumption that the Egyptian social unconscious is currently fixed at a point near the paranoid-schizoid pole of the PS–D spectrum. Most of these themes revolved around grandiosity, tendency for aggression, persecution/suspicion/mistrust, and splitting. Table 1 shows some of those themes.

The PS–D spectrum

It seems to me that most Western countries have displayed some paranoid-schizoid manifestations many centuries ago, when the slave trade and military conquests were prevalent. However, they developed

Table 1. Emerging themes of the Egyptian social unconscious.

Emerging theme	*Examples*
Grandiosity	– Stop! I am the top – The magician – The director – The hawk – The manager – The international – The general – The boss – The legend – Best of men – The prince – The professional – The amazing, one and only – We are original not copies – The gentleman is here so everybody should step aside – Watch and take your lesson – We were and we are still – Do not challenge me – I am above the law – You can never beat me – This is way above your level
Tendency for aggression	– Dracula – The wolf – The scorpion – The hunting panther – Serial killer, living in comfort however – Trouble maker – Mister muscles – The butcher – Mafia – The flood – Shut up, kid – I will cut you into pieces – If you cross your lines, I will terminate your existence

(*Continued*)

Table 1. Continued.

	– Beware of the mountain's wrath – Do not race with me if you want to live – I will do whatever I want to do with you – If you are man enough, try to stand that – If you want to live, don't defy me
Suspicion/persecution/ mistrust	– Leave us alone – Let us live – If you play me, I will play you – If you intend to play me, may God turn you into a lizard – I cannot trust you – You cannot trust human beings – Time of betrayal – Do not trust two kinds of people, friends and women – All friends turned out not to be – Venom of a snake is better than betrayal of a man – I loved you and you betrayed me – I believe no one anymore – People's eyes are destructive – Life is not to be trusted – They envy me – A lion's bite is lighter than an envious look – Their eyes are watching, but God protects us – Don't watch me, this car is rented – Protect us from people, oh God – Nobody is frank enough, I swear by God – No friends exist
Splitting	– Keep off to the left side if you want peace of mind – Many people are left, few people are right – So many bad people that good ones became so rare – God! Help me against them – We are the good, they are the bad – They are not interested in the good one – To end with: We are the ones, they are none

beyond that mentality/position and moved closer to the depressive pole/position (acceptance of others, concern, care, creativity, etc.). What led to such a transition in Western societies but not in Arab/Egyptian ones? The answer to this question needs further study, analysis, and exploration that might be approached in a later work.

In one of his emails to me around this subject, Bob Hinshelwood (2010a), who was my PhD supervisor in the UK, wrote:

> The idea that cultures may be different on the PS and D dimension is interesting ... For instance, taking a depressive culture, it might mean one in which people are cared for and their lives are repaired when they go wrong. You could measure this by looking at the budget spent on health, social services and other welfare. Many Western countries might show a high level of care in this way ... there may be other operational criteria other than concern—for instance, the degree of polarizing into good and bad (i.e., PS).

Cultures seem to oscillate and alternate on the dimension between the two mental positions. For example, Arabs lived a long time closer to the depressive pole/position in an earlier Islamic era (c. 750 CE to c. 1257 CE), during which they showed much community care, concern for others, non-polarisation, and creativity. Many of the mainstream sciences were developed during that era. Philosophers, scientists, and engineers of the Islamic world were credited with a period of creative contribution to scientific knowledge, cultural arts, civilisation, and architecture, both by developing earlier traditions and by relatively rapid and marked innovation. A substantial degree of historic Islamic intellectual innovation occurred in that so-called "Islamic golden age" (Islamic Golden Age, Wikipedia, n.d.).

On the other hand, most Western countries moved towards the paranoid-schizoid pole after 9/11, which might imply that when there is a perceived threat, it is easier to move to the PS position. Currently, President Donald Trump seems to be taking the US some more steps in the PS direction. In another email, Hinshelwood (2010b) continued:

> What you say about the PS and D of cultures, and their alternation and oscillation, is very interesting ... British Empire was created on the basis of the slave trade and of military conquest—more PS than D, I think. And after 9/11 Bush in America was very PS, many of us

> think. And we still have a lot of paranoid suspicion around in our country as well as America. You know, the last time I went to the US (July 2009), they took my fingerprints at the immigration desk at the airport. I asked if the prints were destroyed when I left the country. "No," the officer said, "they are kept and sent to Interpol, and to MI5 in London." I was very shocked. But one can do nothing in that situation.

Being at a point closer to the PS pole does not mean that a society displays no D characteristics at all; it still may display some D manifestations, and vice versa. Hence, the idea of a PS–D scale makes sense. For example, in spite of being at a point closer to the PS pole, Egyptian culture still displays some D characteristics. Being friendly, humorous, and known for hospitality and extended family care are some examples. And in spite of being at a point closer to the D pole, many Western cultures still display some PS characteristics; Hinshelwood's airport example is an obvious one.

Figure 1 tries to clarify the idea of social positions. It shows two poles of a spectrum: paranoid-schizoid (PS) and depressive (D). Both the old

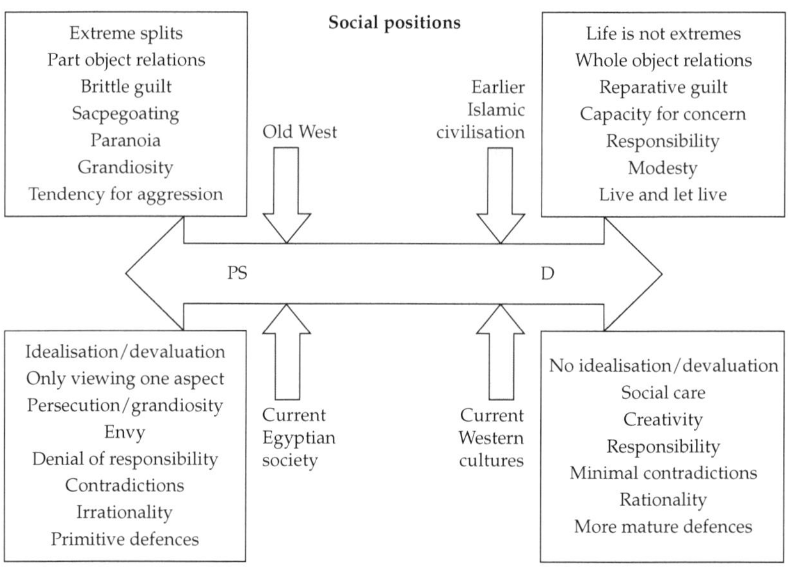

Figure 1. Proposed social positions on the paranoid-schizoid (PS)–depressive (D) spectrum.

Western and the current Egyptian societies seem to be near the PS pole with dynamics of splitting, part object mode of relating, blaming, brittle guilt, scapegoating, paranoia, grandiosity, and tendency for verbal and physical aggression. This leads to idealisation-devaluation of self and other, envy, denial of responsibility, presence of simultaneous contradictions, etc. However, earlier Islamic civilisation and current Western cultures seem to be near the D pole with characters of modesty, responsibility, and reparative guilt. And this leads to notions of "live and let live", movements of social care and concern for others, more creativity, minimal social contradictions, etc.

Conclusion

In this chapter, I have tried—by the means I have—to formulate some theoretical assumptions. To some extent, cultures, societies, and communities seem to apply some of Wilfred Bion's and Melanie Klein's concepts of basic assumptions and psychic positions. The Egyptian revolutions of 2011 and 2013 have been good chances to inspect and analyse some aspects of the social unconscious of the Egyptian people from those perspectives. Examples could support the notions that some cultures may display the dynamics of a certain basic assumption at a certain point in time and that societies can move between the PS and D poles of a suggested PS–D spectrum. Further discussion is inevitably needed.

Notes

We can view Eric Berne's theory of "life scripts" from the same described perspectives as "social life scripts". Berne (1961) defines an individual's life script as an "extensive unconscious life plan" (p. 123) that reflects the "primal dramas of childhood" (p. 116). One source of forming an individual's life script is how children unconsciously choose a common myth or story as the model for their future, and then forget it, leaving the adult acting on a plan for life of which he or she is not consciously aware (Steiner, 1974).

Berne himself considered script analysis as valid in the life of groups and organisations, even mankind in general; hence we may define a "social life script" as how societies and cultures unconsciously choose a common trauma, myth, or fantasy as the motive for their behaviour, then forget it, taking actions based on a plan for life of which their members are not consciously aware.

Connecting this with the theory of basic assumptions, it seems that for each basic assumption there may be a typical life script with certain features. This notion may further deepen the discussion of basic assumptions and their application to societies and cultures. However, the details and examples of this idea will be discussed in another work, for the sake of time and space.

References

Abd-El-Hameed, M. A. (2012, January 30). Notes on the social unconscious. Lecture conducted in Minia University's Department of Neurology and Psychiatry.

Al Aswany, A. (2008, November 19). Why the manners of Egyptians have changed. *Dostor*. Last retrieved July 24, 2016, from http://www.dostor.org.

Al Sharnoby, A. (2013, September 23). Egyptians inventing a new god to worship. *Canada Free Press*. Last retrieved July 24, 2016, from http://canadafreepress.com.

Berne, E. (1961). *Transactional Analysis in Psychotherapy: A Systematic Individual and Social Psychiatry*. New York: Grove.

Bion, W. R. (1961). *Experiences in Groups and Other Papers*. London: Tavistock.

Eissa, I. (2008, September 14). The Egyptian matters. *Dostor*. Last retrieved July 24, 2016, from http://www.dostor.org.

Eissa, I. (2010, August 20). *Our Country in Egyptian* [Video file]. Last retrieved July 24, 2016, from http://www.youtube.com/watch?v=AXjg9x9X3D8.

El Kardosy, M. (2013, August 28). Egypt to Sisi: "I give you myself as your wife". *Al Watan*. Last retrieved July 24, 2016, from http://www.al-watan.com.

El Naschie, M. (2012, January 28). Zewail city: The wrong man, the wrong time and the wrong country. *Al Fath*. Last retrieved July 24, 2016, from http://elnaschiewatch.blogspot.com/2012/02/unhinged-attack-on-ahmed- zewail.html.

Hinshelwood, R. D. (2010a). Personal communication.

Hinshelwood, R. D. (2010b). Personal communication.

Hopper, E. (1997). The fourth basic assumption. *Group Analysis, 30*: 439–470.

Hopper, E. (2003a). *The Social Unconscious: Selected Papers*. London: Jessica Kingsley.

Hopper, E. (2003b). *Traumatic Experience in the Unconscious Life of Groups*. London: Jessica Kingsley.

Islamic Golden Age (n.d.). *Wikipedia*. Last retrieved July 24, 2016, from http://en.wikipedia.org/wiki/Islamic_Golden_Age.

Issa, M. (2013, November 8). Wives are pregnant with your star. *Al Watan*. Last retrieved July 24, 2016, from http://alwatan.kuwait.tt.

Klein, M. (1975). *Envy and Gratitude and Other Works 1946–1963*. London: Hogarth, 1984.

List of battles of Egypt (n.d.). *Wikipedia*. Last retrieved July 24, 2016, from http://en.wikipedia.org/wiki/List_of_Battles_of_Egypt.

Montgomery, C. (2002). Role of dynamic group therapy in psychiatry. *Advances in Psychiatric Treatment*, *8*: 34–41.

Okasha, A. (2009). *The Anatomical Dissection of the Egyptian Personality*. Cairo: Dar El-Shorouk.

Rakhawy, Y. T. (2014, April 30). Are we making a hero or electing a leader? *Al Youm Al Sabea*. Last retrieved July 24, 2016, from http://www.youm7.com.

Sharif, G. (2013, July 25). Sisi, you just need to wink. *Al Masry Al Youm*. Last retrieved July 24, 2016, from http://www.almasryalyoum.com.

Shenker, J. (2010, September 17). Al-Ahram newspaper defends doctored photo of Hosni Mubarak. *The Guardian*. Last retrieved July 24, 2016, from http://www.guardian.co.uk/.

Smith, J. A. (2003). *Qualitative Psychology: A Practical Guide to Research Methods*. London: Sage.

Steiner, C. (1974). *Scripts People Live: Transactional Analysis of Life Scripts*. New York: Grove.

Taha, M., Abd-El-Hameed, M. A., Kamal, A., Hasan, M. A., & Mahfouz, R. (2010). Power of love and love of power in group psychotherapy. *Group Analysis*, *43*(2): 155–169.

Taha, M., Mahfouz, R., & Arafa, M. (2008). Socio-cultural influence on group therapy leadership style. *Group Analysis*, *41*(4): 391–406.

Volkan, V. (2002). September 11 and societal regression. *Group Analysis*, *35*(4): 456–483.

Weinberg, H. (2007). So what is the social unconscious anyway? *Group Analysis*, *40*(1): 319–334.

Weinberg, H. (2014). Commentary on "Social Positions, Scripts, and Functioning Dynamics: Phenomenology of the Egyptian Social Unconscious". *International Journal of Group Psychotherapy*, *64*(3): 345–350.

Young, R. M. (2005). Bion and experiences in groups. Last retrieved June 13, 2012, from http://human-nature.com/rmyoung/papers/pap148h.html.

CHAPTER TWELVE

Fundamental terror of ISIS: the story of a reversed family

Eran Shadach, Shulamit Geller, Yoram Schweitzer, and Einav Yogev

Analysing contemporary Islam through the lens of psychoanalytic theory is a valid method of analysis (Benslama, 2009; Saïd, 2003). Hopper's conceptualisations of the aetiological significance of sociocultural-political factors, and the importance of a transgenerational perspective, enable us to harness the forces of group analytic theory as well (Hopper, 2003a, 2003b, 2009). In this chapter, we will draw upon recent developments in group analytic theory (Hopper & Weinberg, 2011, 2016), and certain psychoanalytical conceptualisations (Meltzer & Harris, 1976) in order to describe the Islamic State in Iraq and Sham (ISIS) as a Salafi[1] jihadi entity.

In order to become a supranational empire, ISIS advocates the imposition of Salafi Islam through violent jihad that rationalises and justifies all of its actions. Through violations of every norm with regard to human rights, laws of war, and the protection of women and children's rights, ISIS defies the Western world and its values, various Arab and Islamic regimes, and non-Muslim minorities that do not recognise its supremacy (Schweitzer & Omer, 2105; Thornton, 2015). It is important to state, however, that the current analysis does not presume to make any claims and generalisations about Islam itself, but rather to describe and explain some aspects of the formation of large groupings of people with a particular mental constellation.

Social regression and social trauma in the Arab world

The history of Islam, and specifically of Sunni Islam, has been marked by continuous successes and by significant territorial expansion. Islam's "golden age" began in the days of Muhammad and the four caliphs, and ended with the fall of the Ottoman Empire, which, relying on its administrative, military, cultural, and religious power, preserved a sociocultural configuration that enabled Islam to fulfil its central role as the leading religion, and has been described as a "chosen glory" (Volkan, 1991). However, after the empire collapsed, the loss of hope for glory triggered a deep sense of humiliation within the Islamic Sunni world. Attempts to regain Islam's superiority proved futile. In fact, the forfeiture of glory pushed Islam further back from modernism and creativity, resulting in the repression of women and the rejection of modern science and literature.[2]

This "regression" of Sunni Islam is even more relevant if seen in the context of the division between Sunnis and Shiites[3] and the rivalry between them (Haivry, 2016).[4] Benslama (2009), in his analysis of Islam, suggests that this crisis stems from the caesura from Islamic tradition, which has unleashed the forces of destruction against "civilisation". Thus, modernity is experienced by the masses as a transgression of the fundamental law of Islam. In the same vein, Stein (2006) suggests that Muslims are in a state of mourning for what they perceive as moral and social decline from better times. However, it is also argued that while a return to traditional Islam is not a magic solution to the threat that the modern era poses to the cultural and social proliferation of Islam, attempts at integration with modern Western culture have proved frustrating (Benslama, 2009).

Charfi (1994), an Islamic scholar, who has analysed the conditions leading to the emergence of the Islamist movement, distinguishes between modernity and modernism. While modernity is a type of civilisation that was invented in Europe and then spread across the globe, modernism is the imitation of modernity, that is, its blind application and, as such, is a misleading ideology of modernity. Charfi's analysis of the genealogy of Islamist despair resulting from modernism rests on the belief that Islamists are the reactive product of modernism, which is seen as a failure of modernity (Benslama, 2009).

As the gap between Islam's current and original statuses becomes larger and more difficult to bridge, social stresses are intensifying, and with them feelings of anxiety, frustration, disappointment, and inferiority, mostly persecutory in nature. In this connection we suggest that social trauma of failed dependency are likely to result in the fear of annihilation and other psychotic anxieties (Hopper, 2003b), as well as "mental pain" in general (Meltzer & Harris, 1976).

Social trauma and the basic assumption of incohesion

The continuous failure of the modern Arab nation states to function properly involves multiple social trauma. When our leaders are felt to have failed and disappointed us, psychotic anxieties, including the fear of annihilation, are likely to arise. These psychotic anxieties are then manifest in the basic assumption of incohesion: aggregation/massification (or (ba) I:A/M),[5] which involves an assertion of identity based on delusions of grandeur and fantasies of omnipotence and omniscience (Hopper, 1997, 2003b, 2009). These experiences of loss, abandonment, and damage cause psychic fission and fragmentation, then psychic fusion and confusion, and finally a defensive oscillation between them, and feelings of shame, envy, and humiliation (Hopper, 2009). Traumatised people feel unconsciously compelled to communicate through interpersonal enactments involving a failure of the symbolic process and the use of various forms of projective and introjective identification (ibid.).

Applying these conceptualisations to actual events, we would suggest that the events known today as the "Arab Spring" were in fact a response to the fear of annihilation and the more general mental pain associated with an immense social and cultural regression following a massive social trauma. Although some forces within the Arab Spring represented progressive democratic governmental change, stronger forces led to a collapse of boundaries between different groupings of people, and to the de-institutionalisation of sovereign structures which steered the development of large group entities (see Taha's chapter on the social unconscious of the Egyptian people in this volume). When the attempts to maintain Islam's superiority repeatedly failed, these large group entities appeared in the form of Salafi jihadi organisations that offered a magic ideological solution, based on the elimination of all that was anxiety-provoking.

Hopper describes and conceptualises these magic solutions in the language of fatal purification, citing psychoanalytical works on attacking all obstacles as comparable to a state of merger with mother's mind and body. Tarantelli (2010), adding to Hopper's ideas, proposes that terror organisations (e.g., the Red Brigades) develop forms of magical thinking that enable their members to eliminate death anxiety. Furthermore, it seems that all fundamentalists share this magical thinking and "refuse to travel between illusion and reality and attempt to keep illusion as their own special reality" (Volkan, 2009, p. 129).

Foundation and dynamic matrices

The foundation matrix pertains to large contextual social systems, such as a society or a nation state with territory, and draws heavily from society's history and traditions. By contrast, the dynamic matrix pertains to constituent groupings within the contextual social system. Such groupings involve day-to-day interpersonal interactions, relationships, and communications between organisations and communities (Fariss, 2003; E. Foulkes, 1990; Hopper, 2003a; Hopper & Weinberg, 2016).

The relations between the foundation and the dynamic matrices are reciprocal. Processes of equivalence exist so that traumatic events within the foundation matrix of the group can be imported into the dynamic matrix and then enacted (Hopper, 2009). The foundation matrix thus serves as a source, a frame of reference, and a context for the traditions, narratives, and myths that are manifest within the dynamic matrix. However, external and internal developments lead to changes within the dynamic matrix, which in turn challenge traditions and myths and create confusion as to the best way to continue following them.

This confusion in turn calls for new solutions within the dynamic matrix, solutions that may be either benevolent or malevolent. While benevolent ones are adapted to accepted cultural norms, and are usually suited to conventional means of governing and leadership, the dynamic matrix that adopts malevolent solutions disregards cultural norms. A prominent example of a malevolent solution is that of drawing on unrealistic magic acts for the purpose of obliterating the boundary between reality and phantasy. Such solutions may be accomplished through processes of idealisation and purification (Stein, 2006). The number of magic solutions needed to defy reality grows as reality becomes more traumatic, and therefore the degree to which the dynamic matrix is malevolent depends strongly on the level of trauma and suffering experienced. It is in this context that ISIS, a multidimensional Salafi jihadi entity of terror, has evolved. As a specific fundamentalist dynamic matrix, ISIS is situated within the foundation matrix of the historic and mythical origin of Islam, and is intended to eliminate mental pain through wishful, unrealistic, and omnipotent salvation. Through a return to the fundamentals of the law of Islam, ISIS works to alter the interrelations between the present dynamic matrix and the past mythological foundation matrix, so as to eliminate the differences between them in the immediate present. Being a fundamentalist entity, ISIS adheres to the notion that nothing is opaque and truly puzzling, nothing needs further understanding; there is nothing new under the sun; everything is self-evident and self-identical (ibid.). These beliefs originate in a history of anxiety, fear, shame, helplessness, a painful sense of smallness, and the feeling of being at the mercy of powers greater than ourselves. The fundamentalism of ISIS offers a means for eliminating these feelings, or for violently transcending them. Such striving for a mystical reunion with the divinity can generate deep faith and powerful hope, but at the same time can be a source of evil (ibid.).

We will now present an illustration of both the dynamic and the foundation matrices of ISIS. At the level of the dynamic matrix, ISIS is a type of "reversed family", characterised by illusional and delusional qualities. At the level of the foundation matrix, ISIS re-enacts the myth of the Abrahamic family, which is a major myth for Islam.

Family structure and the matrices

Group theory asserts that groups often involve the unconscious re-enactment of the family cell (Foulkes, 1964; Yalom & Leszcz, 2005). Although Foulkes did not have a concept for defining the family matrix, several group analysts have subsequently discussed it in terms of both the dynamic (Hopper & Weinberg, 2011) and the foundation matrices (Le Roy, 1994; Skynner, 1987).

At the level of the foundation matrix, transmitted cultural contents are not restricted to the mother–infant dyad: general cultural codes, that is, transgenerational stories, secrets, and pathologies, independent of the individual and common to all members, are transmitted and re-enacted unconsciously in subsequent generations (Le Roy, 1994; see also the chapter by Nitzgen & Hopper in this volume).

In Islam the family is the central institution (Ahmad, 1974, p. 13), the smallest and fundamental cell of society in which the most important basic rules of a community are practised (Mohagheghi, 2006). Furthermore, the tribal mentality in Islam reflects the importance and centrality of the family structure within any Islamic matrix.

By redefining the whole community (*umma*) of believers as the "tribe", Islam created in effect a "super tribe" with tribal warrior ethos that transcends mere blood as the bonding agent (Thornton, 2015). In this context, ISIS offers a viable alternative to traditional tribal society that suits the region's foundation matrix, which has been described as "tribes with flags" (ibid.). "In the absence of a functioning nation with national institutions, only tribe and sect offer identity and protection … only those of (one's) own kind might come to the rescue" (Price-Jones, 2016). For some people, especially disaffected young Salafi men, mortal combat with such a tribal "band of brothers" in the service of a great cause is both an ultimate adventure and a road to esteem.

Meltzer and Harris's (1976) psychoanalytical model of the educational role of the family focuses on the family as an informal educational institution whose ultimate goal is to achieve identity through adequate growing processes. As the family organisation aims to foster learning from experience and to deal with mental pain, the parental function is to provide not answers but "a space where reason can operate" (p. 118). In particular, parents help their children to grow and develop through an increase in self-awareness. The model follows Bion's (1962) ideas concerning the ability of groups to learn from experience, and sees the family as mediating between the individual and the community by defining a social contract that assigns specific social roles to individual members, and between individual members. Family structures can act either in the service of growth and development, or in the service of destructive attack upon it (Meltzer & Harris, 1976). A mature family type fosters love and hope and minimises pain and depressive thinking, but the immature family type arrests such growth and development (ibid.).

We hypothesise that under certain circumstances of conflict and massive changes in the economy and in the social and occupational structure, accompanied by the collapse of traditional hierarchies of power and authority, a radical form of an immature family is likely to emerge, namely, the reversed family (Hopper, 2016). The reversed family is equipped with magic solutions that offer the temptation of an immediate and total elimination of mental pain, and by so doing, negates learning processes (Meltzer & Harris, 1976).

The tendency towards the development of more elementary, tribal family-like structures within the Islamic population in the Middle East can be understood as an attempt to regain and sustain a sense of cohesion, involving increased integration, solidarity, and coherence. We would suggest that ISIS fits the reversed family structure, and as such reshapes the dynamic matrix of a sizable group of people.

The "reversed family" as a specific form of dynamic matrix

The "reversed family" is characterised by engaging in defiant relationships with the community and its values, and by proving unequal to the task of fostering learning from experience, and of dealing with mental pain. Important characteristics of the reversed family include an immature form of learning directed towards controlling the world rather than understanding it, and an unconscious omnipotent phantasy of taking control of internal and external objects. Additionally, mechanisms of projective identification and delusional learning create the magical belief that scientific study is worthless and that only the occult is of value (Meltzer & Harris, 1976). Thus, the reversed family is incapable of reality-oriented translation (Foulkes, 1964) and modulation (Meltzer & Harris, 1976), and instead works to modify reality or evade it (ibid.).[6] By applying such regressive mechanisms, mature thinking, and planning almost cease (ibid.), while annihilation anxieties, weakness, shame, and personal fusion and confusion become prominent (Stein, 2006). As a result, the existence of the group is perceived as being under ever increasing threat, and the group thus enacts the phantasy that it is a collective being that offers its people protection from extreme anxieties (Hopper, 2009).

These characterisations of the reversed family are clearly and tangibly present in ISIS's reversal of values as exhibited in rebelling against the community, political isolation, illegal economy, predatory and provocative relations with neighbours, drug taking, sexual perversion, and violence (Lahoud, 2014; Ryan, 2015; Schweitzer & Omer, 2015). Elitism and exclusivity, as shown for example in the notion that ISIS's Islam is the only true Islam (McCants, 2015), are used to tempt and lead individuals away from mature responsibility and the restrictions such responsibility imposes on the defiant behaviours described above.

Additionally, ISIS tends to invade any existing organisation with the purpose of perverting its ethos and its aims, disguising its own tyranny in flamboyant uniforms and slogans (Meltzer & Harris, 1976).

The community that is associated primarily with basic assumption values becomes a setting for tyranny that reflects and echoes the culture introduced by the reversed family. In such situations of social trauma, individuals' regressive inclination to move into what Meltzer and Harris (ibid.) term "(ba): pairing" is enhanced; (ba): pairing may also be viewed as a paranoid inverted pairing, according to which "Those who are not with (us) are against (us)" (Hopper, 2009), which is typical of traumatised social systems that are subjected to incohesion and the use of pain in the guise of pleasure, leading to their infertility and stasis (Hopper, 2003b).

Reversed family and perversion

The outcome of the reversed family is often a pathological structure that resorts to perverse solutions, in which the bad and destructive social elements have no choice but to react with violence and envy to the pain they cause (Meltzer & Harris, 1976). Perversion is about the abolition of differences that make up reality, for example, between sexes and generations (Chasseguet-Smirgel, 1983). Differences maintain individuality and separation, and thus create obstacles to phantasy and confront one with what is lacking. Perversion is therefore about a universe without obstacles that precedes the introduction of separation, distinction, naming, and of paternal law (Chasseguet-Smirgel, 1986). As the religious terrorist mentality is essentially perverse (Stein, 2006), we refer to ISIS as a terror entity that pursues its task in a perverse way, which is typical of incohesion (Hopper, 2003b).

We will now refer to four prominent aspects of perverse mechanisms characterising ISIS: violence, envy, gender, and time:

1) Like other terrorist groups, ISIS exhibits a dialectical movement between annihilating and fear of being annihilated, between being deadly and being dead (Tarantelli, 2010). Using Freud's conceptualisations of group psychology and the analysis of the ego (1921c), we assume that ISIS turned its fundamental ideology into a sublime object, put it in the place of the ego ideal, and submitted itself (and its victims) to it. Thus, its violent actions, for example, beheadings,

rape, destruction of artefacts, are carried out as a challenge to the supremacy of the destructive forces of those who are considered *wa'l-bara* (outgroup), and are justified as they affirm the ideal of the group's destructivity (Tarantelli, 2010). As Rosenfeld (1987) puts it, such an ideology serves as a delusional object that grants the freedom to indulge in sadistic activity. ISIS's phantasy is to destroy what is perceived as the bad object (*wa'l-bara*), and thus to be freed from annihilation anxiety.

2) Pathological envy embodies hatred of reality, opposes evolution, prevents development and growth, and is aimed at spoiling or destroying the envied object (Bion, 1962; Klein, 1957). As a result, omnipotent infantile parts of the self remain in control, and mature ego ideal functions do not develop. The outcome is a perverse superego characterised by sadism, cruelty, and the desire to destroy things (Mancia & Meltzer, 1981). In the case of ISIS, these aspects of perversion represent both an omnipotent denial of, and passion to eradicate all who are different, and a zealous destruction of traces of earlier cultures, as they all evoke unbearable envy.

   As a defensive development against fear of annihilation, envy can be viewed as directed towards spoiling the resources of people who are perceived as potentially helpful but who will not actually help (Hopper, 2009). With reference to ISIS, it is suggested that such envy is at least one of the unconscious motivations behind the rivalry with the non-Muslim world, specifically the West, as well as sibling rivalries with the Muslim world.

3) Regarding gender, Salafi jihadi organisations are centred on the male warrior and his honour, a tradition rooted in Arab myths according to which the survival and honour of the tribe depends on martial valour. Men and their prowess in war are the means of gaining prestige for the whole tribe[7] (Thornton, 2015). In this context, ISIS can be seen as a men's club in which authority belongs to men, while women are returned to their "natural place". This culture of hyper-masculinity can be regarded as a tool for absolving these men of the need to acknowledge emotional dependency and the need for women (Stein, 2002), hence liberating them from the fear of becoming softened and emasculated (Juergensmeyer, 2000).

   ISIS's extreme ideology of a perverse patriarchal family model that enforces the subservience of women is a prominent expression of the reverse family. For example, although ISIS propaganda portrays women as valued mothers of the next generation and guardians of its ideology, in reality life within ISIS-controlled territory is significantly different (Saltman & Smith, 2015). In a guideline for women entitled "Women of the Islamic State: Manifesto and Case Study", published in 2015,[8] it is stated that men and women are not equal; they have distinctly different roles under Islam, and thus women should remain hidden and veiled. Other examples of female subservience are that it is the fundamental function of a woman to become a mother and serve her husband and children; women can only leave the house in exceptional circumstances, for example, to wage jihad or to study religion. The document further condemns Western society as materialistic, causing women to depart from their role as wives and mothers for a career (Mah-Rukh, 2015).

Moreover, the "sexual jihad" (*Jihad al-nikah*) is a controversial fatwa[9] suggesting that women should offer themselves as sexual servants to jihadi fighters. The purpose of this ruling is purportedly to relieve a man of distracting sexual frustration in times of war. The fatwa gives a man permission to marry a woman for a week or even a few hours in order to have sex (*halal*) with her, so that he may be able to pursue his jihadi mission more effectively on the battlefield.

4) In order to understand current social and political structures, the historic perspective must be considered (Meltzer & Harris, 1976). From this viewpoint, adequate forms of thinking include linear and relative perspectives, while primitive forms of thinking are characterised by timelessness, that is, those that are governed by the pleasure principle and by mindlessness. In this context it has been advocated that ISIS is not a case of resistance to modernisation, but rather a case of perverted modernisation (Zizek, 2006), and that it offers an imaginary "double-edged" solution: a utopia of the future that is at the same time a leap back into a lost golden age (Berman, 2006).

Following these conceptualisations, we suggest that the phantasy represented by ISIS's efforts to erase the difference between present and past, so as to recreate the present on the model of a concrete mythological past, is an expression of perversion. That being said, it has also been suggested that what may be viewed by the Western observer as perverse terrorism, is actually a concrete effort to reinstate tribal warfare in order to prevent a full-scale war (Salzman, 2008).[10] Two more extremely significant expressions of timelessness are the caliphate and eschatological ideology. Concerning the caliphate: the title of caliph holds great historical significance, as it means the "deputy of God". A caliph is capable of making mistakes but is still expected to implement the same system of governance that existed during the Prophet's time. ISIS is unique in its ability and desire to turn its vision of a re-established Islamic caliphate into an immediate political reality (Lahoud, 2014).[11]

Concerning eschatology: ISIS is characterised by a clear and explicit ideology which bears a direct link to Islam's foundation matrix as presented in the 75th Sura, *al-Qiyama*, which addresses the theme of resurrection. By offering a practical way to implement this ideology, ISIS tries both to differentiate itself from other Salafi jihadi organisations like Al Qaeda, and to offer an immediate way to fulfilling the unsatisfied need of Salafi jihadi Islam to hasten the time of the apocalyptic solution. References to the end times fill Islamic State propaganda and are a big selling point with foreign fighters, who want to travel to the lands where the final battles of the apocalypse will take place (McCants, 2015).

The foundation matrix

In an attempt to find cohesion, people tend to look at patterns, myths, and narratives that bind them together; the group draws on a founding myth in order to reconcile itself with its situation, constantly reinterpreting but also reusing that myth as a guide to the meaning of its experiences (Frosh, 2015). The myth is consequently a paradigm for action, but also for understanding what the world might be about, and, because of this, it is a powerful reference point for identity formation (Delaney, 1998; Hassan, 2006). Myths may serve to understand values (Scholz, 2011), certain intense identifications, and identity complexes (Frosh, 2015). In group analytic terms, founding myths may be seen as elements of the foundation matrix of a culture,[12] taken for granted but consciously and unconsciously drawing on a kernel of meaning that gives shape to shared experience. When a transgenerational myth remains unspoken, it tends to be embodied and re-enacted in later generations through the family group (Le Roy, 1994).

In analysing a cultural phenomenon such as a myth, it is essential to work in a non-reductionist manner that does not strip the religious substance of its content and beliefs. It is likely that the primal Abrahamic family serves as a founding myth, which includes themes of rivalry, envy, and competition (Benslama, 2009; Frosh, 2015). There are some prominent illustrations of this myth in all three monotheistic religions. The myth of the Abrahamic family contains five characters: two wives, Hagar and Sarah, their common husband, Abraham, and two sons, namely, Ishmael and Isaac. There are several ways to refer to this myth and different authors attribute different meanings to it (see, e.g., Hassan, 2006, and Benslama, 2009). Thus, according to Benslama (2009), Hagar's expulsion into the desert and out of the Qu'ran led to a situation in which repudiation replaced the union provided by the family, and abandonment of the child replaced caring and education. Benslama goes on to say that in Islam, the problematic issue of abandonment, which is common also to Christianity and Judaism, is radicalised as the mourning derived from it is denied. Similarly, when Ishmael was given the gift of the promise of nationhood, it only served to further separate him from a father who had already abandoned him, and so gift and abandonment became the basis of the monotheistic ontology (Benslama, 2009). Existence may be understood as a gift attached to the experience of abandonment, which in itself reflects a universal human struggle. Consequently, in fundamentalist Islam the figure of the father who was prepared to sacrifice his son Ishmael is perverted, and moreover is perceived as a persecutory father and an inner "gang leader" (Rosenfeld, 1971). It is therefore necessary for fundamentalists to transform Abraham the father into an idealised love object, in order to reverse the rage, discontent, pain, and suffering into glory and narcissistic enhancement (Stein, 2006).

There is another angle to this myth however, whereby Abraham believed it necessary to leave a part of his family in the uninhabited, uncultivated land in order to fulfil the prophetic mission of building the Sacred House of God (Hassan, 2006). Thus, Abraham did not send Hagar and Ishmael away in order to appease the jealous wrath of Sarah, and Hagar does not see herself as a victim of Abraham and Sarah. On the contrary, she is a victor who, by God's and her own initiative, is able to transform a wilderness into the cradle of a new world dedicated to the fulfilment of God's purpose on earth. The possibility of attributing such different meanings to the myth of the Abrahamic family may in itself be an expression of the tension and pain caused by the envy and competition that are represented by this myth.

In summary, it is advocated that under extreme circumstances, such as a social trauma, the denial of abandonment embodied in the family matrix and transmitted down through the generations, is likely to be manifested in later epochs in organised violence and destruction. Similarly, ISIS's conviction of its superiority as an expression of its secret inferiority (Zizek's, 2014), is likely to involve an enactment of these feelings aroused in the mythological family and of a parental inability to cope with them.

Concluding remarks

In this chapter, we have outlined our general understanding of the dynamics of the inconsistent and conflictual relations between the dynamic and the foundation matrices of a large group of people in the Middle East. This pattern follows the experience of massive social trauma and failed dependency. The members of this large grouping of people have developed a variety of psychotic anxieties and in particular the fear of annihilation. These feelings are manifest in the dynamic matrix as the basic assumption of incohesion (Hopper, 2009).

At the level of the dynamic matrix, when various solutions repeatedly fail to satisfy the dependency needs, anxieties are enhanced, and the probability of more malevolent solutions is increased. Under such circumstances a large grouping of people is likely to make use of the family system for restoring cohesion, identity, and belonging, and for reducing mental pain.

It is suggested that Salafi jihadi Islam involves malevolent solutions for the restoration of cohesion, and within it ISIS, which is a particularly cruel terror entity, has the specific characteristics of a reversed family structure, offering a perverse defence against mental pain.

The fate of ISIS is not known, but in terms of the theory of (ba): I:A/M it is likely that its structure will tend towards aggregation. Current evidence concerning the external dynamic forces in the Middle East suggests that this development is highly likely.

Notes

1. Salafism is a strictly Sunni ultra-conservative reform movement that seeks to "purify" Islam of Western influence and centuries' worth of "deviant" departures from the true Islam. Salafists define Islam as anything that was explicitly condoned by Muhammad and that was upheld by his first three generations of Sunni followers (until the ninth century). Anything that appeared after that and anything Muhammad did not

explicitly condone is considered un-Islamic (Olidort, 2015). Within this context, the Salafi jihadists' goal is to raise awareness among Muslims that Islam is in a state of religious, political, military, economic, and cultural decline. Salafi jihadists present a military programme of action, intended to reverse the tide of history and redeem adherents of Salafi jihadist ideology from their misery. Martyrdom is extolled as the ultimate way in which jihad can be waged (Moghadam, 2008).

2. The twentieth century, particularly the second half, brought further humiliation, especially in the Middle East. Muslim countries were falling behind, while the West was the leading civilisation alongside the later rise of other Asian economic powers, despite the wealth many Muslim countries possess through their oil. By all the standards that matter in the modern world—economic development and job creation, literacy, educational and scientific achievement, political freedom and respect for human rights—what was once a mighty civilisation has indeed fallen low. Furthermore, the political culture of the Muslim world has not changed over the centuries, and has remained very much rooted in and led by the codes of a tribal culture (Lewis, 2002).
3. The major split within Islam, which dates back to the seventh century, is between the minority Shiites and the majority Sunnis. Shiite, which comes from the word *shia*, which denotes the party of the fourth caliph Ali, refers to the sect that recognises Ali and his descendants as part of the divine order. Sunni, which comes from the word *sunnis*, denotes the oral traditions and interpretations of the Qu'ran and refers to the sect that rejects the legitimacy of Ali. The two sects are in continuous rivalry over the question of who is a true Muslim (Blanchard, 2009).
4. Among other influences, the collapse of the Ottoman Empire dramatically affected the centuries-old Sunni Arab regional order and the entire worldview that upheld it. In a world where Sunnis vastly outnumber Shiites, this was a crisis of epic proportions. Recently, the Sunni world was again destabilised following the collapse of Saddam Hussein's Sunni regime, which shifted Sunni-dominated Iraq to a Shiite-held state. This shift resulted in growing discrimination against the defeated Sunni majority and the emergence of Salafi jihadist forces under the leadership of Abu Musab el Zarqawi and Al Qaeda elements, who seized the opportunity to revolt against Shiite dominance and the American invasion (Haivry, 2016; Kramer, 2016). A different perspective is that what we are witnessing is not a Sunni collapse, but a Sunni revival after a century of slow but steady erosion. The rise of Al Qaeda in Iraq, the

outbreak of the largely Sunni Syrian revolt, and the rise of ISIS are the most violent expressions of this broader revival (Kramer, 2016).

5. A group-like social system in which the fear of annihilation is prevalent is likely to be characterised by oscillation between aggregation and massification, the bipolar forms of incohesion. While an aggregate is a very simple social formation which is characterised by too much individuality, a mass, not quite a group also, is characterised by too little, as well as by the eradication of subgroups and contra-groups (Hopper, 2009).
6. Translation and modulation are both mature mechanisms for alleviating mental pain through genuine development. Translation provides the "autistic" symptom with meaning (Foulkes, 1964), and has to do with offering a "zone of contact" between the translating culture and the foreign object in order to make it familiar (Venuti, 2000). Similarly, modulation is obtained by understanding and adapting to the external world, or by internalising new qualities into the internal object (Meltzer & Harris, 1976). Modification and evasion, on the other hand, are regressive defence mechanisms aimed at dealing with mental pain through omnipotent fantasies, for example, manic and confusional mechanisms that promote repression and loss of insight (ibid.).
7. The element of loyalty in tribal societies is binding on those within the tribe only, with alliances with other tribes or other peoples being formed only ad hoc, according to the immediate interests of the tribe and being abandoned or betrayed if circumstances or perceptions change (Salzman, 2008). For the importance of *al-wala'* (loyalty to ingroup) and *waa'l-bara'* (disloyalty to outgroup) in disavowing non-Muslims, see Shavit (2013).
8. *Women of the Islamic State—A Manifesto by al Khansaa Brigade* http://www.quilliamfoundation.org/wp/wp-content/uploads/publications/free/women-of-the-islamic-state3.pdf.
9. An Islamic term for a legal opinion given by a mufti or a cleric in a situation in which Islamic law is not clear enough, or can be interpreted in different ways (Mah-Rukh, 2015).
10. What nowadays is identified as terrorism was initially "a tactic of tribal warfare to prevent a full-scale war by so terrorizing enemies that they would give up without a fight … which [was] meant to frighten and demoralize the enemy … [and was] typical of tribal warfare and diplomacy" (Salzman, 2008). Not just the violence of war, but also the cruel torture and slaughter of outsiders, including women and children, are legitimate ways of serving the interests of the tribe (Thornton, 2015).

11. It is interesting to note that Abu Bakr al-Baghdadi took the name of the first of the four caliphs known as the Rashidun, or rightly guided caliphs, who had a personal connection to the Prophet Muhammad. It became traditional to select the caliph from the Quraysh tribe. ISIS's leader, Abu Bakr al-Baghdadi, who is represented as a member of the Quraysh tribe, succeeded in cementing his standing within the global jihad world following the coup d'état he staged by appointing himself caliph, which placed him in a supreme position, above even Ayman al-Zawahiri, the leader of Al Qaeda. ISIS is therefore a throwback to a seventh-century style of governance, while its leader (Abu Bakr) is now known as Caliph Ibrahim, which suggests that his leadership is derived from the path of Ibrahim, that is, from a Salafi jihadist concept of Islam (Ryan, 2015). The designated caliph promises that if the "soldiers of ISIS" remain united and commit themselves to being the "guardians of religion", they "shall conquer Rome and seize the earth" (Lahoud, 2014).
12. See Weinberg (2007) for his definition of the social unconscious.

References

Ahmad, K. (1974). *Family Life in Islam*. Leicester, UK: The Islamic Foundation.

Benslama, F. (2009). *Psychoanalysis and the Challenge of Islam*. Minneapolis, MN: University of Minnesota Press.

Berman, P. (2006). Interrogating terror and liberalism (an interview with Paul Berman by Alan Johnson). *Dissent Magazine*. Retrieved from: www.dissentmagazine.org/democratiya_articl/2016/aug/02.

Bernard, L. (2002). What went wrong? *The Atlantic*. Retrieved from: www.theatlantic.com/magazine/archive/2016/jan/07/what-went-wrong/302387/.

Bion, W. R. (1962). *Learning from Experience*. London: Karnac.

Blanchard, C. S. (2009). *Islam: Sunnis and Shiites*. Washington, DC: Congressional Research Service.

Charfi, A. (1994). Les Islamistes sont-ils les ennemis de la modernisation ou ses victims? *Labinat* (Sud-Édition): 95.

Chasseguet-Smirgel, J. (1983). Perversion and the universal law. *International Review of Psycho-Analysis, 10*: 293–330.

Chasseguet-Smirgel, J. (1986). *Sexuality and Mind: The Archaic Matrix of the Oedipus Complex*. New York: New York University Press.

Delaney, C. L. (1998). *Abraham on Trial: The Social Legacy of Biblical Myth*. Princeton, NJ: Princeton University Press.

Fariss, S. (2003). The resilience of a collective: A Jungian reflection on the American democratic republic. Unpublished diploma thesis, Analyst Training Program, C. G. Jung Institute of Chicago.

Foulkes, E. (Ed.) (1990). *S. H. Foulkes. Selected Papers*. London: Karnac.

Foulkes, S. H. (1964). *Therapeutic Group Analysis*. London: Karnac, 1984.

Freud, S. (1921c). *Group Psychology and the Analysis of the Ego. S. E., 18*: 67–143. London: Hogarth.

Frosh, S. (2015). Born with a knife in their hearts: transmission, trauma, identity, and the social unconscious. In: E. Hopper & H. Weinberg (Eds.), *The Social Unconscious in Persons, Groups and Societies: Volume 2: Mainly Foundation Matrices*. London: Karnac.

Haivry, O. (2016). The great Arab implosion and its consequences. *Mosaic Magazine*. Retrieved from: https://mosaicmagazine.com/essay/2016/jul/16.

Hassan, R. (2006). Islamic Hagar and her family. In: P. Trible & L. M. Russell (Eds.), *Hagar, Sarah, and Their Children* (pp. 149–167). Louisville, KY: Westminster Knox Press.

Hopper, E. (1997). Traumatic experience in the unconscious life of groups: a fourth basic assumption. *Group Analysis, 30*: 439–470.

Hopper, E. (2003a). *The Social Unconscious: Selected Papers*. London: Jessica Kingsley.

Hopper, E. (2003b). *Traumatic Experience in the Unconscious Life of Groups*. London: Jessica Kingsley.

Hopper, E. (2009). The theory of the basic assumption of incohesion: aggregation/massification or (ba) I:A/M. *British Journal of Psychotherapy, 25*: 214–229.

Hopper, E. (2016). Personal communication.

Hopper, E., & Weinberg, H. (2011). Introduction. In: E. Hopper & H. Weinberg (Eds.), *The Social Unconscious in Persons, Groups and Societies: Volume 1: Mainly Theory*. London: Karnac.

Hopper, E., & Weinberg, H. (2016). Introduction. In: E. Hopper & H. Weinberg (Eds.), *The Social Unconscious in Persons, Groups and Societies: Volume 2: Mainly Foundation Matrices*. London: Karnac.

Juergensmeyer, M. (2000). *Terror in the Mind of God: The Global Rise of Religious Violence*. Berkeley, CA: University of California Press.

Klein, M. (1957). Envy and gratitude. In: *Envy and Gratitude and Other Works, 1946–1963* (pp. 176–235). New York: Delacorte Press/Seymour Lawrence, 1975.

Kramer, M. (2016). Revenge of the Sunnis. Sunni Arabs have been losing their grip on the Arab heartland since the fall of the Ottoman empire; the moment of their revival is now. *Mosaic Magazine*. Retrieved from: https://mosaicmagazine.com/response/2016/jul/23/the-era-of-sunni-dominance-ended-a-long-time-ago/.

Lahoud, N. (2014). Metamorphosis: From al-Tawhid wa-al-Jihad to Dawlat al-Khilafa (2003–2014). In: N. Lahoud, M. al-'Ubaydi, D. Milton, & B. Price (Eds.), *The Group That Calls Itself a State: Understanding the Evolution and Challenges of the Islamic State*. West Point, NY: The Combating Terrorism Center at West Point.

Le Roy, J. (1994). Group-analysis and culture. In: D. Brown & L. Zinkin (Eds.), *The Psyche and the Social World* (pp. 180–201). London: Jessica Kingsley.

Mah-Rukh, A. (2015). Isis and propaganda: how Isis exploits women. Reuters Institute Fellowship Paper, Oxford University.

Mancia, M., & Meltzer, D. (1981). Ego ideal functions and the psychoanalytical process. *International Review of Psycho-Analysis, 62*: 243–249.

McCants, W. (2015). *The ISIS Apocalypse. The History, Strategy, and Doomsday Vision of the Islamic State*. New York: St. Martin's Press.

Meltzer, D., & Harris, M. (1976). *The Educational Role of the Family. A Psychoanalytic Model*. London: Karnac, 2013.

Moghadam, A. (2008). The Salafi-Jihad as a religious ideology. *Combating Terrorist Center Sentinel, 1*(3): 15. Retrieved from: https://www.ctc.usma.edu/v2/wp-content/uploads/2010/jun/17/Vol1Iss3-Art5.pdf.

Mohagheghi, H. (2006). Between the ideal and the real: the situation of Muslims in Germany. In: H. Reifeld (Ed.), Marriage, Family and Society—a dialogue with Islam. Sankt Augustin, Germany: Konrad-Adenauer-Stiftung.

Olidort, J. (2015). What is Salafism? How a nonpolitical ideology became a political force. *Foreign Affairs*. Retrieved from: https://www.foreignaffairs.com/articles/syria/2015/nov/24/what-salafism/.

Price-Jones, D. (2016). Is a century of Sunni Arab dominance truly finished? *Mosaic Magazine*. https://mosaicmagazine.com/response/2016/07/is-a-century-of-sunni-arab-dominance-truly-finished/.

Rosenfeld, H. (1971). A clinical approach to the psychoanalytic theory of the life and death instincts: an investigation into aggressive aspects of narcissism. *International Journal of Psychoanalysis, 52*: 169–178.

Rosenfeld, H. (1987). Destructive narcissism and the death instinct. In: *Impasse and Interpretation* (pp. 105–132). London: Routledge.

Ryan, M. W. S. (2015). ISIS: The terrorist group that would be a state. Center of Irregular Warfare and Armed Groups, United States Naval War College. Retrieved from: www.usnwc.edu/ciwag/2016/nov/26.

Saïd, E. (2003). *Freud and the Non-European*. London: Verso.

Saltman, E. M., & Smith, M. (2015). *Till Martyrdom Do Us Part: Gender and the ISIS Phenomenon*. London: Institute for Strategic Dialogue.

Salzman, P. C. (2008), The Middle East's tribal DNA. *Middle East Quarterly, 15*: 23–33.

Scholz, R. (2011). The foundation matrix and the social unconscious. In: E. Hopper & H. Weinberg (Eds.), *The Social Unconscious in Persons, Groups and Societies: Volume 1: Mainly Theory*. London: Karnac.

Schweitzer, Y., & Omer, E. (2015). The Islamic state: a global challenge. The Institute for National Security Studies (INSS), Tel Aviv University.

Shavit, U. (2013). Can Muslims befriend non-Muslims? Debating al-wala' waal-bara' (loyalty and disavowal) in theory and practice. *Islam and Christian Muslim Relations, 25*(1): 67–88.

Skynner, R. (1987). *Explorations with Families: Group Analysis and Family Therapy*. London: Methuen.

Stein, R. (2002). Evil as love and as liberation. *Psychoanalytic Dialogues, 12*: 393–420.

Stein, R. (2006). Fundamentalism, father and son, and vertical desire. *Psychoanalytic Review, 93*: 201–229.

Tarantelli, C.B. (2010). The Italian Red Brigades and the structure and dynamics of terrorist groups. *International Journal of Psychoanalysis, 91*: 541–560.

Thornton, B. (2015). Make the ISIS caliphate a Jihadist kill zone. What committing a serious fighting force to decimate ISIS would mean for Mideast stability. *Frontpage Mag*. Retrieved from: www.frontpagemag.com/fpm/251478/make-isis-caliphate-jihadist-kill-zone-bruce-thornton/2016/feb/15.

Venuti, L. (Ed.) (2000). *The Translation Studies Reader*. London: Routledge.

Volkan, V. D. (1991). On chosen trauma. *Mind and Human Interaction, 3*: 13.

Volkan, V. D. (2009). Religious fundamentalism and violence. In: M. K. O'Neil & S. Akhtar (Eds.), *On Freud's The Future of an Illusion* (pp. 124–141). London: Karnac.

Weinberg, H. (2007). So what is this social unconscious anyway? *Group Analysis, 40*: 307–322.

Yalom, I. D., & Leszcz, M. (2005). *The Theory and Practice of Group Psychotherapy*. New York: Basic Books.

Žižek, S. (2006). *A Glance into the Archives of Islam, The Antinomies of Tolerant Reason*. http://www.lacan.com/zizarchives.

Žižek, S. (2014). ISIS is a disgrace to true fundamentalism. *The New York Times*. Retrieved from: http://opinionator.blogs.nytimes.com/2014/09/03/isis-is-a-disgrace-to-true-fundamentalism/2014/sep/03.

EPILOGUE

There is always some collective and personal fusion—if not confusion—whether a new book is a baby or a tombstone, or both. There is always cause for joyous celebrations as well as mourning. It is important to acknowledge the liminality of the product of two editors and many colleagues from around the world and from different core disciplines. Although this book will be launched at several conferences in several cities throughout the year, and there will be several opportunities to wet the baby's head, it is also the right time to spread some sage smoke. After all, a decade has passed since we began our editorial work, which we hope has helped to foster the creativity of those who share our passion for the study of the social unconscious and its clinical applications, the latter of which will be the main theme of the next volume in this series.

We would, however, be seriously remiss if we neglected at least to mention the political context of the study of the social unconscious. This can be traced to the revisions of classical psychoanalysis, often associated with the work of the Frankfurt school, who emphasised the importance of environmental and nurturing processes as opposed to those which are seemingly innate and "natural", leading to the study of sociocultural restraints and constraints on personal and group development. The group analytic approach emphasises the assumptions of relational psychoanalysis, and, thus, the importance of helplessness over envy, the latter being an emergent defence against the former rather than an expression of the putative death instinct. Co-created social facts and social processes are not merely projected fantasies. In contrast to objective or subjective reality, intersubjective reality is the foundation of socially unconscious processes, which creates a sense of belonging among the members of a particular society, ethnic group, and/or other community, and, therefore, which enhances the connections among them, and enables them to collaborate.

Historically, group analysis has been marked by several preoccupations. S. H. Foulkes himself was certainly concerned with the effects of the Second World War, not only with the obvious horrors of it, but also the transgenerational transmission of dispositions towards violence, malignant child rearing, the centrality of aggression in social character, etc. The work of P. de Maré was situated in neo-Marxist interests and values, which gave birth to the study of large(r) groups. E. Pichon-Rivière shared these perspectives, as seen in his notion of the dialectical spiral. Many colleagues have applied group analysis to the study of inequality in economic and social resources, race and racism, gender identity, anti-Semitism, Arab-Jewish relations in Israel, the dynamics of extremism, terrorism, and fundamentalism, etc. We have been especially concerned with massive social trauma and its vicissitudes, including the development of populist processes in the context of societal regression. We have also become concerned with the profound consequences of information technology on our patterns of relationships, values and norms, styles of communication, and other dimensions of the tripartite matrix.

These issues have become painfully urgent in the contemporary United States and Europe, if not throughout the world. Once again, the boundaries of nation states are challenged. Aggregation processes, as seen in withdrawals from international and national alliances, and massification processes, as seen in forced cultural homogenisation, would seem to be emergent. Scapegoating is increasingly apparent. So, too, are defensive nationalism, Fascism, and fundamentalism.

It is in this context that in the preface to the recent publication of the translation into Czech of *The Social Unconscious in Persons, Groups and*

Societies: Volume 2: Mainly Foundation Matrices, we (Hopper & Weinberg, 2016) have written:

> … we must bear witness to massive social traumas that threaten to engulf the entire Middle East as well as greater Europe, if not the world. The migration of refugees is dominated by their attempts to survive the terrors of war and of migration itself. Although many are given sanctuary, many are lost in their search for it. Once again, the political struggles of inclusion and exclusion, and of racial prejudice and discrimination, have been awakened. The context of the return of the repressed and the suppressed is the inexorable development of a global economy deeply influenced by the rise of political and military power in the Far East. Unemployment, if not rampant inflation, is a constant insult to the integrity of the citizenry of many nations … (p. 8)

The stranger and the foreigner are two kinds of "other". Stranger anxiety is undoubtedly based on insecure attachment to primary objects, which can be displaced onto and into our groupings. Only those of us who are personally and socially secure can tolerate the stranger in our midst, and, thus, have the opportunity to benefit from relations with the "new". It is ironic that as societies become more cosmopolitan, they tend to flourish and develop. This can be seen in such geographically and historically diverse situations as the Golden Age of Athens following the mix of migration from Africa in the south and invasion from Europe in the north, Israel following the search for safety by those who survived the Holocaust, and the United States since its very inception, which might be denied by its current citizenry.

Foreigners and foreigner anxiety are, however, different from strangers and stranger anxiety. The foreigner is not only strange, but also intrusive, usually defined in terms of the early experience of a third object such as a sibling or a father who interferes with the mother–infant dyad. Whereas the stranger is defined in terms of the senses, such as "taste" and "touch", the foreigner is based on the fear that the self and primal relations will be violated. The members of a host society, especially those who are most vulnerable and deprived, are understandably frightened of strangers and foreigners, and most prone to engage in fatal purification, which is sometimes known as "ethnic cleansing".

However, strangers and foreigners are themselves laden with anxieties connected with loss and uncertainty concerning the realisation of their aspirations and their survival itself. Refugees are likely to have suffered additional trauma.

The resolution of these social and political problems depends on an appreciation of difference and diversity. It is essential to make creative use of what is in essence traumatic experience for strangers, foreigners, and their hosts alike. This is always a matter of process and continuous reflective practice. We do not yet know how this will affect the peoples of various regions of the world.

Pleas for the acknowledgement that there is only one "sky" are both helpful and misleading. Yes, there is only one heaven in contradistinction to one hell; but no, there are many skies: big, small, blue, grey, sunny, cloudy, dry, rainy … those that last for a season at a time, and those that change moment by moment. Whereas we share an infinite number of "commonalities" that are rooted not only in our species, but also in the nature of our societies, many features of our humanity are variable, and the basis for division, rivalry, and exclusion, which is precisely why they warrant sensitive appreciation. Our study of the social unconscious is intended to be a contribution to this "project" in the existential sense of the term, which ultimately is in the service of personal and social cohesion as manifest in integration, solidarity, and coherence.

Reference

Hopper, E., & Weinberg, H. (Eds.) (2016). *Socialni Nevedomi U osob, Skupin a Spolecnosti 2: Dil: Prevazne Zakladove Matrice*. Czech language edition. London: Karnac.

INDEX

Printed in Great Britain
by Amazon

76926531R00169